# The Art of Urban Survival
*A Family Safety and Self-Defense Manual*
By Stefan H. Verstappen

Woodbridge Press

Woodbridge Press
Toronto, Canada

Cover Design: S. Verstappen
All Illustrations by S. Verstappen
Copyright © 2010 by Stefan H. Verstappen
All rights reserved

ISBN 978-0-9869515-0-3

The author of this book does not dispense medical advice or proscribe the use of any technique as a form of treatment for physical or medical problems without the advice of a physician. The author does not assume any responsibilities for injures that may occur in pursuing certain exercises. Please consult a physician before engaging in any of the physical exercises.

# The Art of Urban Survival
*A Family Safety and Self-Defense Manual*

The Art of Urban Survival

# Table of Contents

# Introduction

*Know your enemy and know yourself,
and you will win all your battles.*
Sun Tzu, *The Art of War*

Since the invention of cities and by
definition, civilization, man has created
an artificial environment in which to
live. Part of the function of this urban
environment is to separate us from the
rest of nature and protect us from
natural disasters, climate, and the predation of predators. However,
nature is not easily thwarted and the laws of the jungle still apply.

We may have escaped being eaten by a tiger, but the tiger has been
replaced by other predators; the robber, mugger and rapist. As has
the wolf packs, hyenas, and coyotes been replaced by street gangs
and organized crime. In addition, even though we have some
protection from the natural disasters of droughts and floods, we are
now subject to new man made disasters of war and tyranny.

Our pre-civilized ancestors survived all dangers and disasters
because they possessed the ultimate weapon - their intellect.
Primitive man learned the behavior patterns of predators, and the
laws of nature. These patterns have changed little since the coming
of civilization.

By learning to observe and recognize the behaviors of predators,
and the signs of impending turmoil, civilized man can likewise
survive the challenges and dangers of the urban environment.

## How to Use this Manual

This book is divided into three sections: Surviving Predators,
Surviving Natural Disasters, and Surviving Social Disasters.

Surviving Predators covers all threats that come from human
sources. These include psychopaths, criminals, groups, and gangs.

Surviving Natural Disasters covers natural threats that can occur in an urban environment such as storms, earthquakes and pandemics. Finally, Surviving Social Disasters covers the threats from when whole societies become predatory and destructive resulting in anarchy, terrorism, and war.

Like any technical manual, this book contains more information than can be digested in a read through. Instead, read specific chapters as it applies to whatever potentially dangerous activities you are planning to engage in. For example, if you are planning on traveling read Travel Safety. If you are planning on going to a public event or demonstration read Riots. If a storm is predicted for your area read Disaster Preparedness. If there are threats of terrorist or military activity where you live read Surviving Social Disasters. In this way you can plan and prepare your reactions ahead of time and the lessons will truly sink in.

# Surviving
## Predators

The Art of Urban Survival

# Surviving Predators

*Life is nothing but a competition to be the criminal rather than the victim.*
Bertrand Russell

In the urban environment criminals fulfill nature's role of predators. While the strategies criminals use vary widely there is an important distinction between two types of criminal, the psychopathic, and the non-psychopathic.

The non-psychopathic criminal is the type most familiar to the public. For these criminals, crime is a survival mechanism anthropologists call the *Cheating Strategy*. The Cheating Strategy simply refers to the advantage cheating provides in terms of survival. For example, a person may spend eight hours a day working to earn a certain amount of money, but a thief could spend only a few minutes to gain what another spent eight hours to acquire. The thief's cheating strategy is cost effective – the gains far exceed expenditures.

However, man is a social animal and cheaters are seldom tolerated in a reciprocal society wherein everyone works together for common benefits and equal share in the fruits thereof. Society evolved the institution of revenge and punishment as a counter to the cheating strategy. While some question the effectiveness of punishment as deterrent, on a survival level, punishment factors into the cost/benefit analysis of those considering a cheating strategy. A thief who steals another's wages may be acting cost effectively, but if the thief is subsequently caught and forced to serve five years in prison, he will find the costs now far exceed the benefits.

Therefore, crime prevention requires that we make the costs of using a cheating strategy greater than the benefits by forcing criminals to work harder, and increasing their chances of being caught.

The cheating strategy is often used when people are at a disadvantage. Poverty, low intelligence, and poor education are the root causes of much criminal behavior. Most crime safety and self-defense literature focuses on this type of criminal activity, defense against a mugger, preventing theft, home defense and so forth. This type of crime is logical. One person has something another does not, and so the latter cheats to acquire it. While you cannot condone the methods employed, you can understand the motivation for the actions.

Another type of criminal behavior committed by non-psychopaths are crimes of passion. These acts of violence stem from emotional turmoil and our primitive instincts. Many otherwise average people are capable of committing assault, rape, and murder in the heat of passion especially if fueled by drugs and alcohol. While the acts they commit are pathological, they are not themselves necessarily psychopaths.

However, when it comes to the second type of criminal the underlying motivations become surreal. While psychopaths will certainly use the cheating strategy, it is seldom necessary to their survival. A millionaire psychopath would readily rob a starving child. Obviously, the millionaire's survival is not at stake. There is no obvious logic to what motives could underlie such behavior. Psychopaths often elude justice for this very reason. In criminal trials, the prosecution is required to ascribe a motive to the defendant. However, in the case of psychopaths, their motives are so bizarre and alien that even if a prosecutor could explain it, most jurors would not believe it. The psychopath can also assault, rape, and murder, but it is seldom a crime of passion. It is instead a cold and calculated plan to gain what the psychopath wants.

Of all the criminal types that inhabit our society, the psychopath is by far the most destructive, the most successful, and the least understood. For these reasons, any self-defense program must begin with a study of the most dangerous predator on the planet.

## The Psychopath

*The urge to save humanity is almost always a false-face for the urge to rule it.*
H.L. Mencken

Psychopathy [1] infects the full spectrum of humanity irrespective of race, culture, geography, economic class or personality type. It is distributed in a population in a similar way that left-handedness is. One would not notice a person is left handed until you see him write or catch a ball. Similarly, one may not notice a psychopath until you see him do something that requires them to have a conscience.

Most people think of a psychopath as a rare creature found only in the lowest levels of society. However, the reverse is true. They are not rare, but actually quite common, and you are more likely to find psychopaths in the boardroom than on the wrong side of the tracks.[2] The reason is that the more competitive a particular environment is, the more ruthless the use of the Cheating Strategy becomes. Within the highest circles of power and wealth, a lack of pity and remorse is practically a prerequisite to success, and only the psychopathic mentality can thrive.

Because of the tremendous destruction psychopaths reap on society, it is vital for everyone to be aware of their existence and to recognize their behavior traits. Understanding them is the first step to defending oneself against them.

## Key Characteristics

Lack of Empathy: Empathy is the ability to experience within oneself, the feelings and emotions expressed by others. It is what allows us to feel what others are feeling. It is why we are inspired by works of art, music and poetry. Empathy allows us to experience the grandeur of life, to be truly alive, and is one of the defining characteristics of what makes us human.

Psychopaths have no empathy and as a result, they are neither truly human, nor truly alive. When they see 'Normals' admiring a piece of art, or playing with their children, or caring for a pet, or any number of human emotional interactions, they can't understand what all the fuss is about. Psychopaths realize at an early age that they are different, and that they should act as everyone else does in order to be accepted into society. They learn to mimic what they see others do, but they can never understand why they should act this way.

Although they are consummate actors, careful observation will reveal telltale cracks in their façade. They know enough to fake concern when someone is sick, or to pretend happiness when some good fortune befalls a friend, but in situations where the psychopath has no pre-rehearsed act; their adlib often reveals a stunning lack of empathy. For example, if attending a funeral, a psychopath would correctly mimic the same expressions of sadness as the other mourners, but then makes sexual advances towards the grieving widow clueless to the gross inappropriateness of such an action. People with empathy would instinctively understand such behavior as inappropriate. However, the psychopath cannot.

Lack of Remorse: Remorse is an emotional expression of personal regret felt by a person after he or she has committed an act, which they deem to be shameful, hurtful, or violent. This very definition precludes a psychopath from experiencing such a feeling. With no empathy, there can be no emotional expression. Nor can a psychopath feel shame, nor comprehend that anything they do can be hurtful to others.

Psychopaths understand when people are angry with them for their behavior, and as a last resort, they may pretend they are sorry, but unlike most people, they are not the least bit disturbed by feelings of guilt. Remorse is a powerful negative emotion that causes turmoil in those that feel it, turmoil that often results in self-destructive or self-deprecating behaviors. The psychopath may pretend remorse but their real behavior has not changed, they still go shopping, they still go to parties, they have no problems sleeping at night.

<u>Superficiality</u>: Passion drives someone to go further than needed to explore, learn, and master a subject. Most people enjoy listening to music, but it is someone passionate about music that goes on to learn how to play an instrument. Similarly, many people are interested in new technology but only a passionate person goes on to become an engineer. Lacking passion for anything other than themselves, psychopaths can never penetrate beyond the surface of most knowledge. As a result, they exhibit a "superficial" comprehension of some or many subjects but are often seen by true experts as being shallow. This superficiality extends to their attempts at acting normal by exhibiting false emotions through an exaggerated affect.

<u>Grandiosity</u>: Despite being shallow and superficial, psychopaths show no self-esteem issues. Psychopaths live in a falsely constructed worldview in which they are both literally and figuratively god. Often seen as megalomaniacs, they also have an equally overblown sense of entitlement.

<u>Irresponsibility</u>: Psychopaths are irresponsible because nothing is ever their fault. Someone else, or the world at large, is always to blame for all of their problems. This makes sense if you understand that psychopaths think themselves perfect. Nothing wrong can ever originate with them and so logic, the psychopath's logic, dictates that everything bad is always someone else's fault.

<u>Impulsive Behavior</u>: The psychopath's impulsive behavior makes sense in light of their megalomania. In their world, whatever they want now, is good, and whatever they do not want is bad. If a psychopath wants sex and his date will not provide it, then rape is good and the date is bad. If someone has money in his or her pocket, and the psychopath wants it, then robbery is good, and the victim is bad for possessing something the psychopath wanted. If this strikes the reader as insane - it is. One of the earliest writers on the subject of Psychopathy, J. C. Prichard coined the now defunct term, *Moral Insanity* as a way to describe Psychopathy in 1835.

<u>Poor Behavior Control</u>: This characteristic can be misleading since many psychopaths exhibit excellent self control by having to

pretend to be 'Normal' for most of their lives. The lack of self-control comes into play when the megalomania causes them to do and behave exactly as they please at anytime they have an urge. This brings us to the next characteristic.

Lacking Goals: Another characteristic attributed to the psychopathic personality is the lack of goals, but this can be misleading. Many psychopaths have goals, such as murder two victims at once, sabotage a co-worker, or become president. However, often long-term goals are subverted to short-term goals that are, as described previously, whatever the psychopath wants at that particular moment.

Compulsive Lying: Living at the expense of the rest of humanity would be an impossible situation in a rational society. Psychopaths have solved this dilemma through their premier weapon - lies. Lies hold together their view of themselves, their own private universe, and facilitate their need to live parasitically off the rest of society.

Without empathy, shame, and remorse they are free to lie as often and as outrageously as they please. Normal people would blush, or sweat, or tremble, if they dared stretch the truth to the same degree. However, for the psychopath lying is as easy and natural as breathing. This is why they often pass polygraphs. They do not register the physiological reactions that non-psychopaths would when lying. They are so good at lying they can fool trained psychiatrists and even other psychopaths. What is important to know is that given the right circumstances they can fool anyone.

Manipulative: Hand in hand with the psychopath's extraordinary ability to lie comes the ability to manipulate others for their own benefit. Having spent their lifetime studying us, psychopaths are masters of manipulation and experts on knowing how to push our buttons to use our emotions against us. They use this ability to keep those around them confused, unable to think clearly, and off balance.

Psychopaths also learn very early how their personalities can have traumatizing effects on the personalities of non-psychopaths, and how to take advantage of this for purposes of achieving their goals.

Like an electric eel that stuns its prey with an electroshock, psychopath's inhuman personality and uncanny ability to manipulate can psychologically stun their intended victims.

Anti-social Behavior: The very essence of the psychopath is anti-social. Their lack of empathy for other people extends onto society and the environment. Vandalism, pollution, graffiti, animal abuse, environmental destruction, building code violations, reckless driving, and a host of morally and socially unacceptable activities are of no concern to the psychopath.

These then are the basic characteristics that psychopaths exhibit. Bear in mind that few psychopaths will express all of the characteristics, and that non-psychopaths can have many of these characteristics as well.

## Common Types Of Psychopaths

While there are as many variations in the personalities of psychopaths as there are among normal people, the following lists some general stereotypes.

Narcissists: The most benign form of psychopathology is pathological narcissism. Narcissists, like the mythological Greek namesake Narcissus, are so overcome with self-love that nothing else in the world matters but them. They need a constant source of *Narcissistic Supply*, which is attention, adoration, recognition, awards, and praise.

There are two basic types of narcissist, the Somatic, and the Cerebral. Somatic Narcissists take pride in their looks and appearance. They will flaunt their sexual exploits, brag of their accomplishments, show off their muscles, and display their toys. They are often health nuts, hypochondriacs and sex addicts. Much of their narcissistic supply comes from having numerous sexual partners, but the act itself, often flamboyant and exaggerated, is nonetheless merely an empty show put on by the narcissist for his or her own amusement. Because of their barren inner life, they continually need new thrills simply for the rush of adrenaline. These thrills range from criminal activity and substance abuse to increasingly bizarre sexual acts.

Cerebral Narcissists love their own minds. They are arrogant, condescending, and 'know-it-alls' that pride themselves on being smarter than everyone else is. Contrary to the somatic type, cerebral narcissists often regard their body and its maintenance as a nuisance and burden and are physically lazy, unfit, and often celibate. Their narcissistic supply comes from fame, notoriety, awards, and displays of wealth to create envy in others.

The danger to the public from narcissists is the drain on energy, time, resources, and emotional wellbeing. A narcissist is interested in a person only for what narcissistic supply that person can provide. They will gladly accept love, attention, affection, adoration, praise, emotional and financial support, but being without empathy, they cannot reciprocate any of it. Any partnership they enter into will always be one sided. Once a person ceases to be a source of narcissistic supply, or a better source comes along, they are discarded without hesitation or consideration. Thus, do narcissists leave behind them a trail of broken hearts, broken dreams, empty wallets, and abandoned children.

The Victim: Commonly used by female psychopaths, (but by no means unheard of among males) is the professional victim stereotype. Preying on what psychopaths see as a weakness in others, sympathy, the female psychopath appears helpless, pitiful, emotionally fragile, persecuted, and sexually vulnerable. She pretends heartfelt gratitude for whatever small kindness strangers provide her, but behind the mask is a cunning, ruthless, and loveless predator. Often using sex as the hook, they can juggle several victims at a time draining them of life and money until there is nothing left, then skipping town to avoid the repercussions.

Con Artists: Not all con artists are psychopaths, but psychopaths make convincing con artists. Being excellent liars, they put that talent to use by cheating others. Without a conscience or remorse to stand in the way, they are free to cheat old women out of their life savings, sell quack cures to terminally ill patients, or shortchange the blind. They are usually charming, articulate and convincing, and make successful salespersons. Unlike the Narcissist, the con artist is not as concerned about love or attention, as money.

There are two types of cons psychopaths engage in the Short Con and the Big Store Con. The Short Con is probably the one that most often comes to mind when thinking about con artists. These are tricks and cheats that require no great intelligence to pull off, such as short changing, bait and switch, and Three Card Monte to name a few.

Psychopaths that have a higher intelligence level and/or come from a more respectable background are more likely to establish the Big Store Con. These are large-scale frauds that all rely on a basic strategy. Take something of little to no value, artificially inflate the perceived value, sell to gullible investors, take the money and run. Traditional big store cons use real estate, stocks, and bonds as the lure. Even 'reputable' multinational corporations, accounting firms, and banks are all capable of being nothing more than a large-scale con. While the short con can deprive a victim of few to a few thousand dollars, the big store cons are especially destructive capable of destroying an entire nation's economy.

The after effects of the these psychopaths are usually financial devastation along with all the repercussions of broken marriages, suicides, alcoholism, domestic violence, drug addiction, and ruined lives.

Malevolent Psychopaths: More popularly known as Anti-Social Personality Disorder, or Sociopaths, the Malevolent Psychopath is the real life monster of our nightmares. These are the wife-beaters, murderers, serial killers, stalkers, rapists, sadists, pedophiles, gangsters, interrogators, and terrorists. They are usually career criminals and can amass an extensive criminal record while still in their early teens.[3]

Often showing their contempt with a sneer or smirk and with a vacant stare from cold, predatory eyes, they are dangerous, unpredictable, and easily triggered into violence. Cowardly and sadistic they tend to target the most vulnerable in society, women, children, and the elderly and disabled. Often impulsive and opportunistic, sociopaths will not hesitate to commit any type of crime and will use manipulation, intimidation, and violence to get what they want.

The malevolent psychopath can show signs of their illness as early as age three. Early warning signs include compulsive lying, fighting, stealing, bullying, bad judgment, cheating, cruelty to animals, vandalism, truancy, sexual activity, fire-setting, substance abuse, and running away from home. The malevolent psychopath is the natural born killer.

Professional Psychopaths: The malevolent psychopath is the most dangerous; however, it is the Professional Psychopath that is the most destructive. [4] While the victims of the former can range in the dozens, the victims of the professional psychopath can run into the tens of millions. These psychopaths litter history with genocides and the destruction of entire nations and empires. Historical examples include such monsters as Stalin, Pol Pot, Ivan the Terrible, and Caligula. While there are many that make it to the pinnacle of the political stage there are also such historical figures as J.P. Morgan, Randolph Hearst, and Mayer Rothschild, professional psychopaths that reach the pinnacle of the financial stage where they cause no less misery and destruction as their political counterparts.

The professional psychopath is just as malevolent, narcissistic, and remorseless, as the other stereotypes, they are just much smarter. [5] They can be found in any profession but usually governments, corporations, and religions will be thick with them.

In a corporation, the professional psychopaths are ideally suited for advancement. They can masterfully fake their abilities and credentials, us their intellect and charm to manipulate and exploit others, and generally backstab their way to high position. Once in power, their masks slip and they abuse their power and bully and sabotage their coworkers and subordinates.

In politics the professional psychopath's ruthlessness and cunning gives them a distinct advantage over any non-psychopath rival. They make charismatic leaders manipulating and brainwashing the naive, vulnerable, uneducated, or mentally weak. Mastery of lying allows them to make whatever outrageous campaign promises straight faced with, of course, no intention of keeping any of them. A life spent faking being human give them the ability to assume the roles of virtuous public servant, the perfect father, husband, advisor, mentor, and everyman. In addition when things get rough they have no inhibitions in playing dirty and readily resort to murder, assassination, persecution, war and genocide.

The third sphere of power that has traditionally attracted more than its fair share of psychopaths is religion. A quick glance at the history of religion from the bloody sacrifices of the Aztec priests, to the tortures of the Spanish Inquisitions, and through seemingly endless religious wars waged in the name of peace and love, makes their influence plainly visible to all willing to look. Since most if not all 'great' religions are constructed on falsehoods, compulsive liars make the perfect proselytizers. A look at recently created religions such as Mormonism and Scientology show their founders, Joseph Smith and L. Ron Hubbard respectively, were at least compulsive liars, and more likely full-blown psychopaths. Charismatic cult leaders such as Jim Jones and Sung Yung Moon were indeed psychopaths, while televangelist preachers that rake in millions from their gullible flocks are at best con artists of the highest caliber.

Religion's supposed *raison d'etre* of moral education and the veil of 'goodness' it bestows attracts psychopaths that use their membership in the religion as a cover, an extra sugar coating lest anyone suspect their true nature.

When psychopaths dominate and seize control of the major cultural institutions that influence a society a final type of psychopath is created.

<u>Secondary Psychopaths</u>: While the classic genetic psychopath is one who is born with whatever genetic trait that causes this pathology, there is another group of people that behave just like the classic psychopath who were not born that way but were created. Secondary psychopaths are created in two ways, through trauma and through groups.

Trauma from an accident, drug addiction, or severe physical and psychological abuse can destroy that part of the frontal cortex of the brain where empathy and conscience is processed. [6] While such individuals are a tragic reality in our society, they are in most cases just as incurable as their genetic counterparts are. The exception is in drug induced Psychopathy. Most drug addicts will behave like psychopaths since the criminality of their addiction forces them to adopt Psychopathy as a psychological survival mechanism. With drug rehabilitation, they may regain their conscience, provided the drug use did not severely damage the brain itself.

The second way in which psychopaths are created is through groups. There are certain groups that will attract psychopaths because of the opportunities of power and influence membership provides. Usually such groups will quickly become led and dominated by psychopaths. Other non-psychopathic members of these groups would have to become psychopaths in order to survive.

For example, in a street gang, sociopaths make the best leaders and therefore most gangs have a sociopath at its head. Other psychopaths are also attracted to the violence and power of a street gang and so together they create a psychopathic value system. The gang becomes a psychopathic entity. The non-psychopathic youth who must live within the territory of such a gang is given two choices -become a victim of the gang or join them. By joining the gang, the new recruit must also adopt the group's twisted value system and behave accordingly thus becoming a secondary psychopath.

Conversely, at the other end of the scale we can see the same principle at work in corporations. The money and power of a corporation attracts the cerebral and narcissistic psychopaths. In a corporate environment they have many advantages over their non-psychopathic competitors for promotion. Not surprisingly most corporations end up being run by psychopaths. As with a criminal gang, a corporation's culture adopts the twisted values of its leaders. Those who would seek employment must likewise adopt or at least appear to adopt the corporation's essentially psychopathic mindset.

What is important to understand is that a mob has no conscience. Individual members may or may not have a conscience but when they are part of a mob, they will have none. Most organizations from street gangs to corporations are mobs. It would be a mistake to place your trust in them since they can turn predatory in a moment and deprive you of time, money, sanity and livelihood.

## The Psychopath's Modus Operandi

One weakness psychopaths have is that once one studies them and begins to understand them, they become predictable. While tactics vary from one to another, most psychopaths follow a similar strategy when conning either an individual or an organization. Their strategy is as follows.

The Interview: Psychopaths are experts at *Cold Reading*. First used by psychologists to describe what phony fortune tellers do 'Cold Reading', is the ability to guess a person's personality type quickly through verbal and non-verbal communication. The technique is simple, ask questions and watch the responses. Psychopaths will Cold Read you as part of what is called the interview stage. The whole purpose of the interview is for the psychopath to size you up as a potential victim. They make mental notes of different ways they could possibly manipulate you.

Learning to say less and observe more when first meeting people is the easiest way to defend against a psychopath. In social situations, you can be congenial without having to reveal personal information that could be used against you later. Remember that getting to know you is a privilege that should be earned over time.

<u>The Seduction</u>: Should you or your organization be seen as a suitable victim, the next stage is the seduction. Based on the results of their interview the psychopath will tailor the seduction to your personality. If concerned about your appearance, they will flatter your good looks, if insecure about your education, they will flatter you about your intelligence. If greedy, they will have insider information on a get rich quick scheme, and if cowardly then only the psychopath can protect you from your fears.

On a personal level, they will shower you with praise and attention in a whirlwind romance. They make sure that being around them is fun and exciting so that you become addicted to the adrenalin rush they create. On the organizational level, they pretend to be the perfect employee, the most devout follower, the most dedicated public servant. They work to ingratiate themselves first to the doorkeepers, and finally the power holders, often by being shameless sycophants and boot lickers.

At this stage of the game the best advice is the old canard 'If it sounds too good to be true – it is.'

<u>Divide and Conquer</u>: Just as a pride of lions will seek to separate a targeted *Wilde Beast* from the rest of the herd, so psychopaths seeks to isolate their victims from the rest of humanity. They accomplish this through the tactic of divide and conquer. In a personal relationship, the psychopath will sabotage and undermine his or her victim's relationships with family and friends. Exasperated by the negative drama and costs associated with the victim, their friends and family drop out of contact leaving the victim without the support and guidance of their social group.

In an organizational setting, psychopaths are the consummate office politicians. They seek to create factions within the organization and then turn those factions against each other to create as much chaos as possible. Psychopaths swim in chaos and the more the better. Secretly they start to draw the gullible, weak minded, and fellow psychopaths to their side while intensifying their efforts to have the most talented, honest, and incorruptible members, ones that could have the strength of character to expose them, expelled. They poison the environment in a variety of ways so that everyone feels irritable, edgy, and unable to perform their jobs. Control of the organization slips into the hands of the source behind the dysfunction, the psychopath who created it all.

At this stage the only defense is to flee the situation. You cannot win this battle since the psychopath's ruthlessness will trump any counter attack you could conceive of. By the time you smell the smoke, the psychopath has already stolen the fire extinguishers.

If in a relationship, cut bait and run. In an organization, find a new job, in a nation, become an expatriate.

Fear and Tyranny: The final stage of the psychopath's strategy is tyranny, the absolute and sadistic control over his victims.

In a relationship, the honeymoon is over and the mask comes off. The psychopath suddenly becomes controlling, abusive, and violent. Instead of flattery and attention, the tactics are now fear, intimidation, extortion, and emotional blackmail.

On the organizational level, ones see benefits being cut, while time cards, production quotas, and surveillance increases. Employees become slaves, powerless and disposable cogs in a machine run for the sole benefit of the psychopaths in charge.

On the national level, countries ruled by psychopaths become corrupt and brutish police states constantly at war with created and imaginary enemies. The population becomes paranoid, neurotic, and ultimately secondary psychopaths. In a psychopathic culture, everyone must adopt a ruthless attitude as a survival strategy.

At this stage there is little chance to flee and escape safely. Instead, you may be left with few options other than to tough it out and hope for rescue or for the psychopaths to die.

## Defense Against The Psychopath

Facing Evil: One of the greatest advantages psychopaths have is that

average decent people cannot believe that such monsters truly exist.

This inability to comprehend the predator mentality is partly due to popular morality. All societies promote simplistic and idealistic morality through schools and churches that teach such platitudes as, all men are created equal, everyone has some good in them, everyone is special, and so forth. Such ideals more often serve as a cover behind which the true machinations of society can operate without evoking the suspicion of the mob.

Another reason that people cannot face evil is fear. The true nature of psychopaths is the stuff of childhood nightmares. Many people simply cannot deal with the fear this realization causes and so to sooth their nerves they revert to an infantile strategy of denial and magical thinking. If they do not acknowledge the existence of monsters, then the monsters cannot hurt them.

The first line of defense against psychopaths is acknowledging their existence. By doing so, one develops a psychological advantage. Forewarned is forearmed and having braced oneself with knowledge of predatory individuals one is better able to think clearly and thus spot the predator before he can spot you.

Once you accept the reality that human predators populate our society the next line of defense is in identifying them. Because of their abilities at camouflage and deception, psychopaths are difficult to spot. They can fool even mental health professionals. It is important to understand that everyone can be conned. If you feel you are the exception, you only make yourself more susceptible.

Recognition: A psychopath is like a smoking ember. The sooner you can spot the smoke and douse the ember the better, since after the house is on fire it is too late to contain the damage and destruction. Learn to spot the typical psychopathic character traits, and recognize their modus operandi.

Where possible do background checks and/or speak with the suspected psychopath's family and friends. Most psychopaths leave a long trail of destruction and heartbreak and will try to cover their tracks. A lack of background information is therefore as suspicious as a history of betrayals. Another of their fundamental flaws is a lack of patience and the incredible energy they use to maintain their façade. Over time, they drop their masks. Thus, one of the best methods of detecting psychopaths is to wait them out.

Once you identify someone as being a psychopath you have only two options - attack or evade.

What Not To Do: What is vital to understand is that empathy cannot defeat the psychopath. You cannot change them, you cannot reform them, you cannot find the goodness inside them, you cannot show them the way to god, and you cannot teach them about love. All these approaches are doomed to failure since psychopaths can never understand nor can they care about these concepts. While they may lead you to believe that you are getting through to them, in reality, your empathy infuriates them and far from admiring your compassion, they despise you even more. While you try to 'understand' the psychopath, they are secretly calculating how best to cause you the most suffering. One must develop a cold exterior to them and view them from a distance. Do not pity them, feel sorry for them, or sympathize with them. [7]

Attack: As a rule, the only thing that can defeat a psychopath is a bigger psychopath. However, should you feel no other recourse but to confront a psychopath your one advantage is their fear of being exposed for what they are. They have known since childhood that they are different from most people. Their whole advantage lies in the fact that they know what they are and no one else does. Exposing a psychopath takes away his or her advantage and reveals their inner corruption for all to see. However, few people have the strength and intelligence to do this successfully. While the statistical distribution of genius and idiot psychopaths mirrors the general population, even a moronic psychopath can elude and outwit an educated accuser.

Before you attempt to expose and expunge a psychopath you must be in a position of power, and you must choose the time and place. You also need to have your people briefed and ready to support you. This means creating a family and friends support group and/or joining a support group. In an organizational setting you need to have coworkers, managers, the legal department, and human resources on your side before making your move.

The Chinese strategist Sun Tzu warned against attacking an enemy who has no escape and likewise it is best not to corner a psychopath since the fight will likely be more vicious than most people can bear. Instead, use the threat of exposure to drive the psychopath away. The thought that they could be exposed at any time is unnerving and most psychopaths will give up the current game and go in search of more ignorant and vulnerable prey.

In an organization, you may have to offer not to press criminal charges if the psychopath will simply resign and never come back.

Evade: A safer and easier strategy is to evade. Once you have identified someone as a psychopath, you must cut him or her off and out of your life completely. In a relationship, you may need to change your locks, change you phone numbers and block your e-mail account, close bank accounts, get a restraining order, or move. Do not tip your hand that you are leaving. Be aware of the services of the police, law and shelters. Take self-defense and firearms training.

In conclusion, the study of Psychopathy is an important new tool not only in crime prevention, but in understanding the source behind many social ills. The more informed and aware you are of this subject the safer you and your family will be.

## **Lies & Deception**

*Genetic capacities for deception have evolved through natural selection...In conflicts between predator and prey, in struggles over scarce resources, deception confers a selective advantage. For hundreds of generations, the less cunning have left behind fewer offspring, and deceptive qualities have come to dominate the gene pool.*
Bond, Kahler, Paolicelli. *Journal of Experimental Social Psychology* 8

Deception is one of the fundamental strategies of nature. From camouflage to impersonation, the ability to deceive has been an advantage to survival. Modern man has taken this lesson to heart. Our ability to deceive has outstripped our ability to detect deception which gives liars the advantage.

The best defence against liars is to be able to tell when they are lying. Unfortunately there is no fool proof method for doing so. Even a polygraph or 'Lie Detector' is far from accurate, but by understanding the principles behind the polygraph we can get a better understanding of why it is so difficult to discern truth from fiction.

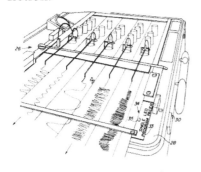

A polygraph uses sensors to record four physiological reactions and transcribe that information in the form of a graph. The reactions monitored are respiration, heart rate, blood pressure, and skin resistance. The theory is that when a person is lying he or she will inwardly feel anxiety, guilt, and fear which will in turn trigger an increase in respiration, heart rate, blood pressure, and skin perspiration (known as the Galvanic Skin

Response). However, there are three situations where lie detectors fail to give an accurate assessment.

First, many, if not most, people become anxious when being questioned or interrogated. Their anxiety may be misread as lying, when in fact it is fear of not being believed. This is known as the Othello Effect - the readings indicate fear rather than guilt.[9] While professional interviewers are aware of this and adjust their methods to compensate, it is nevertheless more art than science; hence the polygraphs' limited viability in the judicial system.

Second, lie detectors don't work on psychopaths. Without a conscience, there is no guilt, and no anxiety that would cause physiological changes. It is natural for normal people to feel some anxiety when being questioned; therefore it is the confident and smooth answers that should raise warning flags.

Thirdly, a lie detector cannot tell what *is* true or false, but only what a person *believes* is true and false. If a person believes he/she is telling the truth, even if it is false, the detector will still indicate that the person was being truthful. There is truth in the saying, 'The best liars are those that believe their own lies'.

In addition, a person can learn to control those physiological reactions that a polygraph monitors through simple biofeedback exercises. Even a person with a conscience can be easily trained to pass a polygraph.

Keeping the above drawbacks in mind, one can duplicate some of the information gathered by mechanical lie detectors through careful observation. Remember that these observations are of discomfort, fear, and doubt - reactions that may or may not be caused by guilt. No one indicator is sufficient to base a judgment on. You must observe the overall behavior and responses, test the logic, and base judgment on your own experience.

## Non-Verbal Clues To Deception

*One can lie with the mouth, but with the accompanying grimace, one nevertheless tells the truth.*
Nietzsche, *Thus Sprake Zarathustra*

Non verbal clues include movements and gestures that may indicate an inner conflict. Known as Body Language and Non-verbal Communication, knowledge of man's peculiar physical quirks have been around for ages. In the martial arts, body language that reveals an opponent's next move is called 'Telegraphing'. In gambling, a gesture that reveals whether a person is bluffing or not is known as a 'Tell'. The following lists common ways in which peoples gestures may reveal deception.

The Eyes: One way in which the eyes reveal inner emotions are through pupil dilation. The eye's pupils control the amount of light that passes through the lens of the eye by contracting under bright lighting conditions, and dilating under low. Pupil dilation is also an indication of increased brain processing. [10] The brain processes more information when thinking over a problem and when aroused or excited. This is why dilated pupils are thought to show desire. Pupil dilation is also an indicator when a person is lying. This is because lying is a more complex process than telling the truth. To tell the truth is simply memory recall, while lying requires both memory of the truth, and memory of the lie used to cover the truth. As lies multiply, the process becomes more and more complex. As a result, the pupils tend to dilate more when someone is lying.

Along with dilation, a person's blink rate will also increase when excited or aroused by visual stimuli. [11] Blink rate is the number of times the eyes blink in a minute. When excited, blinking increases. When viewing unpleasant material, and when concentrating, the blink rate slows down and staring occurs more often. Examples can

23

be found in the flirtatious batting of the eyes, and in the horrified stares of victims of violence. Increased blink rate during questioning may indicate that the topic is creating anxiety.

The final clue the eyes reveal is one that all mothers seem to know, that when hiding something, one tends to avoid eye contact. However, this clue is so universally known that professional liars know to look you straight in the eye every time they lie. Because this indicator is so universally faked, it is a suspect gesture. If someone looks you in the eye and tells you something that still does not feel right, it probably is not.

Hand Gestures: Man's first form of communication was probably a hand language based on the simple gestures the hands make when performing specific functions, for example, holding one hand palm up under the mouth while scooping toward the mouth with the other hand is universally recognized as the symbol for eating. Travelers, immigrants, and tourists still use hand gestures to communicate when no one can speak the same language. This language is so embedded in our psyches that even when speaking our bodies echo our verbal language with accompanying gestures. While the mouth can lie, the body seldom does.

Subconsciously, we sense that if we use our hands when lying their actions may not fit our words and so the use of hand gestures decreases when someone is lying.

Another common gesture using the hands that may indicate lying is a touching of the mouth or face. The hand begins towards the mouth as if subconsciously they want to stop the lie from being spoken. Since this is too obvious, the hand is redirected to the cheeks, chin, eyes, or forehead. The closer the hand comes to the mouth the greater the lie.

Body Gestures: When a person is lying they tend to increase their use of the shrug gesture and raised eyebrows. Using this gesture is a way of saying 'I don't know', or 'It has got nothing to do with me'. This is an attempt to distance themselves from the lies they are telling. The shrug is always a negative gesture to what the person is saying.

Another indicator of lying is a restless shifting or squirming as though the body wanted to escape. Most people control this urge to move but even still, the body will tend to make subtle movements. The restless tapping of a foot, bouncing knee, or raping of the fingers on a tabletop are usually indicators that a person is uncomfortable with the subject matter.

Voice: Natural speech is more than words alone; it consists of auditory tones, rhythms, and cadences. An indicator of how important rhythm and tone are to communication can be seen in those suffering from a rare brain disorder. Known as aphasia, the portion of the brain that processes verbal word meanings is inoperative. As a result, aphasics develop an enhanced ability to detect a "feeling tone" which enables them to recognize when someone is lying. [12] While the average person cannot detect the subtle nuances of another's voice like an aphasic, we can listen for certain clues.

When under stress, people speak a little higher than normal and there is a tendency for the voice to break and become raspy. Voice level or volume lowers when saying things the speaker would rather not say.

If a person is uncertain or nervous about his answers, he may incorporate a rising 'question' tone in his speech especially on the last word of each sentence. This tone is similar to the tone used when asking a question such as 'who?' only less pronounced.

Speech patterns change when people lie. There is a tendency not to use contractions. For example, 'I didn't do it' is more believable then 'I did not do it'. The latter is an indication the speech is carefully thought out, rather than flowing spontaneously. Other clues that indicate a person is thinking out his answers are false starts (whereby he person starts with one explanation and suddenly changes to something else) and frequent pauses and stalling vocalizations: the 'ahs' and 'uhms' between sentences.

Physiological Clues: A polygraph measures physiological changes caused by the fear and shame a normal person would feel when lying. Fear triggers the *Flight or Flight* response in the sympathetic nervous system which increases blood pressure, respiration, perspiration, and heart rate. Some of these effects are visible to the careful observer. These include, increased breath rate, sweating, blushing, a vein that begins to throb on the face, forehead, or neck, and a trembling in the hands or jaw.

## Logical Clues To Deception

When examining information that seems suspicious, look for contradictions in logic such as timeframe, continuity, and probabilities.

Contradiction in Time-line: Unless you have actually experienced a particular activity or event, it would be unlikely that you would know what timetable that event or activity followed. By questioning other witnesses or experts in that field, you can get an approximate timetable and compare it to that given by the suspect. For example, your teenaged son or daughter says they were at the library until ten, but you find out the library closed at nine. Another mistake in time-line is expanding or contracting time, either too much occurred in too short a time, or not enough occurred in too long a time.

Contradiction in Continuity: This is where a person knows something he should not have knowledge of, or does not know something he should. This tactic is used in criminal investigations by keeping secret certain details about a crime. Then when questioning a suspect, investigators watch to see if he reveals knowledge of such details, details that only the guilty party would know. Another ancient tactic is to pretend not to know some piece of information that you have already verified, and see if the person's answers match the information you know to be true.

Contradictions in Procedure: Every job and occupation follows rules and procedures. Anyone describing events that are contrary to the standard procedures are likely giving false witness unless there is a logical reason why those procedures were not being followed. If the enemy is really about to launch an attack where are their baggage trains? On the other hand, if peace overtures are sincere why are they mobilizing troops to the border?

The most obvious flaw in logic is when something is it too good to be true, the solution too easy, and the answer too simple. Age and experience teach that nothing worthwhile is easy, or simple.

## Behavioral Clues To Deception

*The longer the explanation, the bigger the lie.*
Chinese Proverb

When someone is accused of a misdeed, there are three possible responses: redirection, confrontation, and examination.

Redirection: If a person's initial response to an accusation is to blame someone else, he or she is either immature, or has a guilty conscience. This is the tactic children use when accused of a misdeed - "It wasn't me it was Timmy!". A variation is to insist that because some other parties are involved or committed similar transgressions therefore the individual's guilt is absolved. Another form of redirection is mock assistance in finding the 'true culprit' by proposing alternate theories and scenarios.

Confrontation: When the accused responds with indignation and counter charges it may be genuine, or a ruse to draw attention away from the accusation and place the focus onto the accusers. This is common strategy used by defense lawyers whom, rather than dwell on the question of their client's innocence, attack the methods and motivations of the accusers.

Investigation: When wrongly accused, innocent people are interested in exposing the truth because the truth is obviously on their side. They will want to examine details since by careful investigation the truth of their innocence is revealed. The guilty however would prefer to gloss-over the details and try to block any investigation. More often the guilty are revealed through their cover-up of evidence rather than the actual evidence itself.

Learning and applying these simple observations to the people you are dealing with will not allow you to spot all deceptions but it should be able raise a red flag when something is suspicious.

## Anger And Aggression

*The more that is known about the mechanisms underlying aggression, the greater the probability that it will be possible to contribute to the inhibition of hostile behavior in order to protect humankind from destruction. Thus, these are eminently practical reasons for the study of aggressive behavior.*
K.E. Moyer, *Violence and Aggression*

The premier technique of self-defense is to evade conflict, or to influence the course of events to dissipate the conflict before it arises. This is known as 'Winning the Battle without Drawing the Sword'.[13] To accomplish this strategy it is important to understand the causes, and recognize the behavior patterns associated with anger and aggression.

## Causes Of Aggression

Among animals and humans, aggressive behaviors are cause by the following factors. [14]

### Territory

People can become irritable and aggressive if they feel their territory has been threatened or invaded. Each person stakes out and defends several territories. These are:

Intimate Space: Is an imaginary shell extending from the surface of the skin to a distance of four to six inches. This space is reserved for family, and close friends. Only under special conditions are strangers allowed to enter this space, such as doctors, therapists, and sports coaches.

Personal Space: Personal Space extends beyond intimate space another two to three feet depending on cultural norms. For example, the English prefer dealing with strangers at arm's length, while Arabs are accustomed to be in closer, at elbow's length. Personal space is shared with friends, co-workers, and family. A stranger entering personal space makes most people feel uncomfortable even if not considered a threat.

Home Range:  Is the area where one lives. The boundaries of a person's personal living area are proportionate to the person's economic status within a particular society. A homeless person's home territory may extend no further than the space of a sleeping bag, while, at the other end of the spectrum, the home territory of financial moguls can extend to hundreds of miles. The people and possessions found within a home territory are also considered the property of the estate. A mate is territory and will be defended against the threat of other suitors, likewise children are defended against strangers, and possessions defended against theft.[15]

The Hunting Grounds:  Any area that provides enough resources to survive on can be a hunting ground. For hunting and gathering societies, the hunting ground is the amount of territory needed to provide enough game and edible plants to feed the tribe. For pastoral groups the hunting ground would consist of enough grassland to feed their flocks, likewise a farmer's hunting grounds are his fields and so on. In the urban environment, the hunting ground can be the office, factory, storefront or street corner. Executives claim an office, corporations claim a market share, drug gangs claim a neighborhood, and prostitutes claim a street corner. The boundaries are different, but the instinct is the same.

## Inter-Male

Some aggressive behavior is present in all group interaction as a means of establishing group hierarchy. This type of aggression is used to dominate rivals within the group thereby establishing a pecking order. The animal able to dominate all the others becomes the leader, the animal able to dominate all but the leader, becomes second in the chain of command and so on. Confrontations motivated by inter-male aggression usually end the moment one of the rivals withdraws or displays submissive behavior. They seldom end in actual violence. Leadership goes to the most aggressive, in war, this is usually the strongest and bravest, in society it is usually the loudest and most brazen.

## Sex Related

Aggression is also a component in the competition for mating partners. All animals have the instinct to compete with each other for mates to ensure species survival through genetic diversity. Those unable to compete for a mate may be sick or have some genetic flaw that would thus be bred out of the species. In humans, you can observe similar behavior by placing an attractive female among a group of men. Almost immediately, men of breeding age begin to strut and posture more aggressively, talk louder and gestures become more exaggerated. Each man, consciously or not, is competing for the woman's attention by showing off his health, vigor, and machismo, the human equivalent of a gorilla beating his chest. With primates and humans alike, the most dominant males have the most mating partners.[16]

## Fear Induced

It could be argued that all forms of aggression are the result of fear. Fear of losing what you have or not getting what you want, fear of others, and fear of death. Another reason may lie within the brain itself. Pain, fear, and aggression (among others) are regulated by the limbic system. Stimulation of one of these functions may cause a crossover stimulation of the other functions so that pain induces fear and fear induces aggression.

## Maternal/Paternal

Maternal aggression is the instinctive defense of offspring against real or perceived threats. As a result, new mothers have a heightened sense of territoriality. They are also more likely to interpret anyone entering their territory as a threat, and are more likely to respond with greater than normal aggression.

## Irritability

There are a number of factors that will increase irritable aggression such as hunger, thirst, exhaustion, discomfort, frustration, worry, and pain.

## Alcohol And Drugs

Scientists and nonscientists alike have long recognized the association between alcohol consumption and aggressive behavior. Alcohol weakens brain mechanisms that normally restrain impulsive behaviors, including inappropriate aggression. By impairing information processing, alcohol can also lead a person to misjudge social cues, thereby overreacting to a perceived threat. Simultaneously, a narrowing of attention may lead to an inaccurate assessment of the future risks of acting on an immediate violent impulse. Many drugs such as cocaine and methamphetamines have similar effects and in addition to promoting aggression, paranoia and violence can even trigger psychotic episodes. One should always be aware that people under the influence of these substances are more likely to be aggressive and violent.

---

### Alcohol

Based on published studies, up to 86 percent of homicide offenders, 37 percent of assault offenders, 60 percent of sexual offenders, up to 57 percent of men and 27 percent of women involved in marital violence, and 13 percent of child abusers were drinking at the time of the offense. 17

---

## Predatory

In many circumstances aggressive behavior is rewarded, and is therefore more likely to occur. In environments where resources are scarce aggression ensures survival. In such an environment children learn to grab what they can, when they can, or else do without. This applies first to food and attention then, as children become adults, to mating partners, money, jobs, status, and power. In poor and overcrowded environments, only those who fiercely pursue their goals, allowing nothing and no one to get in their way, have any chance of attaining them. Thus, aggression becomes an instrument, a method to achieve goals and gain rewards.

## Signs Of Aggression

*Domination is the goal of aggression, not destruction.*
Desmond Morris, *The Naked Ape*

Animals settle disputes with what is called *Threat Display Behavior*. This includes showing the teeth, puffing up, raising the hair and other actions designed to make the animal look fierce and formidable. Rarely do animals of the same species come to blows and even then the fighting is more symbolic than lethal.

Humans also use threatening displays to intimidate rivals. Like animals, when human rivals come to blows, the injuries are usually minor. It is usually when men are in groups that serious injuries or deaths occur. Nations also use threat display behavior by staging war games and practicing maneuvers near the borders of rival nations, otherwise known as sword rattling. Before hostilities devolve into open violence, one can usually recognize some of the following behaviors indicative of aggressive intent.

Posturing: Like many species, humans attempt to make themselves appear bigger and more fearsome than they really are. This is done by puffing up and expanding the chest, letting the arms hang away from the body and spreading the legs. To appear fiercer men walk with a swagger, often thrusting the head forwards.

Staring: The stare is a universal signal that can indicate either sexual or physical aggression.

Gesturing: Anger stimulates the sympathetic nervous system that triggers the *Fight or Flight* response. If the person does not attack or flee, the energy level will rise to intolerable levels and must be dissipated through what is known as displacement behavior. In humans, this takes the form of mock combat such as sharp sudden movements, punching the air or inanimate objects, jumping and stomping the feet, throwing things, threats, making loud noises, yelling and screaming.

These are the signals for raging anger. When a person is less angry or suppressing his anger, the symptoms are similar, just less pronounced. Instead of grimacing, there may be a facial tick or a scowling gesture. Instead of a wide eyed stare, a reduction in the blink rate. Stomping the feet becomes a tapping of the foot, punching the air becomes a rapping of the fingers.

To recognize the danger signals of imminent attack look for the following: profuse sweating, rapid deep breathing, red face, thin lips drawn back in a grimace or scowl, bulging eyes and intense stare. Body language includes clenched fists, rapid cutting movements, blowing up in size to appear larger.

If dealing with a person exhibiting these signs, stay calm and appear non-threatening. Stay discreetly out of range of a sucker punch, slowly back away and prepare for a charge.

## Preventing Anger

Everyone will lose his or her temper from time to time without really meaning to cause harm. This is a part of the human condition. People may be angry with you even if you did nothing wrong or posed no threat. The following are strategies to deal with the occasional angry outbursts from others.

*Become Like Water.* This oft quoted Taoist maximum works against angry outbursts by calmly absorbing and dissipating the anger. If someone is yelling, do not interrupt. Allow the person to vent his or her anger until its energy has been exhausted. Trying to stop the anger or running away only bottles up the anger. Listen calmly and do not respond immediately to every accusation.

Angry people expect others to go on the defensive and are therefore prepared to press the attack. By remaining calm, you will prevent the conflict from escalating into a vicious circle of mutual recrimination. Eventually the person's anger will subside.

When the anger has been expressed and the person is waiting for a reply, deliberately lower your voice and speak calmly, this forces the other person to tone down their voice in order to hear what you are saying.

Ask the person what you can do to help solve the problem. This shows your concern, which reinforces the person's self-esteem. Afterwards you may calmly agree or disagree on some of the points outlined, so that the person feels he or she is taken seriously and saves face.

Feeding anger with more anger is a waist of time that can never accomplish anything positive and is a drain on your resources of time and energy.

## Staying Calm

*The angry man will defeat himself in battle, as well as in life.*
Japanese Proverb

It is a myth that repressing anger causes it to be bottled up inside only to eventually explode into violence. Research shows just the opposite. The non-expression of anger, and redirection into non-destructive activities, is indicative of intelligence and self-discipline. Anger and aggression are learned behaviors; it controls us only because we learned to let it, we can also unlearn it.

Another reason to learn to control one's temper is that enraging the enemy is a well-known military tactic. This tactic works because an angry opponent cannot think clearly, an inexcusable mistake in any situation where a rational assessment of the situation is required. History records thousands of battles where commanders lost control and charged off to their deaths, dooming their men and country with them. You should not allow personal feelings to put yourself at such a disadvantage.

When you feel you may be on the verge of losing your temper follow these steps:

1) Stop what you are doing.

2) Breath in slow and deep, hold the breath for three seconds, and then exhale slowly. Repeat the breaths two or three times.
3) Relax your face and shoulders. Loosen up.
4) Count to ten. (An old cliché that actually works.)

If this does not work, then leave the situation, go for a walk, exercise, or engage in some other physical activity that will dissipate the excess energy.

Much of the anger and aggression we encounter are the result of the pressures and stress of living in crowded and highly competitive environments. Understanding the causes and recognizing the signals, one can avoid much of the senseless hostility that stalks our personal jungles.

## Fear

*Courage is resistance to fear, mastery of fear, not absence of fear.*
Mark Twain

Fear is nature's guardian that warns and alerts us to real or perceived dangers. Knowledge of fear is essential to survival since fear can sabotage the ultimate weapon of our intelligence making years of self-defense and emergency survival training useless. This is why understanding how to train our response to fear is one of the most important survivals skills.

Fear of a real or imagined threat triggers the autonomic nervous system to prepare the human organism for sudden and frantic activity. Known as the *Fight or Flight* response, this survival mechanism prepares the body to either, flee a potential predator through the hazards of open terrain in a race for survival, or to face the predator in a life or death battle. In either event, the body must be able to call on every ounce of energy and numb any pain that might interfere with running or fighting.

35

The autonomic nervous system consists of the sympathetic and the parasympathetic nervous systems. The sympathetic is responsible for preparing the body for action, while the parasympathetic is responsible for preserving energy.

A threat will cause the sympathetic nervous system to signal the endocrine system to release hormones causing a series of reactions:

- Increased heart rate to increase the flow of blood throughout the body
- Respiration is affected either by hyperventilating or holding in the breath
- Arteries dilate to increase blood flow to the surface to provide the anticipated demand of oxygen from the muscles. (This can be observed by the face becoming flushed)
- Body temperature increases producing sweat, and body hair may become erect
- Blood flow to the digestive organs is restricted to provide more blood to the muscles, the stomach may suddenly feel nauseous, and vomiting is not uncommon

In addition, the adrenal glands increase the availability of blood sugar (glucose) to release stored energy. This process is akin to revving the engine and feeding nitrous oxide into the fuel mixture. Endorphins, whose molecular structure closely resembles morphine, are released into the brain to numb the anticipated pain of injuries and fatigue.

However, the body cannot maintain this heightened state of readiness for long. Soon the parasympathetic system is triggered into action to counter all the changes caused by the sympathetic system: Heart rate is reduced, breathing becomes shallow, gasping, with frequent sighing, and the mouth becomes dry. Blood is drawn in towards the inner body restricting the flow to the brain, which may cause dizziness, spots in peripheral vision, and fainting. The face becomes pale and waxy and body temperature drops. The digestive system may suddenly kick in resulting a bowel movement or release of the bladder.

For a short period the two systems alternate back and forth in a battle for control of the body's nervous system, a battle always won in the end by the parasympathetic. All these opposing responses can take place in a matter of minutes.

Fear prepares the body for action. The accompanying increase in strength, pain threshold, and endurance can be lifesaving assets. It is not something we want to do without. However, too often fear turns to panic and it is then that fear becomes a liability.

The problem exists not in erasing fear entirely, but rather a delicate balance of enhanced awareness and body readiness, combined with a detached self-control. There are three quick techniques to help you lessen fear.

## Breath Control

Fear triggers the instinct to make as little noise as possible and focus on the possible threat. This instinct was a benefit to our ancient ancestors huddled in the bush and hearing a twig snap in the darkness signaling an approaching predator. To make as little noise as possible we do two things, we freeze, and hold our breath.

To reduce system noise made by the respiratory system we either hold our breath or breathe shallowly. However, holding the breath for too long while the sympathetic nervous system is stimulated causes a sudden demand for oxygen. The signal to breathe is overstated and, instead of regular breathing, a person may begin to hyper-ventilate.

Hyperventilating reduces the amount of carbon dioxide in the bloodstream. The body needs a certain amount of $CO_2$ and a rapid drop of it constricts blood flow to many vital organs. Constriction of blood vessels in the brain will cause dizziness, disorientation, and may lead to loss of consciousness. Reduced blood flow to the heart muscle may lead to chest pains. The high oxygen level can make one nervous and edgy, and cause a feeling of `pins and needles', muscle spasms, nervous twitches, and even convulsions. The effect of a lack of $CO_2$ also contributes to panic attacks.

Breath control is the best technique to reduce fear. Simply being aware of the tendency to hold your breath when frightened will help you re-establish normal breathing rhythms.

Whenever you feel frightened or anxious you should establish a regular deep breathing pattern. Focus on your abdomen and take three short breaths holding each for one second before exhaling. On the fourth breath, begin deep breathing at a medium tempo. Inhale as slowly as possible up to a count of five, then hold the breath in for a count of three, then exhale for a count of five. Be sure that the length of inhalation is equal to the exhalation.[18] Abdominal breathing will help you remain calm and reduce feelings of fear.

An old home remedy to treat hyperventilation is to breath into a paper bag. We breathe out more carbon dioxide than oxygen so after a couple of breaths the air in the paper bag will contain more carbon dioxide which in turn will be inhaled back into the lungs and help balance the oxygen/CO2 levels and return breathing to normal.

**Caution:** Medical conditions, like asthma and heart attacks can be confused with hyperventilation. In such cases, reducing oxygen and increasing carbon dioxide can be deadly.

## Relax

The instinct to freeze when frightened results in tense muscles which will interfere with natural reactions and adds to the anxiety by reinforcing fear in a bio feedback loop. To break this loop you need to relax and loosen up. The first place to start is with the shoulders. Most people will raise their shoulders and pull their chins in when frightened. Pull your shoulders down and relax the muscles of the neck and shoulders. Do a couple of quick shoulder and neck rolls then shake out your arms and hands. Pull your head up and chin out. This posture is associated with confidence and will help dispel anxiety.

## Movement

The instinct to freeze when frightened is epitomized in the metaphor of a deer caught in the headlights. Startled by a car traveling down the road, a deer will often freeze in the middle of the road to its demise rather than run off into the safety of the bush. Likewise, many people will also freeze into inaction during a threatening situation. To break this instinct one should simply move. Rather than just wait in dread, go into action. Either go to the rescue or evacuate the scene. Doing something will lessen the dread of fear and help to restore confidence.

Whether you are in an accident, natural disaster or predatory attack, remember to breath, relax, and take action to ensure your and your family's safety.

## Crime Prevention

*In social and professional relationships, the attitude is the same as that of the warrior, even when there is no discord. The mindfulness to observe the dynamic of situations, even in a group, is the art of war.* Yagyu Munenori, *The Book of Family Traditions in the Art of War*

## Awareness

The first step in crime prevention is to develop an awareness and presence of mind to spot potential dangers in advance and take steps to avoid them. Naturally, the degree of alertness you should employ depends on your environment. At home, the workplace and friend's homes you can of course drop your guard, however, when traveling or when out in public your guard should be up.

When out in strange surroundings, stay alert, walk with a purpose, and be attentive to your surroundings. If you feel suspicious of the area or people around you prepare yourself mentally for an attack.

Think of a plan of action you would follow if you were to be attacked. Consider where you could run to for help such as the nearest police station, retail shop or restaurant.

When entering a public area, do a quick scan of your surroundings for possible trouble. Make a mental note of anyone too loud and obnoxious, the drunks, and the brooding loners. Note exits, cull-de-sacks, and always sit facing the entrance.

## Posture

Another component of awareness and deterrent is posture. Your posture is part of your body language. Good posture and a solid fluid walk communicate to people around you a sense of confidence and strength. Criminals often target victims that appear weak and easy to intimidate. Consciously or instinctively, they tend to choose people whose body language communicates a weak and vulnerable disposition. Good posture sends out signals that indicate strength, confidence, and awareness, thereby helping to prevent an attack. Most criminals would think twice about attacking someone with such a confident posture and would simply wait for a more suitable victim to come by. 19

## Safe Distance

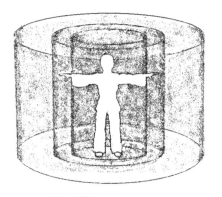

Safe Distance is the minimum distance you should maintain between you and a suspicious person or car. This distance is between four to eight feet away from you. The reason for keeping safe distance is that there is a time lapse in the nervous system between perception and reaction (approximately 0. 5 seconds). This means that if a stranger can come closer than Safe Distance, then that stranger could 'sucker pinch' or 'blind side' (a sudden un-provoked attack) you before you have time to react. However, maintaining safe distance, forces a potential attacker to take two steps towards you first before he can hit you. This gives an alert person enough time to evade and escape or counter-attack.

If a potential attacker moves in close tell him or her to keep their distance. Do not be embarrassed to shout at people to back away if you feel threatened or uncomfortable. If they continue to move closer, keep backing away to maintain the Safe Distance while demanding they back off. Any further advances towards you should then be interpreted as an attack and you would need to react accordingly. (See Hand-to-Hand Combat p. 143)

## Street Smarts

Darwinian socialism dictates that when resources become scarce, there will be a fierce competition to survive. [20] Such environments include deserts, wilderness, swamps and rain forests. In an urban setting these would be the poorer neighborhoods with high unemployment and street crime, towns or rural areas subject to environment depletion and economic depression as well as whole nations subjected to limited or restricted resources under political dictatorships.

The common factor is scarcity and difficulty of acquiring basic survival needs. In such an environment, anyone not part of the immediate family or clan is a competitor and therefore the enemy. The first question for outsiders is always, 'What do you want?' and 'What do I get?'

Based on this cynical if not practical attitude, street smarts is nothing more than understanding that every encounter with another person is a small battle for survival. In such an environment, anyone that acts friendly and takes an interest in your welfare is out to use you. On the street, he may be a mugger, pimp, pickpocket, or rapist. In business, he may be an embezzler, con artist, or crook. In the wilderness, he may be a bandit who will try to lead you into an ambush, or is sizing up your wealth and strength in order to return later with reinforcements. Any stranger making contact for any reason is suspicious and best avoided until you can discover the real reasons for them approaching you.

If you need help from strangers, you must state that you are willing to negotiate compensation for their assistance. To do otherwise would raise the same suspicions you should have if someone approached you under the guise of friendliness or dire need. In such environments, no one will feel sorry for you or take pity on you. If you need help or guidance, you need to pay, or threaten.

## Crime Prevention Strategy

Most crimes follow a four-stage progression: Opportunity, Interview, Positioning, and Attack. Before a predator can attack, he or she needs an Opportunity, a potential victim or target at a time and location that is advantageous to the criminal.

The Interview is the stage in which the predator tries to gauge the level of resistance or compliance the potential victim may offer, or the security measures in place around a potential target. An assertive response at this stage, or the display of a strong defense, will often result in the predator breaking off from the intended target to search for one more compliant or vulnerable.
The Positioning stage is just that, finding the best position from which to launch an attack designed to overwhelm the victim. If a predator has been successful in the previous three stages, he or she will now make the physical Attack. However, a predator may still call off the attack if the victim is able to create enough commotion and put up a stiff resistance.

Interrupting or stopping the predator at any of the first three stages can prevent an attack. The following crime prevention advice uses counter measures to prevent opportunity, avoid the interview, escape the position, and counter the attack.

## Home Safety & Defense

*First, make one's defense impregnable, then wait for the enemy to make a mistake.*
Sun Tzu, *The Art of War*

The first step to denying criminals an opportunity at your home is to prepare some security measures.

Doors and Windows: Doors and windows provide a false sense of security since most can be broken using a good kick. Without the threat of police response, glass windows and sliding doors offer no defense against intruders. In time of civil disorder, natural disasters, or power blackouts, your home will be vulnerable.

The first defense then is to improve the integrity of the home. Foremost is to have solid core, hardwood or metal doors on all exterior entrances complete with heavy-duty doorframes and dead-bolt locks. Even a solid door can be easily opened with a crowbar unless the doorframe is solid as well.

Make sure all potential entrances are secure including neighboring structures such as garages, which are a favorite target for burglars particularly if they have a door connecting the garage to the house.

Even if you have a CCTV (Closed Circuit Television) camera at the entrance, also install a fisheye lens peephole so that during a power blackout you can still check who is at the door without opening the door.

Windows may need burglar bars or grates to prevent entry, but one danger is that they can prevent escape in case of a fire. Consult with local fire safety standards before you install burglar bars. Burglar bars installed on exit doors or windows of sleeping rooms must be equipped with an approved quick release device that allows them to be opened from the inside without the use of a key, separate tool or any special knowledge or effort.

Equip all entrances and garages with motion sensor lights and if possible, have an extra switch for all exterior lights in the master bedroom.

If you have the sliding patio-style doors, install a patio door bar (commonly called a 'Charley Bar'). These doors are easy to jimmy and usually have poor quality locks. Many can also be simply lifted up off their rails and removed.

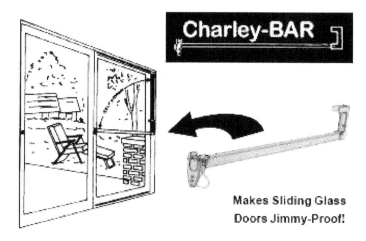

Makes Sliding Glass
Doors Jimmy-Proof!

Leave on a light and a radio or television when you leave the house. Before breaking into a house a burglar will stop and listen for sounds of occupation, the noise from the TV or radio may act as a deterrent. Draw the curtains or blinds at night.

Should you return home and discover signs of entry do not enter the house or call out. Whoever entered your home may still be there, busy either stealing or perhaps waiting for you to return home. Instead, go to a neighbor or public area and phone the police.

Keys and Locks: Change all the locks on exterior doors when you move into a new house or apartment. Previous tenants, their friends, and neighbors may all have keys to your front door.

Do not leave spare house keys under the doormat or in the planter. Burglars routinely check these places.

In many apartment complexes, property management keeps a copy of the key to your apartment. The reason is in case of an emergency or for maintenance purposes; they may need to access your apartment even if you are not home. The danger is that you never know who has access to these keys, and thus can enter your apartment at any time. Building maintenance workers come from the lower economical and educational backgrounds and such jobs are often one of a few employment opportunities for convicted criminals and parolees. Property management companies seldom do background checks and so a recently hired convicted rapist could just walk into the office and steal or make a copy of your door key that he can use days or years later to enter your home.

To protect yourself ask to see where the keys are stored and what security measures are in place. For example, are they stored in a safe or locked cabinet where only the senior manager has a key, or are they hung on pegs in the open or in an unlocked closet.

If the property management company requires a copy of your house key it is usually written into the rental agreement and so if you change your lock without providing a copy key to the management office you will be in violation. However, if you do not think the security seems inadequate to protect you and your family then ignore the rental agreement and change the locks. Your safety outweighs a rental agreement.

At the very least have another strong lock installed that can only be locked from the inside and does not require an outside key. This way you can ensure that while you are at home no one can silently enter with the front door key.

Apartments: In high-rise apartment buildings remember to lock the balcony doors and install a Charley bar even if you do not live on the ground floor since it may be possible to climb from one balcony to another.

Get to know the other people on your floor so that you have someone to run to in case of emergency.

Never remain alone in an apartment laundry room, mailroom, or parking garage.

Do not enter an elevator if you are suspicious of the occupants, wait for the next one. When on an elevator, stand close to the door, if you do not like the looks of the person getting on, you can quickly dash out before the doors close.

If you are attacked in an elevator, push all the floor buttons. This means the elevator will stop at every floor giving you a greater chance of escaping or calling for help. Do not push the emergency stop button. This will stop the elevator between floors with you and your assailant. Most tenants are so accustomed to false alarms they are not likely to be concerned by the elevator alarm sounding again.

Strange Noises: To become accustomed to the strange noises that one hears at night after moving into a new house or apartment do the following exercise: First turn on all the lights and, with a friend if necessary, make sure the house is empty by checking every room and closet. Then lie down in your bedroom with your eyes closed and listen to the various sounds around you. Try to identify unusual or strange noises by tracking the source. In this way, you will be able to recognize suspicious noises from the everyday sounds made by the building. Then if you are awakened in the night by a strange noise of an intruder, you will not confuse it for the everyday sounds made by the building and vice versa.

Strangers: Should a stranger comes to your door asking to use the phone because of an emergency, offer to make the call yourself, but do not allow the person to enter your home. A common ploy is for a disheveled and bleeding 'accident victim' to beg for assistance. Once the door is open, the accomplices rush in afterwards. If the person is truly injured, he or she will be just as safe sitting on your doorstep while you phone for help.

Delivery/Repairmen: Request identification from all delivery and repair men. Phone the company to verify their description. If you feel there is something suspicious then look up the number in the public directory rather than the number that may appear on the I.D. or invoice since there may be accomplices answering the phone.

Valuable items that could be pocketed should be removed from the working area before the repairperson arrives. Lead him directly to the area that is in need of repairs. Do not allow him to wander about the house or follow you around. Be friendly but leave the repairperson alone to do the work.

Do not talk about intimate and familiar subjects. If he makes obvious sexual overtures, then say that your boyfriend, husband, or son, who works as a, firefighter, cop, or professional boxer, will be home shortly. If he continues to make advances, threaten to call his company and lodge a complaint. If still not discouraged, make pretence to slip away and run to a neighbor or safe area and phone police.

---

Statistics show 65.8 percent of burglaries occurred at residences; most residential burglaries (62.0 percent) occurred during the daytime, and that 50 percent of rapes occur within the victim's home. [21]

---

Obscene Phone Calls: There are certain individuals, usually men, who derive excitement and pleasure from harassing innocent victims through the telephone. Most are smart enough to use payphones or prepaid phone cards, so even though the phone company keeps a record of all calls on your phone, they may still not be able to identify the caller.

Most obscene phone calls are not a prelude to actual attacks and are just annoying. However, if threats of violence are made towards persons or property, this is a serious offence and you should call the local police immediately.

Never admit on the phone, or at the door that you are alone. Hang up the instant you realize it is an obscene call. Do not yell, scream, blow a whistle, or engage in any conversation, as this is more likely to encourage the caller. A non-reaction will discourage callers that enjoy hearing fear in, or abuse from, their victims.

If calls continue, keep a written record of the date, time, and what was said. Notify your Phone Company and police. Get call identification, call blocking, or use the *69 button function to trace the last call. Contact your phone company for more information about these services. Do not attempt to call the offender.

Safe Room:  Ancient castles had a redoubt, a place of last refuge in which to retreat and hope for reinforcements. In an apartment or house, one can also build a redoubt or 'safe room' to retreat to if intruders have already entered the home. In addition to defense against intruders, having a Safe Room can also be a lifesaver in the event of a natural or manmade disaster. (See Preparing for Disasters p. 171) A safe room is also a critical requirement for women and families who are being stalked. (See Stalkers p. 91)

The best location to designate a safe room would be in or near the master bedroom, since the most likely time you would be surprised by an intruder is when you are sleeping. A bedroom with a connecting bathroom is best. Be sure to instruct other members of the family and especially children that should any emergency occur when they are home alone that they should run for the safe room, lock the door, dial 9-1-1 and wait until you or emergency personnel arrive. This will give parents some peace of mind knowing that in the event of a serious situation the children would have a plan to find relative safety.

Construction: A safe room needs to be equipped with a strong exterior type door  Most interior doors are useless for preventing entry since they are lightly constructed and can be easily kicked in. Buy a solid wood or steel composite door normally used as an exterior door and have this installed in place of your regular interior door. A door is only as strong as its frame so you will probably have to reinforce your existing doorframe as well. Finally install two strong bolt locks that can only be locked from the inside. Do not bother with door chains and other "Different Distance" locks that allow you to open the door only a couple of inches, as they are useless. Instead, use floor bars and foot locks. The stronger you can make the entrance to your safe room the better.

If your safe room has external windows that can be accessed from the ground or adjoining structure you should reinforce them as well. Also, install heavy curtains to ensure that no one from the outside can see what is happening in your safe room or can tell how many people are inside by watching the shadows on the curtains.

Equipment: The room should have a telephone. A cell phone would be best in case the intruders have cut your landline or if a major disaster has cut power in your area. A Short Wave or Citizen Band radio may work as a last resort if the cell phone services are disrupted.

Store one or more weapons to use as a last line of defense should an intruder succeed in breaking into the safe room. Your safe room is also a good place to store an emergency survival kit in the event of a natural disaster or emergency.

Finally, if you have surveillance equipment installed as part of a home alarm system make sure you have a monitor installed in your safe room so that you can monitor what is going on in and outside your property from the safety of your safe room.

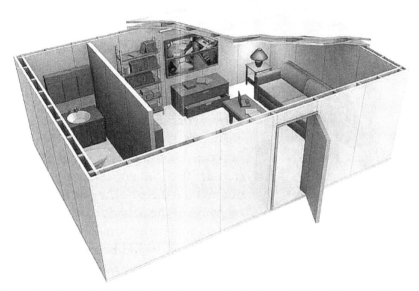

Example of a professional built safe room that is also reinforced to second as a storm shelter.

Defense Against Home Intrusion: If strange noises are coming from outside of the house, and, if it is possible to reach the light switches without being spotted, then turn on the outside lights and phone police.

If you are awake when an intruder breaks in through the front door, quietly run out the back door. Do not allow yourself to be trapped inside your home alone where there is little likelihood of anyone coming to your aid. Screams coming from your house, even if heard by neighbors, are likely to be shrugged off as coming from the television or a domestic dispute.

If you hear noises coming from inside the house, do not immediately turn on the interior lights. The intruder is in unknown territory while you are in your own element, the darkness works to your advantage. Stay hidden, lock the bedroom door or retreat to a safe room. If you have a weapon in the bedroom get it.

If you are alone and you hear movement in the house you can say aloud "John get the shotgun and see what that noise is while I phone the police." this bluff might succeed in scaring the intruder off. Unless he knows your habits, he will not take the chance that 'John' and the shotgun are not real. The surest way to tip off an intruder that you are alone is to call out 'Who's there?' The normal response to the sounds of movement, if there was really someone else living in the house, would be to call out that person's name.

If you awake to find an intruder in your bedroom, pretend to remain asleep, do not get up and confront the intruder. If he believes you are asleep, he may rob the room and simply leave, but if you are awake, you become a threat that may elicit a violent response.

## Bad Neighbors

In survival, the greatest potential threats are usually the ones closest to you. A potential source of danger and misery are your neighbors and chances are that some are either criminals, mentally unstable, or psychopaths. Living next door to these types of people can make your life a living hell and even become life threatening.

If you plan to move to a new home, take extra time to check out the neighborhood and try to find out if there are any good reasons to avoid moving in. Ask your realtor if the neighborhood has a tenant/homeowner' s association or community guidelines that tend to prevent bad neighbors from moving in.

Knock on a couple of neighborhood doors and speak with the locals. Introduce yourself and explain that you are thinking of moving into the area and you were wondering if the neighborhood was safe for your children or for single women. If there are serious problems with some of the people living in the area you will soon find it out.

Drive by at night and see if things change after dark. An area may seem quite innocent during the day but can become a trolling ground for street prostitutes and drug dealers at night.

If you get a bad feeling about the place or neighbors, and you have a choice, then find another place to move. If you have no choice on housing or if new neighbors move in, and you find yourself being harassed or infringed upon here are a few actions you can take.

Diplomacy: The first approach is to be diplomatic. Make sure you have an accurate assessment and that you are not overreacting. Talk to other neighbors to find out if they feel as strongly about the problem as you do. Also, ensure that you are not likewise in some contradiction to community ordinance or standard that would undermine your own claims of being the innocent victim.

Write down a list of your complaints and include times and dates. This will help you to be more organized and better able to communicate your concerns if or when you approach your neighbor. In addition, if diplomacy fails and you need to take a legal course, you will have a much better case if you have written documentation.

If you feel your complaints are justified your next step is to communicate with the offending neighbors. If done under the guise of good neighborliness your initial talk can have a good chance of success. If your approach is angry and accusatory you are likely to elicit a similar response and make the situation worse. In a best-case scenario your neighbor recognizes the problem, apologizes and works to correct it. Some may even react with surprise not realizing they had been disrespectful or annoying.

In a worst-case scenario, the neighbor reacts with anger and threats. Stay calm and do not get into a shouting match. If the animosity increases your neighbor may end up become a vindictive nuisance or even a vengeful stalker.

If nothing improves, the next step is to write them a detailed and formal letter. Make the tone of your letter businesslike. You can cite sections from your homeowner's association or community guidelines, but do not threaten or talk about legal actions you could take. Keep copies of all letters and complaints you file.

Pro Active: If the problem continues or escalates, you will need to step up your defensive strategies. Check with other neighbors to see if you have allies and get them on your side. Chances are that if your troublesome neighbors are bothering you, they are also bothering others.

File a formal complaint with your property owner, property manager, or tenant/homeowner association via a registered or notarized letter. Registered mail is essential for building a legal case if you need to in the future. Demand that your property owner go and speak to your neighbors and that you be debriefed afterward. If there is no improvement, send a second registered letter, specify the disruptions and/or violations, and reference your first letter. Mention the obvious ineffectiveness of that previous effort.

Criminal: If all the previous efforts have failed then you are dealing with either someone mentally unstable or a psychopath.

If you see them vandalizing your property, threatening you, or any other criminal infraction such as parking on your lawn or playing music too loud, then call the police immediately. Establishing police knowledge of these people is important because what will often happen is that they will start to stalk you and vandalize your property. Remember such people have no compunction about destroying your property in revenge for the perceived wrong you have done to them. As far as psychopaths are concerned, you fired the first shot by daring to complain about their obnoxious behavior. Quite often, their behavior that you tried to discuss with them is illegal and if brought to the attention of the authorities it begins to create a paper trail you can use in your favor.

The advice on Home Defense listed above can work to prevent property crime and to warn away such people. Consult the police for tips to help protect your property from vandalism as well as tips that you can do to assist them in making a case against your neighbor in the event of vandalism.

Legal: If by this time the situation has not improved you may consider getting the advice of a lawyer. Do an internet search of tenant and homeowner law and review your lease. Check with local housing clinics to see if there are any grounds for you to withhold paying rent. Withholding rent will help to motivate the property owner to remedy the situation. Leases are usually written with much attention to details that favor the property owners, but, like any contract, it cannot infringe on any legal statutes or your civil rights. If your neighbors are in any way inhibiting you from enjoying those rights, you have grounds to act.

If they damaged your property, consider suing, but only in extreme circumstances. Contact law enforcement if there is damage, and ask for a police log entry to assist with insurance claims.

Finally, as unfair as it sounds moving out may be your best option. Either that or live in a perpetual state of war.

## Travel Safety

*We are not fit to lead an army on the march unless we are familiar with the face of the country and its terrain. We are unable to take advantage of natural terrain unless you use local guides.* Sun Tzu, *The Art of War*

The maxim of military strategy 'know your terrain' applies equally well to personal defense. Know where you are going and what the local terrain will be. Whenever you go on vacation, visit friends, attend a new school, or plan to spend time in unfamiliar areas, find out what the environment is like. Ask locals, such as waiters, bartenders, taxi drivers, police, tourist and travel agents, questions such as is the area known for street crime? Is there a lot of gang activity? Do buses and taxis go there after dark? Is it an area you should avoid entering? If it is, then do not go there. It is that simple.

## Bad Neighborhoods

There is not a city in the world that does not have an area known for crime and poverty. Simply walking or driving through these areas can be dangerous and thus should be avoided if possible. If you are in a strange city and have not had a chance to find out which neighborhoods to avoid, then look for common signs that you may be in a dangerous area. These include:

- Lots of old, beaten-up cars parked on the street or driving around
- Numerous liquor stores, pawn shops, and check cashing outlets in the area
- Businesses and shops that all have heavily barred windows and doors
- A lot of graffiti and empty lots and abandoned buildings

Also remember that there are plenty of areas that are relatively safe during the day but become dangerous at night. These include many of the downtown and industrial parts of most cities.

If you stray into what you think is a bad area, go back out the way you came (if you can) unless you know that there is a quicker way out ahead.

## What To Do If You Get Lost

If you are lost in a bad neighborhood:

- Lock all doors
- Get out flashlights, self-defense weapons, phone, maps,
- Do not get out of the car
- If you sense immediate danger, call 9-1-1. Look for street signs and any identifying points you can tell the 9-1-1 operator

Backtrack: Make a U-turn if you are on a two-way street and go back the way you came. If you cannot make a U-turn, turn right or left at the next intersection, then right or left again to get you headed back to where you came from.

If you are near a freeway look for an entrance ramp. If there is one, take it – even if it only goes in the opposite direction you were headed. Once on the highway, you can turn back at the nearest safe-looking exit. It is better to take a few extra minutes driving out of your way then to remain in a dangerous situation.

Plot a New Course:  If backtracking does not work and you find yourself driving even deeper into the bad area then plot a new course. Find a safe place to stop and look at your map. Get out your cell phone and call a spouse, friend, or relative to alert them to your situation.

Locate your present position on your map. Mark your map with your present position and look for the nearest freeway on-ramp for the direction you want. Make sure that getting there does not take you through more of the bad neighborhood.

If you cannot find an on-off ramp reasonably close, as a last resort, look on your map for any kind of major street that you can head for. The point is simply to get into a safer part of town.

GPS and *OnStar* Users: Turn on your GPS unit, if you have one and it is not already on, so that it can start acquiring satellites. Should you have *OnStar* or other on-board motorist assistance, contact them immediately to explain your situation.

Enter in your GPS unit's destination screen either 1) the destination you were originally headed for; or 2), if that is too distant, look for any destination already in the system's memory that is heading roughly in the direction of the freeway. Follow the directions from your GPS unit back to the freeway or major road you were originally on before getting lost.

Lots of graffiti is a sure warning sign of a high crime area.

## Defense Against Carjacking

Continued advances in automobile anti-theft technology have made it increasingly more difficult for thieves to steal cars. As a result the best way now to steal a car is to carjack one with the driver still inside. In this way, the thief or robber can take the car keys and thus does not have to find a way to override the car's alarm systems. Not surprisingly the incidents of carjacking are increasing and will likely continue to do so.

A carjacking can occur at any location where a car and driver slows down. These include: shopping centers, ATMs, parking lots, self-serve car washes, self-serve gas stations, convenience stores, hotels, fast food drive thru, and driveways as the driver gets in or out of the car.

There are four common tactics used by carjackers.

Ambush: In an ambush, an assailant will wait out of view and suddenly attack as you are either leaving or entering your vehicle. Assaults in public parking areas are not confined to when you are returning to the car. If there is a place where an attacker can lurk undetected, he may choose to make a surprise attack just as you are opening your door.

Defense Against the Ambush: The first defense is to become more aware whenever you are parking or going to your automobile. Be aware of any people within a 30-foot radius around you — front, back and sideways, when you are walking to and from your vehicle.

Always look for the parking spot that has the most potential for safety. In a large garage with elevators, this means parking as close to an elevator as you can. If that is not possible, go for the next closest from an elevator that still has the best illumination.

In an open parking lot, park as close to the mall entrance as possible yet away from structures that could afford a hiding place to a potential attacker. Also, park as close or under a streetlight even in the daytime. If you return after nightfall, you can better see your car and check the area around your car. Remember that many parking areas can be busy and full of people during office hours but can become deserted after hours and ripe for carjackers, rapists, and robbers.

Do not leave any packages or luggage in the car, even if they contain nothing valuable, thieves do not know this and will break into your car causing damage and inconvenience for nothing.

In multi story parking garages you should avoid using stairs because they are often dark and little used. However, there may be circumstances where stairs are safer than an elevator, but that is a judgment call only you can make at the time.

Keep your pepper spray or other self-defense tool in hand when exiting or returning to your vehicle. Also, have your keys in your hand when approaching your car so that you do not have to linger before entering your vehicle.

If you are returning to your car and you see someone or something suspicious in your path or near your car, go no farther. Return to where you came from.

If there is a security office, go there and ask for help. If not, go to the store manager; and ask for one of the stock boys to accompany you to your car. Do not be afraid to ask for help if you feel the least bit suspicious about returning to your vehicle.

If your car has a remote door opener, it probably also has a panic button. This button is usually red or has a special texture. Pushing this button will turn on your car's alarm. If you see a suspicious person or persons lurking near your car you can use the panic button to activate the alarm from a distance to scare off any potential attackers  without revealing your location. In addition, if you are surprised by an attacker as you are approaching your car you can activate the alarm to try to attract attention and assistance.

When you get back in your car, lock your doors immediately. If you are buckling your baby in the car seat, put the baby in the car seat and buckle him/her up quickly. Do not become preoccupied and thus vulnerable with arranging hats, bibs, pacifiers, etc. This can wait until you are in your seat with the doors locked.

If you are outside your car when attacked, try to keep the car between you and the assailant, crawl under the car if necessary. If the attackers want your vehicle, give it to them. Do not get into a possibly lethal confrontation over something you can always replace later. The time to fight is if the carjackers want to take you hostage as well. If your attacker is intent on kidnapping you or hurting you, fight for your life.

If you must get into a car with the assailants, try to keep your hand on the door handle and make sure the door is unlocked. Be prepared to jump out just as the car begins to accelerate, or when stopped at busy intersections.

If the assailant is driving, wait until he stops at an intersection. If you can, grab the keys and escape. If you cannot escape, then try to take the keys and throw them out the window.

If you are carjacked and forced to drive, run red lights honking your horn to attract attention, drive to a police or gas station.

If you are forced into the trunk of your car, feel around for the emergency trunk release. This is a 'T' shaped handle attached to a short cord that will release the trunk when pulled. Open the lid slightly to see out. As soon as the car comes to a stop in an area that is well lit and you can see a safe area to run to, escape. Be aware that an accomplice may be following your stolen vehicle in order to distract from possible police pursuit. If it is the same car following yours, you will have to wait until you are in a heavily populated area before trying to escape. If it appears that you are being driven into the wilderness you may have to jump out even if the car is still moving.

If your car does not have an internal trunk release, feel around for the wires to the rear lights. Pulling out these wires will disable the rear signal and brake lights that may attract the attention of the police.

Bump and Rob: In this scenario, the carjacker rear-ends your car. When you get out of the car to inspect the damage and exchange license and insurance information, the carjacker jumps in your car and drives away or produces a weapon. An accomplice drives the carjacker's car away at the same time.

Defense Against the Bump and Rob: If another driver bumps you in traffic, stay alert. Roll up your windows and lock your doors. In most jurisdictions it is not necessary to call the police and file an accident report if the damage is less than a specified minimum. Often, if there are no injuries, the police may not come out to investigate even when asked to. The type of damage that would occur during a bump and rob is deliberately kept to a minimum so that the victim is less likely to call the police on the cell phone right away.

Look at the driver and passengers of the other vehicle, before getting out of your car to exchange info. Are they young males? Are there other cars close by? If the situation makes you apprehensive, write down in your car notebook, the vehicle's license number and description (color, make and model).

Signal to the other driver to follow you and drive to a police station or a populated, well-lit area. If you get out of your car, continue to be suspicious and make sure you take your keys and purse/wallet with you.

If the other driver wants you to roll down your window when you signal him to follow, do not. Simply write, "Follow me to police station" in your notebook and hold it up so he can read it through the window. If it is an honest accident then the other driver should have no reluctance to follow you and make a report.

The Pullover: The carjackers pulls up next to you and signal you that you have a mechanical problem, or a flat tire. Carjackers have even been known to follow a target vehicle while a passenger throws stones onto the back bumper to make it sound as if there is a real problem before they pull up to signal the driver. When you pullover to investigate they draw weapons and steal your car.

On city streets, it may be someone on the sidewalk that signals you or asks for directions with the same intention. On less trafficked roads the carjacker may pretend to have a breakdown or accident and attempt to flag a victim down under the pretense of requiring assistance.

Defense Against the Pullover: If someone is signaling you to pull over, slow down, turn off the radio if it is playing, then listen and feel for anything unusual in either the sound of the engine or in the handling of the vehicle. If you do have a flat tire you can feel this through the steering wheel and you will notice a tendency to drift either to the left or right depending on which side of the car the flat tire is on.

If you do hear or feel something unusual with the vehicle slow down, turn on your hazard lights and continue to drive until you come to either a busy well lit area or a gas station. Remember you can continue to drive even with a flat tire provided you remain under 25 mile per hour.

Do not stop to offer help to a stranded motorist. Instead, roll down the widow and offer to stop at the next telephone and call for help, or call 9-1-1 from your cell phone. If you do pull over to investigate or lend assistance at a traffic accident, stop behind the other cars. At night keep the headlights directed onto the scene, leave the motor running, and do not get out unless you are reasonably sure there are no signs of danger. Scan nearby vegetation for anyone hiding in the bushes. If the road is flanked by a gully or ditch, check for anyone lying down in it.

If you suspect someone is following you: drive to the nearest service station, drive-in restaurant, or police station and blow the horn.

If you are a single woman, keep a man's style hat in the car that you could wear if waiting for mechanical assistance or if driving alone at night. By wearing the hat, your silhouette will appear to be that of a man's, which will deter anyone looking for single females

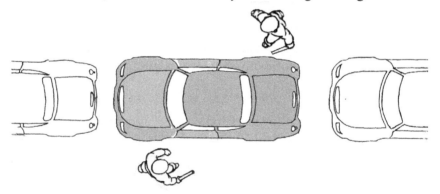

The Box: Carjackers stop at a red light or stop sign in front of your vehicle. The carjackers quickly jump out of their car and run up to your window and produce a weapon to force you out of the car. An accomplice remains in the lead vehicle and they all drive away together. More professional carjackers may have a second vehicle pull up behind so that you cannot back up because you are completely boxed in.

Another variation that can be worked on city streets is to have a pedestrian at either a crosswalk or while you are stopped at a red light, walk in front of your car to delay and distract you while an accomplice runs up to your window from behind a parked car or other cover. The accomplice will either pull you from your vehicle or produce a weapon to rob you of it.

Defense Against the Box: Make it a habit that whenever coming to a stop behind another vehicle you always leave enough space between you and the car in front of you so that you can see their rear wheels. This will give you enough room to sharply turn and go around the lead car either along the shoulder or over the sidewalk if necessary to escape.

If someone is standing in front of the car to prevent you from driving away, continue driving forward slowly, gradually increasing speed.

If an attacker reaches in through the window, then quickly roll up the window and trap his arm, injure the arm in whatever way possible. If the window is broken then wait until he reaches in to unlock the door and again attack the arm.

Your safety must trump the well-being of the car. If you are being boxed in by other cars, and it is obvious they mean you harm, you have to be willing to let them know you will stop at nothing to escape by running your car into the other cars.

## Car Breakdowns

Keep your vehicle in good shape and keep a **Car Emergency Kit** in the trunk. Never allow your gas tank to drop below half a tank.

Everyone old enough to drive a car should learn some basic car repair. Know how to connect the battery, jump-start a dead battery, check the oil and radiator fluid, and change a tire. These simple procedures might get you back on the road again.

Even with a flat tire, you can safely drive without ruining the rim provided you drive five miles per hour or less and you drive along the shoulder of the road with your hazard lights on.

Changing a tire at the side of the road is one of the most dangerous activities you can undertake. If you plan to change the tire yourself, ensure that you are safe from oncoming traffic by moving the car as far off the road as you can.

If your car breaks down on a public road, turn on hazard lights or, if the battery is not functioning, raise the hood and tie a handkerchief or piece of cloth to the radio antenna or door handle nearest passing traffic. Lock the doors and phone for help. If a stranger offers to help, do not get out of the car, ask the person to phone for assistance if you cannot do so yourself.

If you have car trouble in dark or deserted areas, then turn on your hazard lights or raise the hood of your car. Get out your emergency kit and find an area off the road and out of sight of passing motorists where you can safely watch your car and wait for help to arrive. (If you do not have a phone and you see a place within walking distance that would have a phone then go there and call for help.) The reason for hiding off the road is that it is becoming more common for criminals to cruise the roads looking for stranded motorists, especially in isolated areas. If they see no one in the car, they may try to rob or vandalize the car but you will be safe from harm hiding nearby.

## Car Breakdowns In The Wilderness
If you have a breakdown in a remote wilderness area, the following survival tips may come in handy.

If in dire need, cannibalize your vehicle for makeshift survival tools.
- A hubcap or sun visor can be used as a snow shovel
- Seat covers and even the foam seat padding can be used as blankets and as added insulation in your jacket or use the foam to fashion footwear to prevent frostbite.
- Floor mats can be used as shelter to shut out the wind and rain.
- The car's wiring can be used like rope to construct shelters and foam mukluks.

To signal for help
- A car horn can be heard up to a 1 mile away. Three long blasts, 10 seconds apart, every 30 minutes, is the universal distress signal.
- Burning engine oil in a hubcap provides a black smoke signal that can be seen for miles
- A rear-view mirror can be removed to serve as a signaling device
- Burn a spare tire for signal and/or warmth. Release the air pressure first and use gasoline or oil to ignite it

## Car Emergency Kit

An emergency can strike at any time. Keeping some equipment and supplies in your car ensures that you will always have the necessary survival tools with you wherever you travel. The following are some recommended contents for your kit.

- Flashlights
- Self-defense tools such as pepper spray, stun gun, etc.
- Batteries
- First aid kit
- Pocketknife

Keep the above items in your glove compartment or center console where you can access it without leaving your seat. You can store the following in the back or trunk.

- Blankets or sleeping bags
- Mittens, socks and a wool cap
- Extra pair of walking shoes, especially for women who often wear high heels.
- Waterproof covering like a tarp or poncho
- Metal coffee can which can be used to heat water

- Small shovel: even a folding one
- Bottled water - it may freeze so allow expansion room in container: don't use glass
- Booster battery cables
- Emergency road flares and/or warning reflectors
- Energy bars or high-energy food like raisins or nuts
- Bright color scarf to attract attention
- Waterproof matches / waterproof case, cigarette lighter
- Candles: a blanket over your head, body heat and a single candle can prevent freezing
- Tool kit, the more tools the better
- Paper towel or toilet tissue also used as fire starter
- Spare tire
- Rope, tow chain or a strap
- Extra oil
- 8' plastic tube to use as a siphon hose
- Map of the area where you plan to travel
- Small book to keep the mind occupied
- Small hand-held CB radio and it's batteries: channel 9 is the emergency channel
- Pen or pencil and paper
- Toilet kit, soap, washcloth, toothpaste and toothbrush

Except for the spare tire, the above items can fit neatly into a small daypack and can be a lifesaver in any number of situations.

If there are any warnings of either impending natural disasters or threats of social disasters you should add to your car kit a small container of fuel and extra engine oil and engine coolant.

In case you are away from home when disaster strikes, or if you have to search for family members, these supplies can extend your range in case service stations are closed.

## Car Accidents

If you are involved in a legitimate accident in a populous area of the city then leave your car as close as possible to the place of impact without obstructing traffic. If it is a minor accident then pull all the vehicles involved off the road to avoid obstructing traffic as well as the possibility of causing another more serious accident.

Securing the Scene: Make sure there are no other hazards or potential accidents before administering first aid. Raise the hood of your car and use your car's hazard warning lights. Set out flares, warning reflectors, or send someone to warn oncoming traffic to slow down. Put out any fires and get away from fuel spills.

Check if anyone is injured. Give first aid if you are qualified and call for an ambulance. Look around and note the location of the accident before you call for an ambulance. Tell the emergency operator the name and number of the street and nearest intersection if you know it.

Legal Considerations: Call the police especially if someone has been injured. A police report of the accident will help your insurance claim and any liability claims. Take notes about the accident such as the time of day, weather conditions, road conditions, streetlights and length of skid marks.

Also, make a diagram of the accident noting the location of the vehicles, cross walks, stops signs and traffic signals. If you have a camera, take photos or videos of the scene. Date and sign the notes when you are done. These can be invaluable later if you should find yourself sued or having to sue someone else.

Exchange information with the driver of the other car. You should get the following information:
1. Other driver's - name, address, phone number, driver's license number, name of insurance company and policy number.
2. Passengers - name, address and phone number.
3. Witnesses - name, address and phone number.
4. Owner (if not the driver) - name, address, phone number, insurance company and policy number.

When you exchange information with the other driver and give facts to the police, do not admit responsibility for the accident. This means not apologizing even if you think that you were responsible. It may be that a road hazard, mechanical failure, or the other driver was equally at fault. Do not sign any papers or agree to pay for damages. This would imply that you accept responsibility and that can be used against you if there is litigation.

Conversely do not downplay any injuries you may have and do not accept any gifts or money since this would imply that you have accepted such as equal compensation. Your injuries may be more serious than you know.

## What To Do After An Accident
Before you allow a tow truck driver to tow your car, be sure to ask the driver how much it will cost and tell the driver where to take your car. Get the name, address and telephone number of the driver and the towing company.

Even if there are no obvious injuries, both you and your passengers should consider seeing a doctor after an accident. The doctor may recognize injuries, sometimes serious, that are not apparent to you. Do not settle claims from the accident until your doctor has advised you about the extent of your injuries.

Take photos of any damage to your vehicle before you have them repaired. Call your insurance agent as soon as possible after an accident. Your insurance company may have grounds to deny coverage if you fail to give prompt notice of the accident

Follow up the phone call with a written report, including information you noted about the accident, photos of the car damage, and copies of the police report.

Contact a lawyer if you are considering a lawsuit, or expect one to be brought against you. Never sign any legal documents or statements without legal council.

## Public Transportation

Try to avoid waiting or getting off at isolated bus stops when alone. Learn the bus schedule so that you can avoid waiting long periods alone at a stop.

If standing alone at night at a bus stop avoid standing directly underneath the light, by doing so you make it easy for anyone to see that you are alone. Instead, blend into the shadows away from the light or next to a pole so that your silhouette does not stand out. This makes it more difficult to spot you from a distance or from cruising automobiles.

If you are a woman traveling alone on a bus or streetcar, try sitting near other women or near the driver. When using subway trains try to sit in the front car from which the motorman operates the train or in the car with the amber or white light on the side of the car in which the guard rides. Sit in aisle seat so that someone arriving later cannot trap you in.

Never hesitate to tell someone 'stop bothering me', in a loud voice, when others are around. The chances are that your would-be assailant will be more embarrassed than you will.

If someone continues to bother you on the train do not hesitate to press the yellow passenger assistance alarm strips located above the windows. This will activate signals in the Motorman and Guard's cars and will set off indicator lights on the outside of your car.

When the alarm goes off the motorman will alert the transit control who will in turn request police assistance. At the next station, the train doors will remain closed until the guard reaches your car. The guard will come to your assistance.

## Taxi Drivers

Most western nations require taxi drivers to have background checks in order to be licensed. However, even in a best-case scenario, this is rarely done. The independence of being a taxi driver attracts many types of criminals from thieves to rapists. While more common in poorer countries, crimes by taxis drivers can occur anywhere. The most typical crime is overcharging for the standard fare. This can be prevented by having a map and knowing where you are and where you want to go. Question the driver on which route he plans to take and let him see your map so that he knows you are paying attention. Also, ask him how much this trip would normally cost. This will discourage taking long detours and save you some money. However, if there is a dispute in the fare then just pay it. Often taxis drivers have friends among the police and/or local street gangs that would turn any argument against your favor.

Tourists and travelers may become victims of even more serious crimes such as robbery, rape and kidnapping. Taxi drivers have been known to work with gangs and robbers and will drive their passengers to an isolated area where their waiting cohorts can rob them of their money and baggage. Single women face another danger of being driven to abandoned area to be raped or even kidnapped and sold into a sex slave ring. The following can help prevent you becoming a victim of a taxi driver.

Phone a reputable taxi service listed in the phonebook rather than flag one down on the street. Criminals can pose as a taxis service simply by renting or purchasing a used taxi. With listed services, there is a better chance that its drivers are licensed and at least there is a record of your call that police can trace in case you should disappear.

When possible have friends or family see you to your taxi. Have them stand by when the taxi arrives and visibly write down the driver's license number. Make sure the driver sees them do this. Even better, use a phone camera or other digital camera to take a picture of both the driver and the license plate. It is within your right to do this and most taxi drivers know why you are doing it and will not object. (You could also take the photo on your phone camera and then e-mail it to a friend.) If however the driver makes a fuss about being photographed then call another service. This lets a potential attacker know that there are eyewitnesses and hard evidence to convict him if anything should happen to you. A criminal posing as a taxi driver can have his pick of victims so it is very unlikely that he would attack you after all the precautions you have taken. Easier victims are just minutes away.

Make sure you let some friend or family member know that you are traveling by taxi, where you are going, and what time you are expected to arrive. Tell them that you will call them when you arrive. If you don't call to confirm your arrival, the friend should then alert police and friends in your area. This is like leaving a travel plan with park rangers before going on a wilderness hike. If you don't show up at the right time and place they will mount a search and rescue.

Before getting into the cab make sure that back doors have door handles. If not, don't get in. If you believe the driver is going off the regular route tell him to get back to the main streets. If he refuses then tell him to take you back where you came from. If he again refuses, then wait until the vehicle slows down or stops at a stop light and quickly jump out and run in the opposite direction. Get out your pepper spray and find the nearest public area or business, and then phone the police to report the incident.

## On Foot

Plan your route and avoid shortcuts through parks, vacant lots or unlit areas. Remember to stay alert and walk with a purpose.

Walk near the curb and away from dark alleys and doorways, and facing oncoming traffic.

Do not overburden yourself with bulky packages and a bulky purse. Carry only the essentials. However, if you are attacked while loaded down, use the packages to your advantage and throw them at the attacker. It may give you the time to run away or strike back.

When you plan to walk a fair distance, wear footwear and clothing that are comfortable and can allow you to move quickly. High heel shoes make a distinctive tapping sound that is immediately recognizable to predators waiting for a potential victim to walk by. If you jog, try to run in groups or pairs especially if you run during times when there is little public traffic, or in isolated areas.

When traveling through strange neighborhoods be inconspicuous while blending into the background. Dress like the locals, the more different you look, the easier it is to single you out. Never display large sums of cash in public or wear highly visible and expensive jewelry or clothes.

Do not stop to give directions to a driver or a pedestrian. Asking for directions is a common rouse to delay and distract you. However, if you feel you must give directions, always ensure a safe distance between you and the other party in order to avoid being surprised by a sudden attack.

Do not allow strangers to stop you on the street for conversations or stop to give beggars change or to light a cigarette. These are stalling techniques used to set up an attack. If you feel the charitable need to give change, make sure you have some small change in your hand ready. When a beggar approaches, hold out your hand and give him the money without slowing your pace.

If you suspect someone is following you, cross the road and walk back in the opposite direction. If the person is truly following you, they will also have to change direction. In addition, if they are intent on attacking you it is better to see it coming than to be surprised from behind. Head for the nearest well lit or populated area. If people are within hearing distance, do not hesitate to turn to the person following you and say in a loud voice, 'Stop following me'. If the area is deserted: go to the nearest house that looks occupied, or business premises, or service station and call the police, do not go home. You do not want the suspect to know where you live because most attacks occur in the home out of public view.

## Defense Against A Drunk

Dealing with an obnoxious or aggressive drunk depends on whether the drunk is a friend or stranger. If a stranger, then its best to let the authorities handle the situation. In an eating or drinking establishment notify the management or door staff and let them handle it. If not, phone the police or send someone you trust to phone the police while you occupy the drunk's attention. If the drunk is a friend, then gently but firmly maneuver the friend into a cab or onto a couch in the family room.

If all else fails and you find yourself fighting a drunk there is an advantage and disadvantage. The advantage is that alcohol will interfere with his coordination and balance and this will act in your favor during combat. In addition, drunks have a tendency to pass-out because of the depressive effects the alcohol has on the nervous system. A slap to the face may cause just enough shock that the blood pressure will fall rapidly causing unconsciousness.

The drawback is that occasionally the alcohol numbs the senses and the drunk will have little sense of pain, as a result, he may continue

74

fighting long after a sober person has quit because of injuries suffered. If this happens then the only way to stop him is to cause him serious injury since submission holds may not work due to the absence of pain.

## Recovery Position

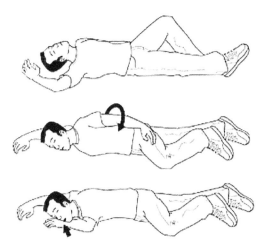

If someone passes out from intoxication do not leave them lying on their backs. Many have died from suffocating on their own vomit while unconscious in this position.

Instead, bend one knee and use the knee as a lever to roll the drunk over and lying on his or her stomach in what is known as the 'Recovery Position'. Should they vomit while unconscious this position will help keep their airway clear.

## Money

Avoid carrying large sums of money or unnecessary credit cards.

Do not carry all your money in one pocket, spread the money about; if you are robbed or pick-pocketed, they will only get one location's worth of money, leaving you the rest. Carry your identification and credit cards separately from your spending cash.

Travelers style waist money belt

75

If traveling through high-risk areas carry a decoy wad. This is a cheap wallet that has a real money bill on the outside but play money or paper cut to size on the inside. A wallet may include phony credit cards. (Cut out credit card ads from a magazine and glue them to cardboard). The decoy should look valuable, and then if you are robbed, you can throw the decoy in one direction while carefully and quickly leaving in the opposite direction.

Carry your real money and cards in a traveler's waist pouch or shoulder holster style pouch that you wear under your clothes.

Do not leave a purse or briefcase unattended in shopping carts, on store counters, in your car, or next to you on the floor in a bathroom stall.

## Defense Against A Robber

If confronted by a robber or mugger co-operate. Listen to what he says. Always answer in the affirmative in a quite, calm, voice. Be polite, while you might feel angry and believe you could overpower the robber, it is nevertheless essential that you pretend to be intimidated. This will allow the robber to relax his guard, then, if you feel you have no alternative but to attack, you can use your calm appearance to launch a surprise attack. Acting hostile and indignant will only encourage the robber to use a weapon that may or may not be visible.

Remember that personal safety is more important than material things. Resist only to protect yourself from harm, not to protect your belongings.

Try to get a good mental description of the robber, afterwards jot down some quick notes. Remember any physical characteristics and distinguishing marks such as scars, tattoos, facial hair, hair and eye color, complexion, age, height and weight, and what clothes he was wearing.

If the demand is for money take out your cash (or your decoy wad) and hold it up for the attacker to see. Then throw it on the ground between you and the assailant while backing away. When he bends to pick up the money, make a run for it. If the assailant is really after only your money then he will go for the wallet rather than you.

If the robber attempts to move you to another location or restrain you, see Kidnapping p. 85.

## Defense Against A Street Gang

The first defense is always awareness. Watch for the telltale territorial markers - graffiti. Most gangs mark their turf with graffiti. Note the increase of what is called tags, badly written words and symbols spray painted on traffic signs and walls. Also, look for other signs that you are walking in a bad neighborhood. (See Bad Neighborhoods p. 51)

Pack affiliation is expressed through symbols of fierceness such as loud and symbolic clothing, elaborate body decoration such as hairstyles, tattoos, piercing or scarring. Gangs may also adopt a group color and its members will all display some item of clothing, usually a bandana, T-shirt, or cap of the same color. If you notice people displaying these symbols, be cautious.

Look for weapons. Anytime you come across a group of men with weapons, whether police, soldiers, militia, or hoodlums, exercise extreme caution. Mistakes happen, but when weapons are involved, those mistakes can become fatal. Another factor for turning a group violent is alcohol and/or drugs. The effects of alcohol include a relaxing of the brain's inhibitions against impulsive and aggressive behavior. An otherwise normal group of people can turn dangerous when alcohol is involved. Beware of any groups under the influence of drugs or alcohol.

If you happen upon a gang loitering near your route - stop and go back in the direction you came. Be inconspicuous as you quietly escape the area. Better to go out of your way then to present yourself as a potential target.

If it appears a gang has spotted you and is moving towards you then move quickly towards any well-lit and public area where there are more people. If there is a retail shop, café or office building nearby you can duck inside and either wait for the gang to pass by or call for help.

If a gang confronts you, keep your head up but do not stare at anyone, say nothing, do not react, and try not to slow your pace.

If they block your progress, your first line of defense is to use your wits. Talk to the leader, find out what they want and if possible give it to them. Be polite and cooperative, but do not grovel. There is a delicate balance between submission and dominance and you do not want to fall into either camp. If you are too submissive, they will only despise you more and interpret your fear as an invitation to escalate the abuse. If you are too aggressive then the pack instinct takes over and they will interpret your resistance as a challenge to their domination requiring the gang to save face by attacking you.

Speak and reason only with the leader, do not try to win over others to your side. As a rule if you fight one person in the gang, you fight everyone in the gang. The scenario of a fair street fight, one against one, is an urban myth.

The Strategy of Feigned Madness: If you are not a fast talker, then play stupid. Say little or nothing or simply nod your head. If you are a good actor and your appearance does not already give you away, then pretend to be mentally unbalanced. Act as though you have no idea what is going on, drool slightly and let mucus run out of your nose. Ignorant people are often afraid of 'crazy' people, as though madness were infectious. In a street gang confrontation, attacking a 'crazy' brings little satisfaction and hopefully they will get bored and leave you alone.

The important thing is to survive, uninjured if possible. Do not be led astray by movie myths of martial arts heroes who beat multiple attackers one after the other. Members of a street gang are likely to be carrying weapons. It may be possible for a highly trained, unarmed fighter to defeat two, maybe three unarmed and untrained attackers, but against multiple armed attackers that is practically impossible.

If there is no other way to escape an impending attack, then try to take-out the leader first. Make a direct and sudden attack at the leader and do not stop until you see an opportunity to escape. If the gang is only loosely connected, then taking out the leader may put an end to the attack. Drinking buddies feel tough when they are all together, but if the leader, presumably the toughest one among them, falls, then the rest cave in as well. However, in well-established street gangs, taking-out the leader will not stop the attack, but it might buy some time as the rest of the gang mentally regroups.

The principle tactic for fighting larger forces is hit and run. If surrounded, quickly attack the weakest point in the circle and try to break through. If, while running, you find they are catching up then stop suddenly, attack the leading pursuer and then run again. Do not let yourself be surrounded, keep moving laterally so that they can only come at you one at a time. While moving, look for a way to summon help or escape.

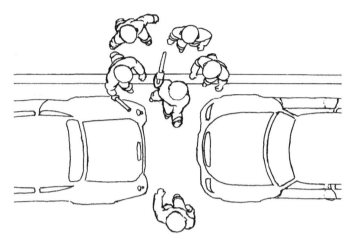

Use the features in your terrain. Where possible, try to fight in small, narrow, or enclosed spaces. Confined areas negate the advantage of numbers. Stand in the hall or doorway, between parked cars, or between tables in a restaurant. If there are no narrow spaces then look to fight with solid objects at your back, such as walls, doors, tables, parked cars, this prevents attacks from behind. Try to make the terrain between you and the attackers more difficult to cross. Knock things over as you run such as garbage cans, mailboxes, signs, tables, chairs, and lamps.

All the time you arr fighting and running make as much noise as possible, set off car alarms, break store windows and set off burglar alarms, break glass since people are more curious about the sound of breaking glass then screams for help, the two together will improve the chances that someone will pay attention and phone the police.

If you are knocked to the ground, lie on your side and use your legs to kick out at the shins and knees of anyone within range. If surrounded on the ground being kicked and beaten, curl up into a ball with the fingers interlaced behind your head so the elbows and forearms protect your head. With the fingers interlaced even if you loose consciousness, the arms will tend to stay in that position offering some protection for your head. Pull your knees into your abdomen and keep your thighs pressed together. The only disadvantage to this position is that it still leaves exposed your spine and kidneys, either of which could easily be broken with a kick. If possible, have your back against the wall or partway under a car. Remember you can also try to crawl underneath a car.

## What to Do After You Are Attacked

First, ensure your safety from a repeat attack. Get out of the area and call 9-1-1.

Do a visual physical examination for possible injuries and apply emergency first aid if needed. Seek medical attention; you may have suffered internal injuries that would not immediately exhibit signs or symptoms. Only a professional medical examination would spot them.

Do not drive yourself home. Arrange for transportation either to the hospital or to your home. Shock can occur anytime after a serious fright such as a car accident or attack even if you were uninjured. You do not want to pass out from shock while driving.

Notify the police. Write down notes about the attackers such as identifying characteristics, what direction they ran away in. If they left in a car, note the color, make, and license number if possible.

Notify the banks and credit card companies if your wallet and ID were stolen. If your keys were taken, change all the locks to your house, office, car, and anything else that was on the key ring.

Beware of phone calls from strangers saying they found your valuables and requesting that you meet them somewhere to pick up your belongings. This is a common ruse to get you to leave the house so that they may burglarize it. To avoid this possible trap, ask for an address or phone number and tell them that you will have someone else come and pick it up at their residence or office.

Finally, you may need to seek out a support group, pastor, or counselor to help deal with the traumatic aftereffects of being victimized.

## Sexual Assault

Rape is an act of violence expressed through sex, but is not primarily about sex. Rapists tend to be cowards and therefore victims are most often those that are the most defenseless - children, the disabled or handicapped, minorities, and the poor.

Sexual assault is most commonly committed by a male upon a female although same sex rapes are not uncommon especially in segregated societies such as prisons, military settings, and single-sex schools. Female on male rape has been reported but is rare.

## Social Situations

Social environments are the hunting grounds for sexual predators. Whenever going out in public you should be aware of this fact and take minimal precautions.

Use caution in conversations with strangers or within earshot of strangers. Avoid giving your name, address, or place of employment.

When entering any public area scan the layout for entrances, exits, and any suspicious looking people. This is not only to help you to spot trouble coming, but also in case of fire or earthquake you can escape more quickly.

In bars and restaurants, sit with your back against the wall preferably with a view of the entrance. Never leave your drink unattended. There are drugs that can be slipped into a drink that can incapacitate your senses and leave you vulnerable to sexual assault.

Remember it is risky to accept a ride home or an invitation for a late night coffee or drink from someone you have just met. This applies to men as well. A common ploy is have an attractive woman meet and pick up traveling businessmen or tourists, then drug and rob them in their hotel rooms. Be careful of whom you are with and where you are when you are drinking alcohol.

## Defense Against Sexual Assault
Try to remain clam. To regain your composure breathe deeply and slowly. This will help you to overcome the panic and sick stomach caused by fear and the lack of oxygen.

Scream only if people are nearby and are likely to come to your aid, otherwise the attacker may decide to silence you. Shout or scream 'Fire', 'Call the police'. Studies show that 75% of attackers take off when confronted by a screaming victim.

To deter the would be attacker you may tell him that you have a venereal disease, herpes, hepatitis B, or AIDS.

If you decide to fight, do so at the beginning of the attack. You have a greater chance of discouraging the attacker if you appear not as easy to overpower as he believed.

If given the opportunity, run. Have some safe place in mind to run to, a place where there are people who can help you. Try to get a good lead on your assailant and run towards lighted and crowded areas. If you are wearing high-heeled shoes, kick them off.  This will give you greater mobility as well as making less noise to track you by. If you are being taken to another location, see Kidnapping p. 85.

## What to Do After A Sexual Assault
Go first to a safe place and call the police. There is always a possibility that the attacker may return. If you are attacked in your home, lock your doors and windows, phone police and then call a friend, family member, or neighbor to stay with you while you are waiting for the police to arrive.

The police will arrange for you to be taken to the hospital for medical attention even if you are not visibly injured. In addition, with your consent, the hospital will conduct a forensic medical examination in order to gather potential evidence. The medical examiner will explain the procedure beforehand. While you are waiting for the police to arrive, do not bathe, douche, change your clothes, or disturb the scene of the assault. If you do, you may destroy useful evidence.

Try to remember points of identification about your attacker such as complexion, body build, height, weight, hair color, length, facial hair, approximate age, scars, tattoos, and type of clothing or jewelry. Write this information down and date it.

Sexual assault can result in serious mental trauma as well and you should seek counseling through any of the Rape Counseling Centers or private counsel. Also have another health exam three or four months later to check for delayed illnesses or disease.

---

### Sexual Assault Statistics

According to most estimates, 80 to 90% of rapes are not reported.

Recent trends suggest that 1 in 3 American women will be sexually assaulted at some point during their lifetimes.

The typical rape victim is a 16 to 24 year-old woman. However, anyone of either sex from infants to seniors can be the victim of rape.

The typical assailant is a 25 to 44 year-old man who usually chooses a woman of the same race. Nearly half the time, the victim knows the rapist at least casually, by working or living near him.

Alcohol is involved in more than 1 out of 3 rapes.

Most rapists plan their attacks, rather than acting on impulse.

Contrary to the admonishment against walking down dark alleys, over 50% of rapes occur in the victim's home. The rapist gains entry by either breaking into the victim's home, or under false pretenses, such posing as a repairperson, salesperson or asking to use the phone.

---

## Kidnapping

A kidnapping occurs when a criminal through fraud, force or threat, moves a person against his or her will to another location as part of another criminal activity such as holding the person for ransom, or to sexually abuse the captive. There are three types of kidnappers, family members who take an offspring, sexual predators, and ransom seekers. If a family member has kidnapped your child the best course of action is to immediately notify police and consult an attorney. The second two types are known as stranger  abductions. The most likely victims of stranger abductions are children and lone females.

Kidnapping can occur as a follow up crime. In the course of a carjacking, mugging, or home invasion, the assailant(s) may try to move you to another location. To help prevent such initial crimes follow the previous advice for home invasion, street safety, and carjacking. It is when an assailant tries to transport you that you must make the decision on whether to fight or cooperate.

## When To Fight

As a rule, anytime an assailant tries to take you to another location it is because the criminal will have a greater advantage, and you will have less chance of being rescued. If you are going to have to fight it out, then do it as soon as it becomes obvious that this is the intention and before the odds are any more in the attacker's favor.

This is the best strategy if the would-be abductor is unarmed, if the attempt is sexually motivated, and if there are other people nearby that can quickly get help. Most abduction attacks in the U.S. and other developed countries, are sexually motivated and usually the intended victim is a woman or child. If you are a woman being abducted your best chances are probably to fight back right away.

Escape and Evade: If given the opportunity, run. Try to get a good lead on your assailant and run towards lighted and crowded areas. If the kidnapper is still following you, make the terrain between you and the attackers more difficult to cross. Knock things over as you run such as garbage cans, signs, tables or chairs.

If attacked on a deserted street, hiding under a parked car can be a final resort. It is difficult to try to drag you out from underneath since you can hang onto the undercarriage and use your feet to kick at the attacker if he tries to crawl under after you.

If you are cornered then you may have to fight it out with everything you've got. Remember you do not need to beat him up but rather just stun him and escape his grip so that you can again run towards safety.

Attract Attention: Scream, yell, run into bystanders, blow a whistle, and bring as much attention as possible to yourself and your attacker. Scream "FIRE!" at the top of your lungs, it will attract passersby. Attracting attention works best in or near public places, where the attacker hopes to remain inconspicuous lest others intervene or call police. You can also attract attention by throwing something heavy through the window of a house if in a residential area, or storefront in a commercial area. The sound of breaking glass is distinct and always rouses interest. In addition, breaking a store window will set off the alarm that will attract attention and the police. Better to pay for a broken window than to risk being injured or killed.

If you find an unlocked car, jump in and lock the doors. Sound the horn to attract attention (Do not hold down the horn continuously since people may interpret this as a malfunction rather than a call for help. Instead, use an irregular sequence).

If you can put some distance between you and your attacker and you have a cell phone, dial the emergency dispatch number for your country. If you don't have a cell phone you can use a payphone to dial 911 without having to deposit any money (It's free to call 911) The chances of the police arriving on the scene in time to prevent a determined kidnapper is slim, but if you can keep fleeing and fighting you know that at least help may arrive.

If you have escaped the attacker, run to a nearby house or business, let them know what happened and have them call 911. This will help ensure that you are in a safe place, that help is arriving, and that you have witnesses.

If an assailant tries to drag you away pretend to faint and go limp, this makes it much more difficult to carry you. If he is still able to carry you away, grab onto anything you can to slow down his progress such as lampposts, fences, tree branches etc. Grab some rocks or handfuls of dirt to throw. If you have been completely overpowered then your next strategy is to cooperate.

## When To Cooperate

An old military adage states that you do not fight battles you cannot win. If multiple armed attackers abduct you for ransom in an isolated or hostile place with little to no chance of escape, you should cooperate right away. Professional kidnap-for-ransom gangs that target executives operate in many underdeveloped countries and are increasing in developed countries. About 95% of people abducted in this manner are released alive. In such scenarios, the odds of being killed are highest in the first few minutes of the abduction, when something goes wrong — usually when the victim tries to escape or fight. If you are abducted by a well-armed ransom for profit gang, your best course of action is to cooperate and use psychology to survive.

Stay Calm: You have every reason to be terrified but the sooner you can calm down the sooner you can formulate a strategy to save your life. Relax and take a few deep breaths.

Stay Focused: From the time you realize you are being kidnapped try to observe and remember as much as possible in order to help you plan an escape, predict your abductor's next moves, or give information to the police to aid in a rescue or to help apprehend and convict the kidnappers.

Gather Intel: Even if you are blindfolded, you can still use the senses of hearing, touch, and smell to gather information. Try to find out:

- How many abductors are there?
- Are they armed? If so, with what?
- Are they in good physical condition?
- What do they look and/or sound like? How old are they?
- Do they seem well prepared?
- What are their emotional states?
- Where are you being taken? Make mental note of turns, stops, and variations in speed.
- Where are you being held? Try to find out where the exits are, if there are surveillance cameras in place, locks on the doors or windows.
- If you are restrained discreetly test your bonds, but do not struggle too much or you could injure yourself.

Look for patterns and routines that the kidnappers follow. Note times when they come and go, when they change guard shifts, and meal times. Knowing their routines will figure into any escape plans you make. Learn to cold-read your captors to determine their moods and commitment. Remember the techniques to placate anger and reduce aggression. The information you gather is vital should you need to plan an escape.

Analysis: The most important information you need to know is the reason why you were kidnapped. Try to ascertain whether you were kidnapped for ransom, political reasons, or sexual assault.

If you were abducted for ransom or to negotiate the release of political prisoners, you are most likely worth far more alive than dead. However, if a serial killer or sexual predator has captured you, or if you have been abducted in retaliation for some political or military action, your abductor likely intends to kill you. In the latter cases, you should attempt an escape as soon as an opportunity presents itself.

## Psychological Tactics

Stay positive: Most kidnapping victims survive so the odds are in your favor that you will eventually be released unharmed. However if you are being held for political reasons then you may be held for a long time. Take it one day at a time.

Put Your Captor at Ease: Remember the rule for dealing with armed men is to keep them as relaxed and calm as possible by posing as little threat to them as you can. Cooperate (within reason) with your captor. Do not make threats or become violent, and do not attempt to escape unless the time is right (see below).

Create Bonds: Non-psychopaths have to de-humanize their intended victims in order to kill, rape, or otherwise harm a captive. Attempt to establish a rapport with your abductors but be careful to avoid insulting them or talking about potentially sensitive subjects such as politics or religion. If you can build some sort of bond with your captor, he/she will generally be more hesitant to harm you. Instead, look for commonalities such as family, food, sports, or entertainment. If you have children and your captor has children, you have a powerful bond already in place. If you have pictures of your family with you, consider showing one or more of your captors if the topic comes up.

If your captor is a psychopath, remember that they despise you even more for being a victim. Do not grovel, beg, or become hysterical and try not to cry. With a psychopath you need to flatter their ego to placate their wrath. Tell him how smart, brave or strong he is. It may seem an obvious lie but remember psychopaths have no empathy to tell them when you are being insincere. The most outrageous flatteries seem normal from their perspective.

Join Forces: If you are held with other captives, try to make contact with them if it is safe to do so. In any dire situation you are always better off making friends and allies so that you can pool resources, look out for each other, have others to talk to, and if the time is right, plan an escape together. Quickly develop and establish covert codes and signals to use amongst yourselves.

<u>Stay Sharp</u>: Captivity can be boring and mind numbing. It is important to challenge your mind so you can remain sane, but also so you can think rationally about escape. Do math problems, think of puzzles, try to remember movies you have seen. Do whatever you can to keep yourself occupied and mentally sharp.

Also stay fit. It can be difficult to remain in physical shape while in captivity, especially if you are restrained. Being in good physical condition can aid in your escape and boost your confidence. Exercise whenever you can even if it is just doing jumping jacks, pushups, or isometrics such as pushing your hands together and tightening your stomach muscles.

<u>Ask for Small Favors</u>: This is a subtle form of manipulation. By asking your captors to do something for you, you help reinforce that you are a human being with needs and rights. It will also begin to acclimatize your captors to the idea of doing things for you. Start by asking for something simple like a drink of water, or a blanket. Keep requests small, at least initially, and space them apart. Depending on the degree of resistance you receive, begin to ask for more favors such as a radio, newspaper, and extra food. The radio and newspaper may provide you with outside information on your kidnapping and/or the political conditions that may affect your situation. The extra food should at first be eaten so that you regain your strength and health, and then stockpile some extra in case you need to make an escape attempt into a wilderness area.

## When To Attempt An Escape

If your captors decide to kill you, you need to know as soon as possible so that you can plan an escape. If your captors suddenly stop feeding you, if they treat you more harshly (dehumanizing you), or if they suddenly seem desperate or frightened, (signaling that law enforcement is closing in or that the ransom demand has not been met) all are warning signs that your time is limited. If you are reasonably certain that your captors are going to kill you then attempt to escape even if your chances are not good.(Also see Escape and Evade p. 249)

## If You Are Rescued

The second most dangerous situation for a kidnapping victim is during a rescue by police or military forces. Victims face the twin dangers of being killed by both the captors and the rescuers. If the kidnappers see security forces moving in they may become desperate and use the hostages as human shields, or even just kill them out of spite. Even if the kidnappers are taken by surprise, the hostages could be killed by the actions of police or soldiers, who may use explosives and heavy firepower to enter the building.

If there is a sudden commotion and running around by the captors followed by gunfire or explosions, it is a sure sign that a rescue attempt is underway. You should duck and take cover. Try to get away from your captors during the commotion and find a place to hide that would provide some cover such as under a desk or behind a sofa.

If armed rescuers burst in do not make any sudden moves. Follow the rescuers' instructions carefully. Your rescuers will be on edge, and they will most likely shoot first and ask questions later. Obey all commands they give. If they tell everybody to lie down on the floor or put their hands on their heads, do it. Remain calm and put rescuers at ease.

## Stalkers

There are three basic types of stalkers, Delusional Stalkers, Vengeful Stalkers, and Intimate Stalkers.

Delusional Stalkers: These are easy to spot crazies who suffer from a major mental disorder such as schizophrenia, manic depression or erotomania. They usually have had little if any contact with their victim but due to the peculiarities of their illness they believe that they have some sublime connection to their victims. In the cases of erotomania, the stalker may actually be convinced that their victim loves him or her and that they have a relationship, even if they never met. In another variation, the stalker knows that he and the victim do not presently have a relationship, but that god and/or destiny has deemed that they should and the stalker is merely carrying out god's design by stalking the victim.

Unlike the next two types of stalkers, delusional stalkers are seldom psychopaths although they are no less dangerous. Typically, they are unmarried and socially immature loners, who are unable to establish or sustain close relationships with others. They rarely date and have had few, if any, sexual relationships. Since they are both threatened by, and yearn for, closeness, they often pick victims who are unattainable in some way such as someone already married, or someone in the public eye like a sports or entertainment celebrity. Delusional stalkers often come from emotionally abusive or barren backgrounds, and seek to support their fragile identity by having someone from a higher status, such as celebrities and successful professionals, love them.

These types of stalkers often target social and heath care professionals such as therapists, clergyman, doctors or teachers. The understanding and kindness shown to all patients and clients by these professions is blown out of all proportion in the mind of the delusional stalker and they interpret professional courtesy shown them as a sign of an intimate relationship.

As a rule, the less of a relationship that actually existed prior to the stalking, the more mentally disturbed the stalker.

The Vengeful Stalker: The vengeful stalker is someone that becomes angry with his or her victim over some real or imagined insult however slight. They are mostly low-level psychopaths whose grandiosity and paranoia causes them to either interpret everyone's actions as a confirmation of, or direct threat to, their identity. These range from the sociopath who will break a bottle over someone's head that "looked at him wrong' to disgruntled ex-employees who target their former bosses, co-workers or the entire company.

Like all psychopaths, the vengeful stalker especially sees himself as the victim and that their stalking is just "getting even" for past injustices. The vengeful stalker can be more malicious and dangerous then the other two types of stalkers since the others still mean to establish or re-establish a relationship, while the vengeful talker is not interested in a relationship but rather to punish the victim.

Intimate Partner Stalkers: Well over half of all stalkers fall into this 'former intimate partner' category. These are typically men whose partners have ended the relationship and they refuse to let go. They may play the innocent lovelorn victim to garner the sympathy and support from friends and family but in reality, they are most likely psychopaths that had been abusive and manipulative during the relationship. Their refusal to let go is not out of any sense of love because they are not capable of love. They refuse to let go because they believe the victim is their private property subject to only their whims.

## Defense Against Stalkers

If you become a victim of a stalker, your first line of defense is to educate yourself. There are several national organizations that provide information on stalking. These groups can also help you with your next line of defense, building a support system for yourself. Also, go to the police, go to a lawyer, go to child and family services as well as family, friends, co-workers, your boss and neighbors and let them know what is going on. Bear in mind that often none of these avenues will be of any assistance but you need to try because chances are you will not be able to handle the situation alone. By building a support system you can bring other tools such as, tactics and training, security measures, and legal and law enforcement to bear on the situation.

Tactics and Training: Your primary tactic in dealing with most psychopaths is to escape and cut the offender out of your life - period. Remember there is no reasoning, negotiating or appealing to their sympathy with psychopaths or delusional individuals. You must say 'No' once and then never speak to the stalker again. For stalkers, like obscene phone callers, even negative attention is still attention.

For the Vengeful Stalker the same rule applies. When you encounter someone whose reaction to you is way out of proportion, then simply back away. Non-reaction is the best way to prevent giving any more fuel to the fire. (See Anger and Aggression p. 28) Remember you are dealing with a lunatic; you gain nothing by counter-attacking at this point.

Take a self-defense course. This is different from martial arts training which may or may not be geared to personal self-defense. A good self-defense course can train you to be more aware and tactical in your thinking that can aid in dealing with a stalker. Traditional martial arts training can also benefit if it is in addition to a self-defense course.

Another consideration is to carry a weapon. Pepper spray has varying degrees of effectiveness but is at least legally neutral in most places. However, depending on both the legalities and personal attitudes, more dangerous weapons such as firearms may be considered as well.

Security Measures: Upgrade your home security by installing an alarm system, surveillance cameras, entry prevention devices and building a safe room. You might also want to get a dog. This is one of the least expensive but most effective alarm systems.

Block your address at DMV and Voter Registration. Never give out your home address or telephone number. Get a post office box and use it on all correspondence. For those places that will not accept a post office box, then simply change "PO Box" to "Apt." Put this address on your checks.

At your place of employment, have co-workers screen all calls and visitors. Do not accept packages unless they were personally ordered. Remove any name or identification from reserved parking at work. Destroy discarded mail.

Equip your gas tank with a locking gas cap that can be unlocked only from inside the car. Acquaint yourself with all-night stores and other public, highly populated places in your area. Get a cell phone and keep it with you at all times, even inside your home, in case the stalker cuts your phone lines.

If you think you are being followed while in your car, make four left- or right-hand turns in succession. If the car continues to follow you, drive to the nearest police station, never home or to a friend's house.

Consider moving if your case warrants it. No, it's not fair, but nothing is fair about stalking. If you stay and fight through the legal system, you might get some justice, but you almost certainly will not get safety. There is no possibility of life imprisonment for stalkers.

Law Enforcement: As soon as you find yourself the target of a stalker you should start documenting the situation. This means writing down incidents and encounters, keeping letters, e-mails or gifts, taking pictures or video of the stalker near your home or workplace, recording harassing phone calls, and keep a caller ID record of incoming calls from the stalker's number. If there is any hope that law enforcement can do anything to help, you must provide solid evidence. The onus is on the victim to do all the detective work.

Most states and municipalities have stalking laws, and if you have gathered enough concrete evidence the police can and will arrest him especially if he is violating a restraining order on top of that. The stronger the evidence you gather, the stronger the case.

If the stalker tries to enter your home or vandalize your property, call the police as soon as possible. Even if the stalker ran away, insist on the police coming and filing a police report. If the stalking escalates, you need a paper trail. That is why you need to insist on a written report.

<u>Restraining Orders</u>: Many people believe that if they are being stalked the first thing they should do is get a restraining order. They often assume that by doing so the stalking will finally end, either because the stalker will stop on his own, or because the police will stop him. Neither of these outcomes are likely.

Only about half of all stalking cases are reported to the police and of these, only a quarter result in an arrest. About a quarter of stalking victims obtain restraining orders in which two-thirds of these cases the restraining order is violated.

A restraining order does not provide police protection and rarely police action when it is violated. Furthermore, the likelihood of police preventing a stalker from attacking you is close to zero. While a restraining order does little to stop the stalker and nothing to prevent an attack it can have a negative effect.

Because of a psychopath's grandiose ego, a restraining order is often seen as an open rejection and declaration of war. The restraining order is a direct attack and the psychopath is again the victim for which he quickly becomes the vengeful type stalker bent on punishing the wrong doer.

Restraining orders are most likely to be violated by the delusional and intimate partner type of stalkers. Delusional stalkers, by definition, cannot be reasoned with. They just don't get it and never will. A court order is just a piece of paper to them.

Former intimate partner stalkers are less likely to adhere to a restraining order the more they have invested in the victim. They feel that nothing should interfere with their retrieving of the debt they think their victim owes them.

With the above pros and cons in mind, give careful thought before deciding which course of action to take. First, research how these orders are enforced in your jurisdiction. You can find such information through support groups, domestic violence programs, etc. Find out if a restraining order violation is a misdemeanor (as it is in most jurisdictions) or a felony. If it is a misdemeanor, it is much less likely to be enforced and/or the consequences are insubstantial. This could make matters worse. If a violation occurs and the police just go out and talk to the stalker or even give him a citation, they merely prove to the stalker that nothing will happen to him, and he can act with impunity. If being issued a ticket is the worst that can happen to him after violating the law what more can the victim do?

Finally, learn the awareness, crime prevention, and empty hand sections of this book in case, as a last resort, you end up having to defend yourself in an attack.

## Children's Safety & Self Defense

Self-defense for children is the responsibility of every parent. It is so simple to teach children a few life saving crime prevention and survival skills that there is no excuse not to do so. Parents should begin to teach basic survival knowledge as soon as possible. In the beginning, teach simple skills such as having them memorize their home address and telephone number. As they mature, teach them what to do if they become lost, or have to stay alone in the home. This should be a continuous and on-going educational program.

## What To Teach Children

- Their home address and telephone number (including area code) as soon as it is possible for them to learn
- Phone numbers where parents can be reached when they are not home, or a trusted neighbor or relative that they could call for help

- How to phone with operator assistance
- How to reach you in an emergency
- How to use the telephone number 911 for emergencies or how to use operator assistance
- Make sure that your child understands that adults do not keep secrets with children

- That it is all right to say 'no' to an adult if the person wants them to do something you have taught them is wrong
- That no one has the right to touch any part of his or her bodies that a bathing suit would cover
- To tell you if someone has asked them to keep a secret from you
- To report to you, school authorities, or a police officer anyone who exposes their private parts

## House Rules

Establish and explain to your kids a set of house safety rules. These should include:

- If someone knocks on the doors, do not open it. Only let those people in that parents have approved. If anyone else tries to come in, to call the police
- In the event of fire, or if the smoke detector goes off, leave the house immediately. Go to a trusted neighbor's house, and call 911 for the Police or Fire Department
- In the event of an emergency, to call you at work, or a trusted neighbor, or the police
- Never to say they are alone if they answer the phone
- Have your child call when they get home so you will not worry

Make sure your children can reach the phone. Put a list of your work, trusted neighbors, and emergency numbers near the phone.

## Rules For Going Out

In addition to safety rules for the home, also institute the following safety rules for children when they go out.

- To tell you where they will be at all times
- Not to enter anyone's home or isolated areas without your permission
- Not to accept gifts or treats from strangers
- Never to approach or enter a stranger's car and to move away from a car that pulls up beside them if they do not know the driver
- Never to take shortcuts through empty parks, fields, or isolated areas
- Learn about the Block Parent Program and logo
- That if they are being followed, they should run home or go to the nearest public place and yell for help
- Always travel in pairs or in groups with more mature children
- That if they become separated from you at a grocery store or shopping mall, to go directly to a cashier of checkout-counter clerk

## What Parents Should Know

- Develop a password with your children and tell them if anyone ever claims they were sent by you to pick them up, that person must give them the password
- Know where your children are, whom they are with, and when you expect them home.
- Make a point of knowing who their friends are, where their friends live, and write down their friend's telephone numbers
- Do not allow children to wear their names on T-shirts, lunch boxes, jackets or jewelry in public. A child is likely to trust someone who addresses him or her by name
- Do not provide personal information about your children on surveys and questionnaires unless a very good reason is given.
- Make sure you are familiar with all baby-sitters. Check their references
- Always accompany children to the bathroom in a public place, and advise them never to loiter in or around the area.
- Create and keep a child identity kit (See Below)

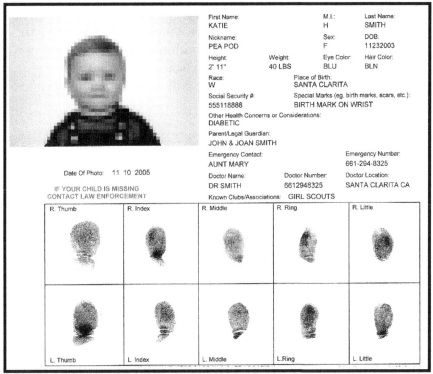

Example of Child Identity Card

## Child Identity Kit

A child identity kit contains important information on each of your children that can be vital to search efforts in the event your child goes missing. The kit should contain:

- An up-to-date color photograph of each child. Up-date the photo at least once a year
- Your child's fingerprints
- Vital stats such as name, age, birth date, hair color, eye color, height, weight, and any medical conditions such as asthma or allergies.

All of this information should be placed on a single sheet of paper or card so that it can be easily photocopied or scanned and sent out to searchers and law enforcement should your child go missing. Also, keep a lock of each child's hair in a sealed baggie that could be used to do DNA comparison checks.

## What To Do If A Child Is Missing

If your child goes missing, or you sense their absence is unusual, then immediately notify police. It is within the first few hours of a kidnapping that police have the best chance of finding the kidnapper and your child. The police will instruct you on what to do.

## Actions You Can Take:

- Make a careful search of your home and surrounding property
- Check with playmates
- Check favorite play areas
- Call all friends, neighbors, and relatives
- Call or visit local the police station. Be prepared to give the following information:
  - full physical description
  - birthmarks or other marks of identification
  - most recent photograph
  - fingerprint record card
  - description of clothing worn at the time of disappearance
  - describe and medical conditions your child might have
  - recent problems at home, school, with playmates etc.
  - possible/probable abduction by spouse or former spouse
  - possible runaway: are favorite clothes, possessions missing?[22]

## Defense Against Child Abduction

All predators, both in the wild and in society, will only pursue prey as long as the caloric gains exceed the caloric expenditures.

Similarly criminals will engage in criminal activity only for as long as the perceived benefits outweigh the perceived risks. Time is the enemy of criminals since the longer it takes to commit a crime, the greater the risk of capture.

**Kicking Tiger** teaches children to become extremely difficult to handle so that a predator would need to expend extra time and energy during the attack stage. Although there is nothing a child could do to prevent a determined adult from carrying them away, the longer a child can delay the predator, and the greater

commotion that child can cause, the riskier it becomes and thus more likely for the predator to break off the attack.

Kicking Tiger teaches kids that if anyone grabs a hold of them and tries to take them away, they should become like a fierce tiger and do the following:

- First, they should drop to the ground, this is to make them a dead weight and more difficult to drag or carry away.
- Next, position their body so that their feet are towards the attacker and kick out at the shins of the attacker.
- Then, make as much noise as possible and to yell, "HELP! This person is a stranger!"
- Finally, if the attacker is still holding on they should bite the hand holding them.

## How to Teach This Self Defense Technique

To demonstrate Kicking Tiger to your children it is best to have another adult or older child to play the role of attacker since young kids do not realize the potential danger of this technique and may accidentally walk into a kick.

Lie down on your side and ask your 'assistant' to attack you. Keep your legs towards the attacker and kick out against the shins as soon as he comes within range. Have the attacker try to run around and come at you from the side. As he does so, pivot on your hip and elbow so that your feet track the attacker and are always pointed towards him. You will see that no matter how fast someone tries to run around you, he can never get ahead of your feet provided you keep pivoting along with his movements.

### Role-Playing: 'Circle of Power'

For this game, only you or another adult should play the attacker and be sure to wear protective soft foam shin pads since the kids can deliver a painful kick to the shins if you are not careful. You could improvise by wrapping a cushion or exercise mat around one shin and hold it in place with a couple of cloth belts. Then keep that padded leg forward to act as a kicking target for the children.

Create a ring or square approximately 10 feet in diameter using belts, skipping ropes, or tape on the ground. Choose children to come up one at a time and instruct them to stand in the middle of the ring. You will then grab them by one wrist. When you say, "Go" you will try to pull the child out of the ring. Tell them that if you can pull them out of the ring, you win. The child should then drop to the ground and start kicking at your shins. As soon as the child lands a good kick on the target, let go and try to run around him or her slowly at first, and then faster. (Allow each child to 'win' this game) Kids learn this one quickly and you will see how it is nearly impossible to outflank those kicking legs.

Tip: While Kicking Tiger makes it very difficult for an adult to drag away a child, if used by an adult against an adult attacker in a self-defense situation, it becomes almost impossible to drag you away. This is also an excellent rape prevention technique for women. Even full contact professional fighters use this technique.

## Police and Law Enforcement

*Man is a tribal animal. We must fully appreciate this fact if we are to understand one of the most important facets of human nature. To ignore it -as so many priests and politicians do- is to court disaster. The tribal qualities of the human species color almost every aspect of our social lives. They are so basic to us, that were we ever to loose them, it would mean that we have mutated into another species altogether.*
Desmond Morris, *Tribes*

### Dangers Of Dealing With The Police

In an ideal society, the police are public servants that prevent crime or capture and punish the criminal after the act. However, this is not always the case. Even the most effective police forces seldom prevent crime. That they may capture the criminal afterwards is a distant concern for the victim being raped, assaulted or murdered. This is why it is essential for everyone to learn crime prevention strategies since relying solely on the police for protection is a statistically foolish gamble.

Like a street gang or a hunting party, police forces are a tribal group of armed men, and occasionally, women. Armed groups are always dangerous for a number of reasons. First, armed men are more likely to resort to force and violence. Weapons can escalate misunderstandings and miscommunications to lethal levels instantly. Second, the tribal nature of a police force tends to create a strong 'Us' and 'Them' culture whereby anyone not a visible member of the authoritarian hierarchy is automatically a criminal. When this mind-set predominates, innocent people can be arrested, imprisoned, and occasionally shot and killed.

Finally, the power, authority, protection, and special privileges afforded by membership in a police force attract psychopaths. When psychopaths infiltrate a police force, they usually succeed in turning that group into another criminal organization. Throughout history and in many different cultures, police forces were as corrupt and dangerous as the most notorious street gangs or organized crime families. In addition, when a nation's government becomes dominated by psychopathic personalities they always seek to transform local police forces into what amounts to an occupation army to be used against civilians.

To complicate matters even more, many psychopaths have impersonated police officers in order to get their victim's compliance and lure them into a trap. For the above reasons one should always approach and deal with the police with caution.

## Calling 911

When calling 911 during an emergency the most important thing is to stay calm and do not yell or scream at the operator. Be prepared to provide the following information

Describe the Nature of the Emergency:  911 operators first need to know whether to direct your call to law enforcement, medical professionals, and/or fire fighters. In certain areas, the dispatcher or a computer will tell you to dial certain numbers to help them know which department to connect you with and with whom you should talk.

Describe What happened: Describe the most life threatening situations first. Is someone shot and in need of an ambulance, or is the intruder still in the house and police assistance is the priority? The purpose is to have the correct emergency responders dispatched for the emergency.

Your Phone Number: The dispatcher will need instructions on how to get to where you are, and may need to call back for more information. Know the phone number of the phone you are using to call for help.

Your Location: Know the address of the emergency and the nearest intersection (cross street), or be able to provide directions for the dispatcher to relay to the emergency responders.

Listen for Instructions: Do not hang up until instructed to. The dispatcher may also give instructions to secure the situation until help arrives. Remember that even if the dispatcher is still asking questions or giving instructions, help is on the way.

Tips: If you call 911 accidentally without an emergency, do not immediately hang up. Stay on the line and let the operator know that it was an accident, giving your name, and address. The operator may interpret that somebody else did the hang-up and he or she will try to trace the call and will send police to investigate.

In a home invasion and hostage situation, you can dial 911 and then discreetly leave the phone off the hook without speaking to the operator. Again, the dispatcher will attempt to trace the call and send police to your location but they can also listen in and try to assess the situation. All calls are automatically recorded which can provide evidence later.

If you use a cell phone, be prepared to give the location of the emergency. Not all cell phones can be traced to your exact location.

---

## International Emergency Dispatch Numbers

Emergency numbers will vary from country to country. If you are traveling, then be sure that you know what the number is for the country you are traveling to. The following are some Emergency Dispatch Numbers used abroad.

| | |
|---|---|
| USA and Canada | 9-1-1 |
| United Kingdom (England) | 9-9-9 |
| Australia | 0-0-0 |
| New Zealand | 1-1-1 |
| Mexico | 0-8-0 |

European Union member states and many other countries use 1-1-2

---

## Greeting The Police

If you called the police to report criminal activity stay calm and identify yourself as the caller as soon as they arrive. Even after identifying yourself as the caller or victim, be aware that they will still regard you with suspicion until they have secured the scene and corroborated your identity. Keep your hands in view and do not make sudden movements. Avoid passing behind them, and never touch the police or their equipment such as vehicles, flashlights, animals, etc.

If you have a photo identity card such as a driver's license or passport present them to the police right away so that you can alleviate their suspicions and thus make it less likely that you would be mistaken for the suspect.

Provide only information concerning the immediate emergency. Do not try to make a legal case, or offer your detective services. Most police will want you to leave the immediate vicinity so that they can focus on the more pressing details of the crime scene. Do not try to help unless asked to.

## Dealing With The Police

There are three basic types of encounters with the police: Conversation, Detention, and Arrest.

Conversation: If the police are trying to get information, but do not have enough evidence to detain or arrest you, they may try to obtain some information by starting a "friendly conversation". If you talk to them, you may give them the information they need to arrest you or your friends. Whenever a law official asks you anything besides your name and address, it is legally safest not to answer any more questions. Ask if you are being detained. If not, you can leave and say nothing else to them.

Never agree to go to the police station for questioning. Simply say, "I have nothing to say."

No matter how you may feel about being stopped or inconvenienced, never bad-mouth a police officer. Stay calm and in control of your words, body language and your emotions. Always keep your hands where the police officer can see them. Do not run away and never touch a police officer!

Detention: Police can detain you only if they have reasonable suspicion that you are involved in a crime. Detention means that, though you are not arrested, you cannot leave. Detention is supposed to last a short time and they are not supposed to move you. During detention, the police can pat you down and go into your bag to make sure you do not have any weapons. They are not supposed to go into your pockets unless they feel a weapon.

Police have two reasons to detain you: 1) they are writing you a citation such as a traffic ticket, or 2) they want to arrest you but they do not have enough information yet to do so.

A detention can easily lead to arrest. If the police are detaining you and they get information that you are involved in a crime, they will arrest you, even if it has nothing to do with your detention. For example, if you are pulled over for speeding (detained) and the officer sees drugs in the car, he or she can arrest you for possession of the drugs even though it is not the reason you were pulled over in the first place.

If you are being detained, the police are allowed by law to pat down or frisk your outer clothing to see if you have any weapons. If the police officer feels something that could be a weapon, then he can go into your pockets and pull out the suspicious item. Otherwise, a police officer cannot go through your pockets or tell you to empty your pockets. By law, the only time a police officer may go through your pockets is if you are under arrest.

Never consent to a search. If the police try to search your house, car, backpack, pockets, etc. say, "I do not consent to this search." This may not stop them from forcing their way in and searching anyway, but if they search you illegally, they may not be able to use the evidence against you in court. [23] To protect yourself make it clear that you do not consent to a search and ask the police officer why he is searching you.

Never physically resist police when they are trying to search you, your vehicle or your home because you could be injured and charged with resisting arrest or assault.

## Traffic Stops

The most common reason for a traffic stop is when an officer observes your vehicle breaking a minor traffic law (there are several hundred of them) and by law is required to give you a citation documenting the violation.

Usually, the officer will follow your vehicle for a short time and then signal you to pull over by activating the emergency lights and/or siren of the police cruiser. The law requires that you pull your vehicle to the right and stop.

Never stop on the left side of the road even if you have to cross several lanes of traffic. Use your right turn signal and carefully change lanes until you are off to the right side of the road. Try to find a safe place to pull over if you can see one within a block or so. For example, do not pull over on a narrow bridge or on-ramp if traveling a block further will provide a wider road and shoulder to stop on. You may be asked to move your vehicle to a different location if the officer believes the current location is unsafe for you, the officer, or passing motorists.

If you are a woman alone in the vehicle that is being signaled to pull over by flashing lights and/or siren and you are in a deserted area, do not stop. Especially suspicious would be an unmarked police vehicle that displays only a flashing light that anyone can purchase. However, though unmarked police cars should arouse concern, even legitimate police officers driving marked police cruisers have been known to assault vulnerable women in remote areas. Turn on your emergency blinkers and drive slowly to a well-lit public area or police station. You may face a moderate misdemeanor charge in some jurisdictions but this would be a small price to pay for your safety.

The officer will stop a short distance away from your vehicle. If the traffic stop takes place at night, the officer may activate the cruiser's spotlights in order to see who is in the car. More police officers are killed each year while conducting traffic stops than during any other police function. A traffic stop is statistically more deadly than a bank robbery, a domestic disturbance or even a bar fight. Officers tend to be a little on edge when approaching a stopped vehicle. Remember, armed men that are nervous are also dangerous and your best strategy is not to do anything that could increase the tension.

It is important that you do not get out of your vehicle. Turn off your radio, and do not go into your glove compartment or under your seat to retrieve anything. Leave both your hands on the steering wheel until the officer has spoken to you for the first time. If the traffic stop is taking place at night, turn on your interior or dome light to show the officer how many people are in the car and what they are doing.

The police officer will first ask you for your driver's license, registration and proof of insurance. By law you are required to carry these on your person or in some easily accessible place in your vehicle at all times while driving and you must surrender them to a police officer upon request. The officer is also not required to tell you why he/she is stopping you until your documentation has been confirmed.

The officer will usually return to his/her cruiser for a short time to contact the dispatcher and check your license and vehicle information to make sure both are valid and that you are not missing or there are warrants out for your arrest. Once the officer has returned your documents he/she must tell you the reason for the traffic stop.

The officer may ask you a few questions about the offense such as "Do you know why I pulled you over?" Always answer that you don't know why you were stopped since saying anything could be taken as a confession.

Should an officer ask you "personal" questions such as, where are you going, where have you been, who did you see, or how long did you visit, you are not required to provide such information. The officer may be trying to find out if there are any other possible criminal offenses to charges you with. To protect yourself it is best to say as little as possible.

If you are issued a citation, you will be asked to sign your signature. It is not an admission of guilt so simply sign it and take your copy. Refusing to sign, or arguing with the police about the offense or the law is futile since once a citation is written it cannot be destroyed and it must be issued. If you do not think you committed the offense you are accused of, you can contest the citation later in court.

Once you have received either a warning or your copy of the citation, the detention is over and you are free to go on your way. Do not try to read the citation while parked at the side of the road. There is nothing on the citation you need to know immediately anyway. Sitting at the side of the road is always dangerous so wait until you get home to read it thoroughly.

If an officer asks to search your car, do not give your permission. If the officer insists on searching your vehicle you cannot stop him. Law enforcement officers are permitted to conduct a warrant-less search of a car if the officer has probable cause. This "probable cause" is based solely on the officer's opinion and so at any time an officer could simply lie and make up a probable cause.

Tell the officer repeatedly "I do not consent to this search." Many people believe that if they have done no wrong and have nothing to hide, there would be no reason to deny permission for a search. This would be true in an ideal society, but as we have already learned, there are many reasons not to trust a police officer any more than you would trust any other stranger. Corrupt police have been known to plant evidence or narcotics during a search. Also by repeatedly saying you do not consent to a search, under US law, any evidence the police might find, or plant, could be ruled as resulting from a warrant-less search and thus inadmissible in court.

If you refuse a search, the officer may offer instead to detain you until a drug-sniffing dog is brought to the scene to conduct a drug search. Opt for the police dog. The officer may be bluffing about calling in a police dog in the hopes that you believe a police officer is less likely to find drugs hidden somewhere in your vehicle than a dog is. By opting for the police dog search, you call the officer's bluff and he may decide not to pursue the search further.

## Arrest

Police can arrest you only if they have probable cause that you are involved in a crime. This means the police must be able to describe criminal related behavior based on what can be observed. They cannot just stop someone because they do not like the way the person looks, they need to be more specific. For example, if there was a robbery at a nearby store and you are seen walking away from the scene this is not enough to arrest you. However, if you were seen running from the store with a bag of money in one hand and a gun in the other this would be probable cause.

In theory, probable cause is the criteria under which the police can arrest someone, in reality the police can arrest anyone, anywhere, and for any reason they like. The police do not decide your charges. They can only make recommendations. The prosecutor is the only person who can actually charge you. Remember this if you are ever threatened by police rattling off all the charges they are supposedly "going to give you."

If the police knock and ask to enter your home, you do not have to open the door unless they have a warrant signed by a judge. Letting police into your home voluntarily means that your encounter with them will likely last longer, and they can also look for evidence of criminal activity. The judicial codes of most countries are so bloated that practically everyone is guilty of some criminal offense at any time.

If the police come to your door with an arrest warrant, go outside and lock the door behind you. If you go back into the house for any reason they can follow you in and search any room you go into.

If they have an arrest warrant, they are allowed to force their way in if they know you are there. It is usually better to go with them without giving them an opportunity to search your home.

In some emergencies such as when a person is screaming for help inside a home, or if someone has called 911 from that address, officers are allowed to enter and search the home without a warrant.

When you are arrested, the police can search you to the skin and go through your car and any belongings. By law, an officer strip-searching you must be the same gender as you.

---

### Miranda Rights

A Miranda warning is a warning given by police in the **United States** to criminal suspects in police custody, or in a custodial situation, before they are interrogated. They are variations of what is exactly spoken but generally the warning is as follows:

*You have the right to remain silent. Anything you say or do can and will be used against you in a court of law. You have the right to an attorney. If you cannot afford an attorney, one will be appointed to you. Do you understand these rights as they have been read to you?*

In **Canada**, equivalent rights exist under the **Charter of Rights and Freedoms.** The Canadian Charter warning reads as follows:

*You are under arrest for _____ (charge), do you understand? You have the right to retain and instruct counsel without delay. We will provide you with a toll-free telephone lawyer referral service, if you do not have your own lawyer. Anything you say can be used in court as evidence. Do you understand? Would you like to speak to a lawyer?*

England, Australia, New Zealand, Europe and most other developed countries have similar rights.

---

## Interrogation

The police have to read you your rights (also known as the Miranda warnings) whenever there is an interrogation by a police officer or other agent of law enforcement while you are in custody. An officer may handcuff you or put you in the back of a police cruiser

114

placing you "in custody" before being formally arrested. Even if you have not been read your rights, what you say can be used against you.

Knowing your rights and demanding them will help you to exercise those rights. Otherwise, the police will think they are dealing with a fool and will try to take advantage of you. The best response is always to stay silent and demand to have a lawyer present. If you do not have enough money to hire a defense attorney, the state is required to provide you with a public defender. When you request a lawyer, all law enforcement officials are legally required to stop asking you questions. They probably won't stop, so just repeat your request for a lawyer's presence and remain silent until they realize they cannot take advantage of you.

Some police officers may become aggressive and hostile if they think you "know your rights." Police often use intimidation to make suspects nervous and more cooperative. If you run into a bad cop, standing up for your rights might get you beaten up or killed. Your rights are not something you can realistically depend on when locked in a windowless room with no witnesses. Police are armed men with virtual impunity to use those weapons. They are potentially the most dangerous members of our society. Always be non-threatening and cautious when you talk to them.

Common ploys to make you talk:
- "You will have to stay here and answer my questions" or "You're not leaving until I find out what I want.
- "I have evidence on you. Tell me what I want to know or else." (They can fabricate "fake" evidence to convince you to tell them what they want to know).
- "You are not a suspect. We're simply investigating so just help us understand what happened and then you can go"
- "If you don't answer my questions, I won't have any choice but to take you to jail."
- "If you don't answer these questions, you'll be charged with resisting arrest."
- "All of your friends have cooperated and we let them go home. You are the only one left."

- "All of your friends have cooperated with the police for lighter sentences and you will take the full brunt of charges unless you cooperate as well."
- "We already know what you did so confess or face more dire consequences."

Good Cop/ Bad Cop: This is the classic ploy whereby one cop pretends to be your friend (Good Cop) while the other cop is aggressive and menacing (Bad Cop). The idea is that the Bad Cop will threaten you and out of fear, you will put your trust in the Good Cop who is usually the same race and gender as you. The Bad Cop may tell you that they have all the evidence they need to convict you while the Good Cop tells you that if you "take responsibility" and confess the judge will be impressed by your honesty and remorse and go easy on you. What they really mean is, "we don't have enough evidence yet, please confess."

Any actual evidence the police have gathered on you may or may not be admissible or relevant in court and thrown out by the judge. However. a personal confession while under interrogation will be next to impossible to retract later.

## Search And Seizure

Police may engage in "reasonable" searches and seizures. To prove that a search is reasonable, the police must generally show that a crime has occurred, and that if a search is conducted it is probable that they will find either stolen goods or evidence of the crime. [24]

If they do have a search warrant, ask to read it. A valid warrant must have a recent date (usually not more than a couple of weeks), the correct address, and a judge or magistrate's signature; some warrants indicate the time of day the police can search.

Police may get a search warrant based on firsthand information, or tips from an informant to search your property. If they use an informant, they must show that the information is reliable under the circumstances.

If the police find evidence or contraband they will ask you if it belongs to you. As with any questions the police may ask you, your response should always be that you refuse to speak unless you have a lawyer present. In many jurisdictions the police can seize your property, your vehicles, and even your homes under the pretext that they are ill-gotten gains. The state can then sell those items and pay bonuses to the arresting officers. With such incentives there is every likelihood that the police will quickly come to abuse their powers for personal gain.

## No knock Warrant

In the US, a no knock warrant is a warrant issued by a judge that allows law enforcement officers to enter a property without knocking and without identifying themselves as police. It is issued under the belief that any evidence they hope to find can be destroyed during the time that police identify themselves and the time they secure the area.

Having armed men wearing black masks that do not identify themselves as police and who break down your door is a terrifying experience. Many innocent people have been shot and killed when they thought criminals were invading their homes and they sought to defend themselves. [25]

This military commando style raid would make most defensive actions futile, even if they were criminals and not police. In either case, your best bet is to stay still and put your hands up in plain view. Do not try to reach for the phone or anything else once the armed men are in your room as this could be mistaken as you going for a weapon.

As in any instance when faced with a group of armed men the first thing you want to do is reduce the tension. Stay calm, don't say anything, and listen. If the intruders are police they will want to handcuff you immediately. Do not resist.

Once the area has been secured and things have calmed down, use the same strategy as in all other such encounters, do not answer questions and demand to speak to a lawyer.

## Undercover And Secret Police

When psychopaths dominate the government of a country itself, they inevitably use the police as the enforcement arm of a political machine. Anyone that disagrees or disapproves of a government's criminal activities automatically becomes a criminal, subversive, or 'terrorist'.

The enforcement of political compliance is usually carried out by 'Special' law enforcement agencies that work under varying degrees of secrecy, hence the secret police. In the US, these would be the FBI, INS, NSA, CIA, and a host of other clandestine forces. In England, this would include MI5, MI6, and Scotland Yard. Each country has its own versions of the secret police each with varying degrees of secrecy. With the public police your civil rights are respected to some degree, but with secret police your civil rights will be violated proportionate to the degree of secrecy these forces operate under.

Ostensibly, these law enforcement agencies are chartered to prevent international criminals from operating within the country and/or counter espionage and counter-terrorism functions. In reality, each secret police force found in every country in the world has been used to investigate their own citizen's political and social activities, despite the fact that these activities are protected by the constitutions of their countries.

You may think that if you do not belong to some radical or subversive political group you would not have to worry about being arrested by the secret police, however, this is incorrect. Almost any group or organization can be deemed a threat by the authorities, politicized, and become targets of the secret police. These include, unions, craft guilds, community service groups, charities, protest and environmental groups, gun and sports clubs, religious groups, advocacy organizations, and political parties, all have been targeted at one time or another by their own governments' secret police.

Often you may be completely unaware that your group or organization is under investigation until after you are arrested. It does not matter whether, in fact, your group is politically subversive or even politically aware for you to be targeted for

118

reasons that may be incomprehensible. For example, a nature group comprised of homemakers and public school teachers that are working to preserve a local woodland may seem the most innocent of organizations. However, if a corrupt government official has already signed a deal with a corrupt corporation to exploit the woodland in question, then these homemakers and teachers automatically become "subversives". Undercover police will be sent in to investigate and then sabotage the group using the typical tools of intimidation, extortion, and subversion.

Undercover/secret police can lie about anything they please including about being police, even if asked directly. Undercover police can even break the law and encourage others to do so as well. For example, undercover narcotics officers get hazard pay for doing drugs as part of their cover. If an undercover agent manages to convince some or all members of your group to commit increasingly criminal activities then the group is soon to be arrested. In a worst-case scenario, the undercover officers may plant evidence and provide false testimony.

## Defense Against The Secret Police
Beware of new members that join your organization especially if they seem to have unusual resources and are advocating a more radical or violent approach. For example, undercover police have been used to mingle among peaceful protesters to throw rocks and commit violence and vandalism in order to discredit and criminalize the peaceful protestors. An undercover officer may introduce drugs or weapons into your organization and should any of your members avail themselves of these items they endanger the entire organization. Isolate, expel, or disassociate any new members immediately upon the first instance of criminal activity.

If you suspect you or your organization may become a target of political intrigue and persecution, pool the groups' resources and retain a law firm that specializes in defending against civil rights violations. Make sure all members have and carry the firm's contact information with them.

If any member of your group is approached or arrested by the police he or she should, as soon as possible, notify all other members. Make sure everyone understands his or her civil rights and how to safely deal with police contact.

Whenever you interact with or observe the police, keep a record. Write down what is said and who said it. Write down the officers' names, badge numbers, and the names and contact information of any witnesses. Record everything that happens.

If you or your organization is being subjected to a harassment campaign by police, then carry a small tape recorder or video camera with you and record your encounters with them. Be discreet. Some (most) police do not like being recorded or filmed, especially if they are planning to violate your civil rights. Recording police actions may cause them to respond aggressively and seize or destroy your recording equipment. However, if there are more witnesses around, filming the police may prevent them from abusing you or your friends. It is important to know your legal rights, but it is also important for you to decide when and how to use them to protect yourself.

Make sure that when you are arrested with other people, the rest of the group knows their right to remain silent. If anyone breaks and talks, you all go down.

## Incarceration
Remember that if you are arrested and cannot afford an attorney you have the right to a public defender. Within a reasonable time after your arrest, or booking, you have the right to make a local phone call: to a lawyer, bail bondsman, a relative or any other person. The police may not listen to the call to the lawyer. If you are on probation or parole, tell your parole office you have been arrested, but nothing else.

Do not talk to the inmates in jail about your case. They could be informants or undercover officers and your jailhouse talk could be used against you in a court of law.

You may be released with or without bail following the booking. If not, you have the right to go into court and see a judge the next court day after your arrest. Demand this right! When you appear before the judge, ask for an attorney. An attorney has a better chance at convincing a judge to let you out on a lower bail then you could.

## If A Friend Or Family Member Has Been Arrested

If you get a call from a police officer or a friend or family member saying that he or she has been arrested and incarcerated the first things you need to know are; where they are being held , by what police agency, and what the actual charge is.

If you are speaking with your friend, tell him or her that you are finding a lawyer and not to answer any questions or make any statements until that lawyer arrives. Do not discuss any details of the crime over the phone since anything they say, even to you over the phone, can be used against them in court. If the arrested is an adult, the police are not required to tell a friend or family member anything.

Find a criminal defense attorney. If you have a family or business attorney you already use then get him or her to recommend a good defense attorney for you. Having another lawyer refer you helps your credibility and the defense attorney may not require as much money up-front than if you just cold called them. If not, then search the internet and/or yellow pages for one nearest you or the place your friend is being incarcerated. Brief the lawyer on the situation including the address of the police station.

Gather as much money as you can to pay the lawyer in court and to post bail. It is more important to get a good lawyer on the case early than to immediately get your friend out of jail. Once a lawyer has been retained follow his or her direction, but do not relinquish critical thinking. Even highly recommended lawyers can be complete idiots. If you feel there is something wrong about the defense proceedings get another opinion. If need be fire the attorney and hire another.

## **Weapons**

*Weapons are instruments of ill omen, they are only to be resorted to when there is no other choice.*
Liu Ji, *Commentaries on the Art of War* 26

No study of the art of survival is complete without a rudimentary knowledge of weaponry, since it is often the type and quality of a weapon that determines combat and survival strategy.

As a rule, a weapon is preferable to empty hand in a struggle for survival. However, carrying a weapon for self-defense has several drawbacks. The first is accessibility. Unless the weapon is carried in the hand, you may not be able to retrieve it from a purse, pocket, boot, or waistband in time to use it. Criminals know to use the element of surprise, which means there may be no time to go for your weapon.

Another drawback is the skill required to use a weapon effectively. Under the stress of combat, even a handgun is only effective at close-range. While traditional martial arts weapons such as *Nunchakus*, *Kobutans*, and *Tonfas* appear lethal in the Dojo, under the stress of a street fight they can be awkward and difficult to handle.

The third drawback to carrying a weapon is the legal ramifications. In most countries, carrying a concealed weapon is illegal and the penalties for carrying a weapon can be serious. Even if you are attacked and you use the weapon to defend yourself, you will find yourself under suspicion because the act of carrying a weapon implies that you must have had the intention to use violence. The attacker may successfully sue you for medical and other costs even if he had provoked the attack.

A weapon is a tool used to accomplish an objective. The most important tools are your mind, and your senses. However, you may also need to resort to the use of weaponry. The following lists different types of weapons according to their classification as Commercial weapons, Improvised weapons and Anatomical weapons.

## Commercial Weapons

<u>Self-Defense Sprays</u>: There are several types of chemical spray dispensers that employ a variety of chemicals. [27] Commonly labeled 'Pepper Spray' they are marketed as self-defense against dogs, bears, and humans.

The advantage to carrying a Pepper Spray device is that it is inexpensive, requires no training, and is legal in most areas. (However. they are not allowed on airplanes). They can be effective at keeping an attacker at a safe distance. The drawbacks are they may not work on someone that is on drugs, in a psychotic rage, or has a high tolerance to pain.

When choosing a spray unit there are two important factors to consider. One consideration is the spray pattern. There are two types, one shoots a stream of liquid, and the other shoots a cone of mist. This is like the two settings on a plastic spray bottle. With the stream dispensers, you get greater distance (15 to 20 feet) and are more effective under windy conditions, but you need to be more precise in aiming. The mist spray has a shorter range (4 to 6 feet) and is easily blown away by the wind, but is easier to aim.

The other factor is the trigger mechanism and/or size of the unit. Choose a model that you could easily fit in a pocket or handbag and that when you grab it you can tell instantly which direction the nozzle is pointing without having to look at it.

Like any weapon, it is only effective if you can employ it successfully. If you are traveling through a high-risk area such as an empty parking garage, or high crime neighborhood, then carry the spray in your hand and keep your hand hidden in a pocket. Also, keep it handy when driving.

Since the spray cannot physically stop an attacker, the strategy to use is hit and run. Spray into the eyes of an attacker and while he or she is adjusting to the pain and watery eyes, you use that opportunity to run to safety.

Stun Guns and Tasers: Stun guns are handheld electronic devices that work by sending an electrical charge through an attacker that temporarily disrupts his nervous system. They typically have two or four electrodes that you must make physical contact with the attacker in order to work. The advantage is that stun guns require no training and can incapacitate an attacker under ideal conditions. The drawbacks are they are illegal in most areas, and like pepper spray, may not work all the time. Since you are required to make contact with your attacker to employ it, there is a greater danger to your person.

**Tasers** are stun guns that also shoot out two small darts attacked to wires to a distance of about fifteen to twenty feet. These darts penetrate the attacker and can thus deliver the shock from a safe distance.

Disadvantages of the Taser are that they can be expensive, illegal, and they are a one shot weapon. If you miss or there are multiple attackers, then they work like any other stun gun with the same drawbacks.

**Impact Weapons:** There are several types of commercial made impact weapons such as police batons, extendable steel batons, and heavy-duty flashlights. The advantage is their low cost, easy availability and effectiveness in causing serious structural injury to an attacker. Swinging a club is an almost instinctive skill so most will be able to strike with a baton. The disadvantage is that one needs more strength to use and you need to be close to the attacker. Close-in fighting is the most dangerous method of dealing with an attack.

**Edged Weapons:** Knives are inexpensive, easily available, easily concealed and, depending on the circumstances, legal to carry. Knives require less strength to use than impact weapons and even a small person could inflict incapacitating wounds with one. A knife is also a useful tool in a disaster/survival situation.

The drawback is again the fact that you would need to close with an attacker to employ a blade. In addition, to be truly effective, some training would be required as well as knowledge of anatomy.

Many knives sport fierce looking or military style blades but all the flash is unnecessary, impractical, and a liability should the police find one on your person. Since in many areas carrying a knife with a blade of five inches or longer is illegal, the best bet for a carry around knife in an urban setting is a working knife. This would be a locking folding knife with a regular looking blade between two to four inches in length. Many come with a thumbscrew that allows you to open the blade with one hand and a locking mechanism that is a vital safety feature to prevent the knife from folding back onto your fingers during a struggle.

Firearms: Firearms are the best self-defense weapon in terms of intimidation and stopping an attacker from a distance. In many cases, simply presenting the firearm will prevent an attack.

As with all weapons, there are disadvantages. Firearms are heavily regulated everywhere in the world, and illegal in most places. Extreme care must be taken when using a firearm, since even slight miscalculations can maim or kill an innocent person. In addition, they are lethal weapons, in that you cannot just use pain or discomfort to stop someone, you must be prepared to kill the attacker and deal with the legal and emotional consequences afterwards.

If you are able to acquire a firearm then you also need to be properly trained on how to use the firearm in a defensive scenario and then maintain proficiency through regular practice.

Handguns: Handguns are small, easy to conceal and carry, and ideally suited for close quarters combat. However, handguns require the most practice of any firearm to use effectively and safely. There are a wide range of handguns and choosing one that is right for you requires time and effort to learn what the options are and what will be the best handgun for you.

Shotguns: If you live in an urban area where owning a handgun is illegal your next option is usually a long arm such as a rifle or shotgun. Shotguns are available in many jurisdictions where every other firearm is illegal. The advantages a shotgun has over other firearms are its stopping power and versatility. Shotguns have the most stopping power against man-sized targets than any other firearm at effective range. Also the wide variety of shell loads allow the shotgun to be used in many application from bird and game hunting to sports like trap and skeet shooting.

Shotguns are typically effective up to 100 yards, which is adequate in an urban home self-defense scenario. The drawbacks to the shotgun include its limited range and accuracy compared to rifles. They also have a strong recoil that intimidates many novice shooters.

Rifles: Rifles are much easier to shoot than any other firearm. They are easier to aim, lighter, and have less recoil than would a shotgun. The drawback in a self-defense scenario is the penetrating power of rifle rounds that can easily penetrate walls and doors and travel up to a mile possibly injuring innocent people. They are usually longer than a shotgun and thus even more unwieldy in a cramped urban self-defense scenario.

Finally, shotguns and rifles are strictly home defense weapons; you cannot go to the mall with a rifle slung over your shoulder. In this case, a Pepper Spray you can use is more practical than heavy firepower you cannot.

## Improvised Weapons

*Well then, the accomplished man uses the sword but does not kill others. He uses the sword and gives others life. When it is necessary to kill, he kills. When it is necessary to give life, he gives life.*
Takuan Soho, *Letter to Yagyu Munenori*

In a life or death battle, a weapon, any weapon, will help to improve your odds of survival. If you are unable to acquire a commercial weapon, or the one you have is unavailable, then your second best option is to improvise one. The following briefly describe ways of improvising and using an assortment of everyday items as weapons.

## Penetrating Weapons

These weapons cause injury by piercing the skin and/or body cavities. Classical examples include stabbing weapons such as swords, spears, and daggers.

Pen, Kobutan, Small Stick: Held tightly in the fist, any solid tubular object can deliver serious destructive energy with no injury to the hand. A four to six inch piece of doweling, pipe, tubing, or such everyday objects as pens, markers, or lighters can be used. Techniques are limited to hammer fist strikes to nerve clusters, the temples, and jaw.

Umbrella, Walking Stick: Instinct says to use these as bludgeoning weapon, but these are more lethal when used in a two handed thrusting motion. The narrow metal tip found on most umbrellas can penetrate through clothing, skin, and muscles like a sword. Targets include the solar plexus, temples, and throat. Use the centre section between your hands to block incoming attacks (especially effective against knife attacks.) and in thrusting horizontally against the throat.

## Cutting Weapons

A sharp edge is used to inflict damage by slicing sinew and blood vessels, which may stop an attacker due to loss of blood, intimidation at the sight of blood, or impairment of physical functions by cutting major blood vessels and tendons. Traditional cutting weapons include the knife, sword, axe, and halberd. Most kitchen knives are just as lethal as specialty fighting knives and are more readily available.

Keys: Held in the fist with the pointed ends of the keys protruding between the fingers, they can be used to scratch and cut. Directed

towards the face the wounds themselves would not be serious enough to stop an attacker but the blood from facial wounds could blind and distract the attacker.

Broken Glass: Using a broken bottle top as a cutting weapon is a cliché improvisation but beware that bottles are more difficult to break than you think. Make sure you hit it against a hard surface to break it. This weapon is only useful for intimidation purposes since its slippery grip, irregular shape, and fragility, makes it an unreliable weapon. A bottle makes a better projectile or club.

## Bludgeoning Weapons

These weapons rely on their mass to generate force and inflict damage. Classical bludgeon type weapons include probably man's first improvised weapon; the club and its more evolved descendants, the mace and war hammer.

Bludgeoning weapons are difficult to block against since their strategy is to smash through a person's defense. Bludgeoning weapons require little skill to use effectively and are therefore more suitable for those with little training.

Baseball Bat, Tire Iron, Metal Pipes: One or more of these can usually be found around the house. The basic method is to simply grasp in both hands and swing against an attacker without any specific target. The baseball bat is one of the best weapons for home self-defense especially for women since it is light enough to swing easily but solid enough to injure a larger attacker. Keep one under the bed and another beside the front door.

Stick, Cane, Broom Handle: Best used either in a thrusting manner like a spear, or laterally, holding both ends to 'clothesline' an attacker's throat. Another method is to hold the stick in one hand and whirl the stick in a circular 'figure-eight' pattern to intimidate attackers. However, a stick is usually too light to have real 'stopping' power. The average person can easily take a hit from a stick without suffering debilitating pain or injury. Extensive training in stick fighting can increase its effectiveness as a weapon.

Rolled Magazine: Tightly roll a magazine into a tube and grasp firmly in fist with the bottom of the tube protruding about an inch from the bottom of the fist. The tightly compressed paper around the butt end is solid enough to deliver a heavy blow. Most effective when using the butt end in a hammering action aimed at the bridge of the nose, temple, back of the neck or collarbone. The forward section can be thrust at the eyes or throat, or in a striking action, like swatting a fly, to the nose and ears.

Bottles and Bar Stools: When in restaurants and bars these are readily available weapons. A bottle makes an effective club for close range while picking up a chair or stool is effective at long range and against multiple attackers. Don't swing them over your head since this would leave you wide open to a tackle, rather use them to thrust and slash like a lion tamer to keep your attackers at bay as you carefully back-out of the situation.

### Flexible Weapons

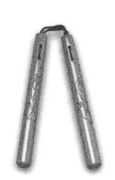

Flexible weapons deliver destructive force through speed that can crush or cut. Classical weapons include flails, whips, and weighted chains. The biggest advantage to flexible weapons is that they are difficult to block since their flexibility allows the weapon to whip around a block to strike from the side and even from behind. There are several ways to improvise flails and whips.

Belt and Buckle, Dog Leash, Key Chain: With a belt, wrap the end around the fist once to make a tight grip and use the weight of the buckle as a flail. With a piece of rope, tie a couple of knots at one end to act as a weight. With chains such as a dog leash or a key ring and chain combination, again wrap one end around the fist and use the heaviest end to swing the weapon. The basic method of using flexible weapons is to use swinging strikes. Another tactic is to swing the weapon in a whirling figure-eight pattern in front of your body to drive back or discourage an attacker.

Sock, Pantyhose, Stocking, Woolen Ski Hat, Pillowcase: Any of these can be stuffed with something solid such as; loose change, a tin can, or a handful of stones, and, holding it tightly by the open end, swung around as a flail. With lighter material such as socks and pantyhose first tie a knot at the toe before adding the weight, this provides a little more strength so that the weight does not rip through the fabric on the first strike.

Purse, Briefcase, Gym Bag: These make somewhat larger and slower flails but their extra weight compensates for the lack of speed. Grasp by the handles and swing in an arching motion against the attacker's head. For a heavier impact, carry a hardcover book in your purse or school bag, or a pair of shoes in your gym bag.

## Throwing Weapons

In ancient Japan, the poorest soldiers were armed with nothing but a sack of smooth, heavy stones that they simply threw at the enemy. Primitive as this may seem the stone-throwers, at close range, where accurate and effective in stopping even amour-clad infantry.
Though less lethal than arrows, this was compensated for by a rate of fire that was three to four times that of archers. Against larger or multiple attackers this ancient tactic can be surprisingly effective; simply pick up as many objects as you can and throw them at your attacker. Common objects that make handy projectiles include; rocks, dirt, sand, bottles, ashtrays, salt and peppershakers, pop cans, furniture, and shoes.

## Chemical Weapons

Most chemical weapons irritate the eyes and the (mucus membrane) tissues in the nose, mouth, throat, and lungs. Chemicals are administered through either a spray or a powder that is aimed at the face. Commercial self-defense chemicals include pepper spray and mace. However, when these are unavailable, some items found around the house can be used as a chemical weapon.

Irritant Powders: Common irritant powders include; salt, pepper, chili powder, drain cleaners, and sand. These can be secretly carried in the hand or a pocket and thrown at close-range into the face to temporarily blind an attacker.

Spray Paint: Alternatives to pepper spray is a can of oil-based spray paint that will irritate the eyes and throat as well as mark and identify the attacker to police. A loud florescent color is best since it will attract unwanted attention to the attacker. Once 'marked' it is hoped that an attacker will be more concerned about scrubbing off the telltale paint than continuing the attack.

### Fire Weapons

Fire is one of man's oldest weapons and there are numerous variations in its use. The most common strategy is the use of fire as a distraction in order to escape. Set fire to something of value to your opponent and he would have to break off his attack to rescue the items from destruction. A fire is something that cannot be ignored.

Gasoline and Match: Throw a glass of highly flammable liquid such as gasoline, paint thinner, or lighter fluid onto the attacker and then use a lighter or match to prevent the person from coming any closer.

Aerosol Can Torch: Many aerosol hair sprays, air fresheners etc, contain flammable liquids. Holding a lit match or lighter two to three inches away from and below the nozzle will ignite the liquid creating a short-range flamethrower. Use only short bursts being careful to keep the flame away from the nozzle so that the heat will not melt the plastic tip.

Boiling Water: Traditionally thrown over the parapet onto besiegers it can also be used in home defense. If you are trapped in the bathroom, you can run the hot water until hot and fill a bowl or other container. Should the attacker succeed in breaking through the door you can throw the water on him and take advantage of his shock and surprise to counter-attack and escape.

## Anatomical Weapons

*Since we have no swords or spears, we shall make our hands into swords and our fingers into spears.*
Motto of the Shaolin Temple

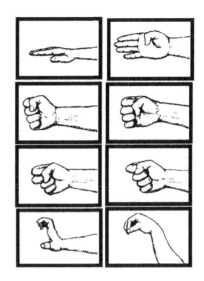

Compared to the teeth and claws of other predators, man's anatomical arsenal may seem inferior, however, our lack of weaponry is more than compensated for by the ingenious methods of turning almost every part of our anatomy into a weapon. Martial arts teach that the body is itself a weapon. Science has shown that the hand of a martial arts expert can develop a peak velocity of 10 to 14 meters per second; even the average person can move their hand faster than a King Cobra can strike. The rupture modulus (breaking point) of human bone is more than forty times that of concrete and is thus capable of breaking wood and concrete.28 The following will examine some anatomical weapons, and give a brief description of their general application.

Head: The human head weighs approximately eight pounds and can deliver a devastating blow because of its size and mass. The best technique is a head butt. Drop your chin to your chest and use the top of the forehead, along the hairline, as a striking surface. Target the nose as this will break the delicate cartilage and cause extreme pain, bleeding, and watering of the eyes. It is often used as a type of 'sucker punch' since the hands can be held relaxed at the sides to reduce suspicion. The head butt is also effective when grappling and both your, and your opponent's arms, are neutralized.

133

Shoulder: The shoulder can be used in a forward 'tackle' technique using the upper side as a striking surface to crack ribs and knock the wind out of an opponent, or when standing, a sideways motion using the outside of the shoulder to knock an opponent off his feet or crush him against a solid object. The drawbacks are its short range and limited application.

Elbows: Because of its solid boney structure, the elbow can deliver a powerful blow easily capable of fracturing bones and rupturing internal organs. Used offensively, the elbow can be swung in an arching movement to strike forwards and backwards, as well as to the side. Used defensively, the elbows are held in close to the body to defend against attacks to the ribs and abdomen, or used to block against kicks and punches. Broken hands, feet, and shinbones are common sparring injuries that occur when an opponent's attack lands against the hard bone of an elbow instead of the target.

Forearms: The forearms can also be used in both defensive and offensive roles. In defense, the forearms block or deflect incoming attacks. As an offensive weapon, the outside edge of the forearms (along the ulna bone) can be used in a chopping action against an opponent's arms when he attacks, or to strike at the shoulders and neck. Using the upper forearm (along the radius bone), the forearm can be used in a sweeping or 'clothesline' technique against the throat.

Fist: The fist/punch is a fast and effective long-range weapon when used against soft tissue targets such as the nose, tip of the jaw, and solar plexus, and as a 'setup' for a final technique. There are two targets you should never punch - the head, and the mouth. The thickness and mass of the skull is sufficient to break the bones in the hand,  while a punch to the mouth often results in the opponent's teeth severely cutting the hand while the human saliva in the resultant wounds are more likely to cause a serious infection.

Knee: The heavy bone structure of the knee, like the elbow, can be used as a powerful short-range weapon. Even women and children can inflict severe pain and injury against a much larger attacker using the knee as a weapon. Traditional targets are the groin, the inside or outside of the thigh, and the face as a defense against a leg dive.

Feet: The use of the feet as weapons has almost as many applications as the hands. Several parts of the foot can be used as a striking surface. These include, the ball, ridge, heel, and instep, all heavily boned surfaces that can deliver crushing energies. Able to generate more power, and have a longer range the feet, however, are slower and have one major disadvantage; you sacrifice stability when kicking since you are standing on one foot. For this reason, a good kicker will withdraw the leg as fast as he kicks it out, reducing the time in which he is vulnerable. Best targets are the groin, knees, shins, and top of the foot (instep).

## Sonic Weapons

*Yelling is very important, because yelling encourages us, we yell at things as fires, and also at the wind and waves. Yells show spirit.*
Miyamoto Musashi, *The Book of Five Rings*

Often overlooked is the use of sound as a weapon. Best used as a fallback or supplemental weapon, sound can deter an attacker through discomfort, by drawing attention to the scene, and as a tactic in combat.

In lieu of commercial produced weapons such as a pepper spray, you can carry a compressed air sound horn. These come is sizes small enough to carry in a pocket or purse and they emit a loud piercing blast of noise that at close ranges can startle, stun, and cause pain and even injury to the ears of an attacker. In addition, the sound can be heard up to a mile away and can attract the attention of passersby and cause the attacker to break off his attack for fear of being discovered in the act.

Another sonic device is a rape whistle. These can produce the same effects as the sound horn but being lighter they are best carried on a lanyard around the neck so that they are even more accessible.

Our final sonic weapon is the voice. Human vocal cords can generate a sonic burst that, at close range, can cause pain, disorientation, dizziness, and even rupture an attacker's eardrum. At medium range, a loud yell can shock and disorient your attacker and upset his concentration.

In Japan, the war cry is called a *Kiai* that aptly means 'Spirit Yell'. Musashi describes three types of yell; pre-attack yell, attacking yell, post attack yell. The pre-attack yell is used to intimidate, and place fear and doubt in your opponent's mind, 'spooking' the enemy. In self-defense, the pre-battle yell works as a deterrent by showing your determination to resist with force. In addition, the yell may draw attention and summon help. The attacking yell is loud and sudden to startle and confuse the opponent. The attacking yell also helps you to focus your own concentration and energy into the attack. The post attack yell is one of victory and release to dissipate excess energy and calm the nerves, ready for another possible encounter.

Another effective use of a yell is during close-in fighting. If being restrained in a bear hug or on the ground on your back and you are able to get your mouth close to your opponent's ear, then use a sudden blasting scream directly into the ear at the same time as you execute your escape technique.

## Psychological Weapons

Feigned Insanity: This is an ancient tactic used to discourage attacks, or cause the attacker to underestimate you. During a sexual assault, feigning insanity can deter an attacker since many people are superstitious and feel uncomfortable around 'crazy' people. (Start talking to an invisible friend and see how many people come near you.) If it does not look as if the insanity act is going to deter an attack, it can nevertheless give you the element of surprise, by suddenly transforming from a drooling idiot into a focused and determined fighter.

Feigned Seizure: This tactic works to dissuade an attack since it appears that you are going to die anyway. Practice the following method a few times so that you will be able to give a convincing performance if you should need to. (Best done alone so you will not be disturbed or cause others concern). Begin by tensing the muscles until they begin to tremble with fatigue, then drop to the ground and contract the abdominal muscles spastically. Facial expressions include, rolling the eyes, drooling from the mouth, and holding your mouth open as in a silent scream. While real epileptic seizures seldom look like this, remember you will probably be dealing with ignorant criminals who will not know the difference.

Contagion: Calmly warn your attacker that you suffer from a rare but highly infectious incurable disease and that if any of your blood or saliva should make skin contact it will surely infect others. Few criminals would know if this were true or not, but, if someone told you they were diseased and highly infectious, would you want to take the chance the person is bluffing?

## Defense Against Weapons

If an attacker openly displays a weapon, it is usually intended to intimidate the victim. If the intention were to harm or kill, then the best strategy would be to keep the weapon hidden until within effective range. A weapon that is displayed is a threat to illicit your cooperation.

As a means of self-defense, a weapon is likewise best used to intimidate and dissuade an attack. By displaying a weapon openly, you increase the perceived risk of injury to a potential attacker. An easy target is an invitation to cowardly assailants, but, someone armed and therefore obviously willing to fight tooth and claw to the end, is another matter altogether.

The best defense is prevention, using learning, experience, awareness, and quick thinking. However if all else fails and you find yourself fighting an armed attacker, then the following principles may improve your chances or surviving.

### Defense Against A Knife

Defending empty hand against an attacker armed with a knife requires trickery and caution. The first strategy is to improvise your own weaponry to equal the odds. If you have a chance to evade, delay, or distract the attacker long enough and you have an available weapon in mind, then go for the weapon. Improvised weapons can either extend your reach or act as a shield. To extend your reach use chairs, brooms, sections of pipe or sticks, or a rolled magazine. A belt and buckle can be used as a flail. For a shield use a coat, jacket, or tablecloth wrapped around the arm to use for parrying thrusts, or use a briefcase, purse, or gym bag to block against a hacking attack. Projectiles can also be picked up and made obvious to the attacker. Threaten to throw the object if he comes any closer. Do not throw unless he really attacks and then always aim for the eyes. Watch for fake lunges to test your resolve.

If it is not possible to obtain a weapon then you must use extreme caution. Try to stay out of critical range, you want to keep the knife in sight at all times, which you cannot do if you are wrestling on the ground. Assume a crouched position with the arms held out in front and use the forearms to deflect incoming attacks and to keep the body's vital organs as protected as possible. Block or parry against the attacker's forearm and elbow, stay clear of the hand and wrist holding the knife. Unless you are an expert in empty hand combat do not attempt to go for the knife hand, at best you will lose a few fingers.

Do not try to kick the knife out of the hand, no matter how good you are. However, kicking to the attacker's knees and shins is very effective since it does not overly expose you, and because they seldom expect it. A person who holds a weapon in his hand is focused on that weapon, and tends to be offensive rather than defensive. This means there is an attention deficit somewhere. Usually they do not expect an attack anywhere else but their weapon hand. Take advantage of this inattention and attack vital targets, such as the eyes, throat, groin, knees. Wear the attacker down using evasion and tactical strikes to his blind spots. If there is an opportunity during this to escape and run, then do so. Only when the attacker is injured and exhausted, and there is no escape, should you attempt to disarm.

Any attacker that displays a knife is using lethal force and your response should be as lethal as possible. Do not waste time on fancy restraining techniques and disarms, they probably will not work anyway. Instead attack the most vulnerable targets; the eyes, nose, and throat.

139

## Defense Against A Club

The club is not as dangerous as the knife and the strategy for dealing with a club-wielding assailant is opposite to dealing with the knife. In a knife fight, you want to stay away, in a club fight you want to move in close. The effective range for a club is quite specific; out of range and it is useless, too close and the attacker has not enough room to swing. It is at arm's length the club is its most lethal.

The strategy for dealing with a club attack is stay out of range of the swing, and then come in fast and stay close. Timing is important, you must move in either before the attacker has a chance to raise the club, or just after the first swing. Once you are in past the effective range, forget about the club since it is not a threat as long as you stay in close. The assailant will expect you to go for his weapon, so while he is preoccupied holding on to his club, you take advantage of his inattention and strike the assailant directly using your most powerful short range techniques such as elbows, knees, or head butt.

## Defense Against Flexible Weapons

Chains, belts, and whips are difficult to defend against since the tactic of flexible weapons is to strike around a block or to ensnare the arms. The best strategy is to try to remain outside the weapon's effective range until you can pick up something solid to throw at the attacker or to ensnare the weapon. For example,

a bar stool with the legs held towards the attacker can ensnare the chain or flail. Alternatively, you can improvise a shield from a garbage can lid or backpack or briefcase to block while Attacking the Corners. (see Combat Strategies and Tactics p. 164)

When the weapon is ensnared, the attacker's first response is to disentangle his weapon, at that moment drop your shield and charge or escape. If there is no time or room to maneuver out of range, then go in low and take out the attacker's legs. This can be done with a tackle, a forward roll, or a sliding kick, like sliding into home base but targeting the opponent's ankles or knees.

## Defense Against A Gun

Defending empty hand against someone armed with a handgun is extremely dangerous but not impossible. Because of the risk involved, attempting to escape from or disarm a gunman should be a last resort used only if you feel certain that cooperation will still result in being shot.

If a handgun is displayed or aimed at you from a distance of more then twenty feet, and if there is a place of safety where there are a lot of people around, then make a run for it. There are several reasons for this: first, it is unlikely that the assailant will shoot since this would attract unwanted attention, and since you saw the gun, its purpose was more to intimidate you than to kill. Even if the assailant does shoot at you, at a distance of twenty feet or more the chances of hitting a moving target is less than one in ten and the chances decrease the farther away you run. Even if you are struck by a bullet, the chances of it being a lethal wound are low, and it is far better to be wounded near possible help and rescue than to be taken away to a remote location to be robbed, raped, and then shot with no chance of crawling to safety or calling out for help. 29

When running, run in a zigzag pattern, which makes it much more difficult for a shooter to target you. Try to turn a corner as soon as you can and put as many obstacles between you and the attacker.

If you are confronted with a gun at from six to ten feet then cooperate, you are too far away to make a play for the weapon and too close to run away fast enough. The strategy is to survive by cooperating while subtly trying to maneuver yourself in or out of this critical range. However, if at any time the gunman becomes distracted and you have somewhere safe to run to, you should run.

If the gun is so close that you could easily reach out and grab it, wait until the assailant's attention is distracted before making a move. Do not look at the gun before you make your move since this will telegraph your intentions. Instead, try to distract his attention and then go directly for the gun hand. Grab the wrist with both your hands and push the muzzle away from you. Remember that there is always a slight delay between perception and reaction. With the aid of a distraction, this should allow enough time to grab the weapon hand before the assailant can aim and pull the trigger. Again, this is only possible if you are already close enough to touch the weapon. If you have to cover ground first to reach the weapon this will negate the advantage of this time gap. Once you have gripped the gun hand you must literally hang on for life, use a head butt and knee strikes against the opponent's body or a grappling type elbow or shoulder break against the arm holding the gun.

Armpit elbow lock.

142

# Hand To Hand Combat

*Most sorts of diversion in men, children and other animals, are in imitation of fighting.*
Jonathan Swift

The worst case scenario in defending against human predators is to have to defend yourself against physical assault.

Up to this point we have examined every possible tool and tactic to avoid this scenario, but should all these fail, then knowing a couple of basic of hand-to-hand combat principles will provide you with an edge to survive. The following describes the basic physical techniques, and tactics used in combat and is intended as an introduction and supplement to a real life self-defense or martial arts training program.

In hand-to-hand combat, almost all techniques can be classified under two broad categories, Punch and Strike, and Grappling. Most styles of martial arts employ a variety of techniques from both categories. Only a few styles incorporate techniques exclusively from one category such as Western Boxing and Greco-Roman wrestling, but these have evolved into a sport and have therefore lost many of the practical techniques of self-defense. The following is a brief description of the different approaches to hand-to-hand combat.

## Punch Kick Techniques

The mechanics behind punching and kicking involves generating momentum through the limbs and transferring the energy into the opponent's body. The body's numerous natural weapons and the wide range of possible motions produce a vast number of different techniques and accompanying strategies.

## Fighting Stance

In combat your stance must be firm and solid, and yet, flexible and fluid. Your feet should grip the ground as you lower your centre of gravity and sink into your stance. The higher your centre of gravity the more susceptible to losing your balance you are. When you move, do so deliberately, but softly. Too fast and too rigid and again you will lose balance.

1) Step one leg in front of the other and bend knees slightly.

2) Keep your back straight, mouth closed and chin down.

3) Raise one hand in front of the face, and another hand in front of the stomach. This position forms a protective "cage" around the body, so that if you are suddenly attacked, your arms and hands protect most of your vital points.

## Blocking

Integral to punch and kick systems are the blocks and parries. There are several strategies using blocks. At it simplest, blocks intercept incoming attacks, while more advanced applications include simultaneous block and counter combinations.

Blocks can also be used offensively by using them to injure the opponent's arms and legs. For example, using a dropping elbow block against an incoming kick will often fracture the small bones in the attacker's foot or the shinbone. Another example is a forearm block applied to the outside elbow of an opponent's punching arm that can fracture and/or dislocate the elbow joint.

Offensive blocks are also a practical strategy against knife attacks since coming in close an attacker would be too dangerous. Offensive blocks applied to the arm and elbow of the knife-wielding arm can cause the attacker to drop the knife while allowing you to stay outside the range of lethal wounds.

## High Block

1) Make a fist and raise arm across chest and face until it is above your head.

3) Make sure the elbow is bent about 45 degrees.

High block as defense against Hammerfist.

## Low Block

1) Bring arm across body to opposite shoulder.

2) Swing arm downwards past stomach.

3) Finish with fist above knee.

Low Block as dcfense against front kick.

## Outside Block

1) Bring arm across stomach and swing the arm outwards and across your face and chest.

Outside block as defense against reverse punch.

2) Finish with arm in front of shoulder.

## Inside Block

1) Chamber your fist near ear level with the elbow out.

Inside block as defense against lead hand punch.

2) Bring the forearm inwards across face and chest.

3) Finish with the fist in front of your opposite shoulder.

## Striking Techniques

### Lead Hand Punch (Jab)
From a ready stance…
1) Punch out at nose level with the lead hand. (i.e. if the left foot is forward, the left hand is the lead hand)

2) The rear hand maintains a block position.

### Reverse Punch
From a ready stance…
1) Punch out at chest level with the rear hand. (i.e. if the left foot is forward the right hand punches)

2) At the same time turn your hips and shift forward.

## Hook Punch
From a Ready Stance…
1) Chamber you rear hand and bend at the elbow about 90 degrees.

2) Swing the arm inwards in a hooking fashion, keeping elbow bent. Fist ends in front of face at about chin level.

**Back Fist**

From a Ready Stance...
1) Chamber your lead hand back and across your body to the opposite shoulder.

2) Swing the arm back outwards like a backhand with a tennis racket. The back of the hand and knuckles strike the target.

**Side Elbow**

From a Horse Stance...
1) Pull your lead arm back across your chest and clasp both hands together.

2) Strike sideways with the point of the elbow.

# Kicking
## Stomp Kick

From a ready stance…
1) The rear (back) leg kicks forwards at shin height.
The foot is turned slightly so that the toes point outwards. The striking surface is the heel or side of the foot.

## Front Snap Kick

From a ready stance…
1) The rear (back) leg kicks forward with the knee bent.
The leg snaps out at groin or stomach level. The striking surface is the ball of the foot.

## Back Kick

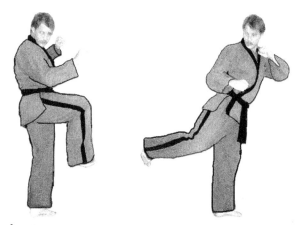

From a ready stance…
1) The front (lead) leg lifts up with knee bent.

2) The leg then stomps backwards like a donkey. The striking surface is the heel and bottom of the foot.

## Grappling And Escape Techniques

The second classification of combat techniques is known as grappling. Grappling includes throws and joint locks and can be used both offensively and defensively. When used defensively, grappling techniques are typically used to escape from an attacker's hold.

All of the following escape techniques start with a distraction technique first, followed by an escape and a finishing technique. The most common and easiest distraction is to stomp or kick low to the attacker's instep or shins. When practicing the joint locks it is important to have a Stop Signal that lets your training partner know when he or she feeling pain. This is called 'Tapping Out' and it means that you must slap your thigh or shoulder two times to signal your partner to ease up on the pressure.

## Escape From Straight Hand Grab

1) Attacker - Stand in front of your partner and use one hand to grab your partner's wrist.

2) Defender - Distract the attacker by stomp kicking his/her shins.

3) Defender - Don't try to pull away. Move in, bring your body close to the arm being grabbed, and clasp your hands together.

4) Defender - Turn away from the person grabbing you by twisting at the waist and using your whole body to break the grip.

5) Defender - Suddenly reverse the escape move and hit the attacker with a Back Fist strike to the nose.

Tip: Make sure the forearms are kept tight across the abdomen and that you twist your body quickly to escape.

151

## Escape From Double Front Hand Grab

1) Attacker - Stand in front of your partner and use both hands to grab both your partner's wrists.

2) Defender - Distract the attacker by stomp kicking his/her shins.

3) Defender - Move in and bring your body close to one of the arms being grabbed. Turn your body sideways as you step in and bring your arm across your stomach until the attacker's grip on that arm is broken.

4) Defender - Strike sideways towards the attacker's solar plexus using a side elbow.

Tip: Make sure the forearm is kept tight across the abdomen and that you turn sideways or perpendicular to your body.

# Escape From Double Hand Grab From Behind

1) Attacker - Stand behind your partner and grab both arms by the wrists.

2) Defender - Step forward with one leg and then use the forward leg to kick back against the attacker's shins until he lets go.

3) Defender - Step forward and bring your elbows up across your chest.

4) Defender - After stepping forward, swing back in either direction and strike with a back elbow aimed at the attacker's jaw or nose.

Tips: This is the simplest technique for this situation. Keep kicking back until the attacker lets go.

# Escape From Front Hand Choke

1) Attacker - Stand in front of your partner and put both hands on your partner's throat. Never apply pressure to the throat!

2) Defender - Distract the attacker by stomp kicking his/her shins

3) Defender - Swing one arm over top of the attacker's arms

4) Defender - Simultaneously turn your whole body sideways and bring your upper arm down on the attacker's arms.

5) Defender - Use the same arm to swing back using the bottom of the fist or the elbow as a striking surface aimed against the attacker's nose.

Tips: This technique could easily break someone's nose. Defender should only practice the return blow in slow motion and must stop short.

## Escape From Hand Choke From Behind

1) Attacker - Stand behind your partner and gently grab his/her neck from behind.

2) Defender - Lift one arm straight over your head.

3) Defender - Turn in the direction of the raised arm so that your shoulder and body weight press against the attacker's forearms. Turn around completely while bringing your arm down deflecting the attacker's arms away from you.

4) Defender - Finish with a stomp kick to the shins or knee to the groin

Tip: Make sure you turn tight so that you bring your whole body and shoulder against the attacker's forearms.

## Escape From Choke From Behind [Arm Bar]

1) Attacker – Grab your partner from behind across the throat using an arm bar. Do not apply any pressure against the throat.

2) Defender - Drop your chin and hunch your shoulders. Stomp on the attacker's instep and kick back against the shins.

3) Defender - Turn in the direction of the attacker's elbow and use the arm closest to the attacker to strike the groin.

4) Defender - Continue to turn towards the attacker's elbow and bring your leg behind the leg closest to you.

5) ) Defender - Bring the arm closest to the attacker up and under his chin while using the leg behind the attacker's leg to sweep back throwing the attacker on the ground.

Tip: Escape from an Arm Bar Choke is one of the most difficult escapes. Keep stomping against the shins until the attacker relaxes his grip enough to start turning.

156

## Escape From A Hammerlock

1) Attacker - Stand in front of your partner and use both hands to grab one of your partner's wrists and twist the arm inwards so that your arm is forced up behind your partner's back.

2) Defender - Do not fight against the twisting action. Turn you body around in the direction of the pressure until you arm is across your lower back.

3) ) Defender - Turn to face your attacker and use your other hand to push against the attacker's chin

Tip: By turning the body in the direction of the twist, you are able to put the weight of your whole body against the attacker's arm. It is very difficult for the attacker to apply any pressure and so you will not feel any more pain from the hammerlock. In serious situations, instead of a push, strike using the heel of the palm against the attacker's nose.

## Escape From Bear Hug From Behind [Under arms]

1) Attacker - Wrap your arms around your partner's waist from behind and under the arms, clasp your hands together.

2) Defender - Use one of your legs to kick back against the attacker's shins.

3) Defender - Clasp you hands together and sink your weight down.

4) Defender - Use two or three back elbow strikes aimed at the jaw in rapid succession alternating from left to right by twisting at the waist.

Tip: Be extra careful in practicing the three back elbows. Go slow since it is easy to hit your partner and cause serious injury. Practice slow motion at first and then increase the speed. The 'Attacker" must lean far back and away to avoid the elbow strikes. Defender must make sure to twist far enough at the waist each time.

# Escape From Bear Hug From Behind [Over Arms]

1) Attacker - Wrap your arms over your partner's arms and shoulders from behind and clasp your hands together.

2) Defender _ Use one of your legs to kick back against the attacker's shins.

3) Defender - Raise your arms up in front of you body as if lifting a heavy pail. At the same time, bend your knees and slide down through the attacker's arms.

4) Defender - Use a back elbow to the attacker's stomach.

Tip: Make sure you coordinate lifting the arms with sliding down so that it is one single action. If an attacker is still able to hold on slightly, then use the elbows and the legs to strike back against the attacker until the opportunity to escape.

159

## Escape From Front Bear Hug [Under arms]

1) Attacker - Stand in front of your partner and wrap your arms under your partner's arms and around his or her waist.

2) Defender - Use a stomp kick against the attacker's shins or top of the foot.

3) Defender - Cup you palms and slap the attacker's ears.

4) Defender - Bring the heel of your palm up under the attacker's chin or nose and push up and back until he lets go.

Tip:  Slapping the ears is an extremely dangerous technique that traps air in the auditory canal and can cause the eardrum to blow. This is also very painful. In practice with a partner, go slowly to avoid trapping the air since even a light slap can be painful. The heel palm to the nose is more painful than to the chin but both are very effective.

## **Escape From Front Bear Hug** [Over arms]

1) Attacker - Stand in front of your partner and wrap your arms around your partner's waist over his or her arms. Clasp your hands together.

2) Defender - Use a knee strike against the attacker's groin.

3) Defender - Simultaneously slide down while lifting your arms. You should be able to bring your hands up behind the attacker's arms, then, using your thumbs, dig them in under the jaw line close to the ears, push up, and back until you break the attacker's hold.

Tip: When learning to dig the thumbs under the jaw line you may have to help your partner on how to position their thumbs to inflict maximum pain. Have your partner apply pressure gradually and do not tap out until you are on the threshold of pain.

## Escape From Hair Grab From Behind

1) Attacker - Stand behind your partner and use one hand to grab a hold of his or her hair.

2) Defender - Use both hands to grab the attacker's hand. Press his hand tight to your head

3) Defender - Hold the hand tight to your head, bend forward and turn to face the attacker. His hand should now be palm upwards.

4) Defender - Raise your body up bringing pressure to the attacker's wrist forcing him to stand on his toes.

5) Finish with a stomp to the knee or kick to the groin.

Tip: Done properly you should be able to cause pain in the wrist joint. Go slowly at first and gradually rise up increasing the pressure slowly so that your partner does not get a sprained wrist.

## Escape From Side Head Lock

1) Attacker - Stand to the side of your partner and wrap your arm around your partner's neck in a side headlock

2) Defender - Bring the hand closest to the attacker down and behind the attacker. Strike upwards into the attacker's groin

3) Defender - Bring your striking hand back and use both hands to grab the attacker's forearm.

4) Defender - Pull down on the arm and slip your head backwards out of the hold.

5) Maintain your grip on the attacker's forearm then pull up and then forwards executing a hammerlock

Tip: The strike to the groin should succeed in releasing the grip. Remember to practice this one in slow motion.

163

## Combat Strategy & Tactics

The first rule of survival is to have a plan. Without a plan of action, confusion and panic will result. In combat, a plan is a strategy, an outline of possible responses to a situation. Tactics are the details of the plan, the individual components of a strategy. The following combat strategies can be applied to many situations.

### The First Attack

To attack first, before the opponent has readied himself for battle, has several advantages. First, it puts the opponent on the defensive; he must react to your attacks and the slight delay in reaction works against him. Second is the element of surprise. It is estimated that surprise in warfare improves the odds by a factor of three; one man could defeat three; ten defeat thirty. 30

On the streets, this is called the 'Sucker Punch' and is one of the most often used tactics in bar room and street fights. The sucker punch is any technique thrown without warning while your guard is down. Alternatively, an attacker may simply walk up to you and strike without warning. To guard against the sucker punch, beware of the distance between you and a potential antagonist. If he moves into your safe range, suspect a first attack. Also, beware of anyone walking towards you in a direct line.

### To Destroy

This strategy means to use a relentless forward assault using multiple techniques in rapid succession. This is to overwhelm the opponent with too many areas to defend and no time to contemplate a counterattack. Where the motivation for attack is anger, fighters often attack each other in a blind rage using a flurry of wildly swinging punches

and kicks. As sloppy and unskilled as this may be, it is nevertheless

164

difficult to avoid or defend against. If both fighters use this method then victory will be the result of size, strength, and dumb luck.

### Injuring the Corners

This strategy is best used when fighting a larger or more powerful opponent. The idea is to injure the attacker's hands, arms, or legs and wear him down through multiple injuries – a war of attrition. [31] For example, if the opponent kicks, use your foot to jam down on the knee or shins of the incoming leg. If the opponent throws a punch, use a forearm to not only block, but also to injure the arm or elbow. If he reaches out to grab you, grab his fingers and break them.

### Evade & Counter

This is the classic guerilla strategy used when faced with a stronger enemy. When you are being attacked, the enemy's greatest force is aimed directly at you. Standing your ground to fight it out would pit you against your opponent's best techniques and allow him to use the advantage of size and strength. This situation can be avoided through evasion.

Most attackers will throw only a few punches or kicks in a row. By initially retreating you use up the attackers time until he runs out of moves. Then there will be a gap in his strength and awareness, when he reconsolidates his energy to launch a new attack. This is his weakest moment; this is the time to counterattack fast, hard, and persistent. This is the strategy used by bullfighters. The Matador does not attempt to stop or kill the bull but continues to evade until the bull is exhausted and near collapse. Only then does the matador approach to apply the *coup de grace*.

The key to applying this strategy effectively is dependent on timing. One cannot retreat or evade too quickly nor too far or the opponent will anticipate your movements. You must always appear within easy reach and evade the attack, as it is launched, not before. In this way, the attacker will continue to expend energy believing his next technique will finish you.

### Distraction

Distraction can by applied in different ways to upset the opponent's concentration. Kick sand or dirt into his face, spit, knock over garbage cans or furniture, or yell suddenly. The feint is also a form of distraction whereby the opponent is fooled into believing you are attacking in a certain manner and when he reacts, you change your attack to strike somewhere unexpected. For example if you move forwards and then bring your back leg up cocked, your opponent will believe you are about to kick him and will drop his arms down to block the kick. At that moment throw a punch at his face and he will be unable to defend in time since his guard is down. The permutations are endless but follow a simple principle, if you wish to attack high, first feint low, if you wish to hit the left, first feint to the right.

### Time And Terrain

Time and terrain both offer advantages to those who know how to use them. To use terrain in combat is to position yourself where you have the most freedom of movement while forcing your opponent onto terrain that causes the most difficulty. It is best to fight in surroundings you are familiar with and the opponent is not. When possible, try to maneuver the opponent into a situation that puts him at a disadvantage such as on slippery ground like an ice patch or slick floor, or on tangled ground such as amongst tables and chairs, or tall grass and hedges. Fight with the sun at your back, and open spaces behind. Maneuver your opponent into cramped or narrow spaces that restrict his ability to move. Take advantage of elevation forcing the opponent to fight uphill or up the stairs.

When possible, choose when a confrontation occurs. If the opponent is ready and willing to fight, then this is not the best time to fight. Everyone's emotional mood fluctuates, there are times when someone will be eager to do battle and other times when he wants to rest and eat. It is when the enemy's spirit is low that you should choose to fight.

## Intercepting

Intercepting is an attack launched at the moment the opponent begins his attack. This advanced tactic requires that you anticipate the moment your opponent attacks and then attack quickly before he can complete his move. This takes advantage of the  opponent's '*Suki*', a gap in concentration. Moments before an attack is launched, the mind is frozen for an instant as it readies itself for the attack. Attacking at that moment catches the opponent off guard with no time to switch from attack to defense mode.

## Three Points to Remember

1. Breath: fear and stress work to stop breathing.

2. Relax: start with the face and then shoulders and work down in one relaxing wave; when tense the body is more susceptible to injury.

3. Focus: head up, look at what is going on around, and scan your surroundings in a side-to-side motion of your head.

# Surviving
## Natural Disasters

# Surviving Natural Disasters

*Better to light a candle, than to curse the darkness.*
Chinese Proverb

Natural disasters can occur at any time and any place. Technology provides some advance warnings of disasters such as hurricanes, tsunamis, brush fires and volcanic eruptions but with or without foreknowledge, you will only have two choices; to either evacuate and head for safety, or dig in and shelter in place. Your best chance of surviving any natural or manmade disaster is to spend a little time and money to prepare a plan, and gather some equipment and supplies.

## Preparing For A Disaster

Contact your local emergency management, civil defense office, or Red Cross chapter to find out what types of disasters are most likely to occur in your area. They will be able to provide you with information on how to prepare for each.

Find out if your community has emergency warning signals, what they sound like, and what you should do when you hear them. If you have children attending local schools, find out about the disaster plans at your children's school or daycare center.

Make sure every family or group member has each other's contact information including telephone numbers for home, work, pager, cell phone and e-mail addresses. Post a copy of these contact numbers somewhere in the home such as on the fridge or bulletin board and give a copy to you children's school administrators. Learn the location of your home's main electric fuse box, water service main, and natural gas main. Learn how to turn these utilities off and keep an adjustable wrench nearby in case the valves are rusted or stuck.

171

Inspect your home for other potential hazards. Look for objects that could fall or tip over during an accident and which could cause injuries or block exits. Heavy objects such as bookshelves, dressers, and hot water heaters may need extra support or restraining straps.

During a disaster, it is important that you work as a team to increase your chances of survival. Once you have organized your home and family disaster plan, make contact with your neighbors to plan how the neighborhood could work together after a disaster. If you already belong to a neighborhood organization, such as a home association or neighborhood watch group, introduce the subject of disaster preparedness at the next meeting

Pool your talents and learn what special skills your neighbors have such as medical, technical, or emergency responder expertise. Work together to plan how to help neighbors who have special needs, such as the disabled and elderly persons. Also designate who will supervise childcare in case parents cannot get home.

Purchase and store a fire extinguisher (ABC type) and instruct each family member how to use it. Be sure to test and recharge your fire extinguisher(s) according to manufacturer's instructions.

Teach children how and when to call 911 or your local Emergency Medical Services number for emergency help. Show each family member how and when to turn off the water, gas and electricity at the main switches.

A few simple preparations can go a long way to increasing one's chances of surviving any emergency. As with all survival situations, information, knowledge and skills are more important than tools, equipment, and supplies. Investing the relatively modest time and effort it takes to participate in first aid courses, outward bound and wilderness survival weekends, and self-defense classes will pay huge dividends in increased confidence, leadership ability, and survival savvy. At the least, you should keep a first aid/home treatment manual, a wilderness survival manual, and a Farmers Almanac in your home.

## Disaster Plan

If you do not have a plan, your chances of survival drop. Have a family meeting and discuss why you need to prepare for disaster. Explain the possible threats unique to your environment such as wild fires, severe weather, earthquakes, floods etc. Discuss the types of disasters that are most likely to happen and outline a plan of action for each scenario. Plan how to round up any young children and how to take care of your pets. Determine the best escape routes from your home. Plan to share responsibilities and designate specific responsibilities to each member. For example, one person put in charge of collecting food and water, another, the one with the most medical experience, in charge of monitoring medical supplies and treating injuries.

Also put someone in charge of communications to ensure that everyone is accounted for, knows what the next stage in the plan is, and that outside family members and authorities are alerted to the situation. If you have school age children, designate which family member is in charge of picking them up.

If there are elderly or disabled persons in your group, plan to secure their specific needs during a disaster. This could include special transportation, additional medicine or medical equipment, and extra assisted care. If you have pets, designate someone to ensure they have shelter, and a supply of food and water available.

Ask an out-of-state friend or family member to be your "family contact". After a disaster, it is often easier to call long distance than locally. This person would act as a Call Center where other family members who have been separated could call this person and tell them where they are, their condition, and what help they need or can offer. Make sure everyone knows this contact's phone number and address.

## Rendezvous And Fallback Locations

When a disaster strikes you and your family may be in different locations, with children at school, adults at their jobs and seniors in the home. For this reason, it is important to meet with your family and decide on two places to meet in case an emergency prevents you from returning home.

Rendezvous: The Rendezvous location should be close to your home and is used in emergencies that prevent you from entering your home such as fire, gas leak, or crime scene investigation. Choose a place such as the corner convenience store, or a neighbor's home that can also provide relative safety and access to communications, food and water.

Fallback: The Fallback location should be outside your neighborhood and is used if you cannot return to the area because of wild fires, floods, landslides, or earthquakes. A close relative's home in a nearby town would be an ideal destination. Other possibilities could include a favorite hotel, resort, all night diner, cottage, or camping site. Make sure everyone in the family has a personal copy of the rendezvous and fallback addresses and phone numbers.

Commercial home emergency kit stored in two plastic storage containers that can second as makeshift toilets.

## Home Emergency Kit

The first question in a natural disaster is whether to stay or go. You need to make some simple preparations that would allow you to survive either decision. If your best choice is to stay in your home, then a few supplies set aside can ease the hardships.

A **Home Emergency Kit** should provide the tools and necessities to allow you and your family to stay safe and sheltered in your home in the event that an emergency cuts you off from outside aid. It should contain food, water, and medicinal needs for everyone in your home for a minimum of three days. Supplies to include in the kit are as follows.

## Clothing

Keep one full change of clothing in the kit. These should be rugged long sleeve and long pants, which offers the most protection. Choose thicker winter style clothing if you live in colder climates. Also essential is an extra pair of comfortable walking shoes or boots. A pair of work gloves can come in handy when having to clean up broken glass and clear rubbish or doing emergency repairs. Include a couple of bandana-type hankies. These can serve several functions such as head covering, dust mask, sling, sweatband, and emergency bandage.

## Toilet Kit

Include toiletries such as soap, toothbrush and toothpaste, mirror, brush, washcloths, toilet paper, feminine products, and baby powder and diapers if there are infants in the home. Staying clean is an important component in survival to prevent infections and diseases and improve morale.

## Maps

Get a recent and detailed map of your area in case you have to move or find an evacuation shelter nearby.

## Money and Documents

Keep a small amount of both cash and coins. In some emergencies, ATMs, cash machines, and credit card scanners may not be functioning. You may need cash to purchase extra supplies or fuel for your automobile.

It is also a good idea to include copies of important family documents (birth certificates, passports and licenses) in your kit. In the event your home and or personal possessions are destroyed, you will have a much easier time having important documents re-issued if you have copies of the originals.

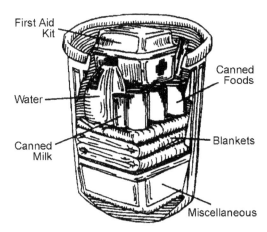

First Aid Kit

Canned Foods

Water

Blankets

Canned Milk

Miscellaneous

Store all of the above items together in a sealable plastic storage container since you may not have time to collect all these items from separate areas of the home. Keep the kit in an easily accessible cool, dry, dark place such as a storm cellar or walk in closet.

Home made emergency kit stored in sealed plastic storage container.

## Water

Drinkable water is an easily overlooked necessity because of its everyday availability, but in emergencies water can quickly become a rare commodity.

The average adult will loose 2 to 3 liters of water per day during modest exertion at room temperature. Therefore, 2 to 3 liters would be the minimum requirement of fresh drinking water per adult per day. However, if you live in a hot and arid environment you could lose up to loose 2 to 3 liters of water per hour. In this type of climate, you would need to drink 14 to 30 liters of water per day.

Factors such as extreme weather, intense physical activity, injuries or illness, can cause your body to lose even more water. If you do not replace this water, you will begin to suffer dehydration. Dehydration is a serious danger in a survival situation since it decreases your efficiency and ability to think and will increase the effects of injuries and shock. You should replenish fluids even when you are not thirsty. By the time you feel thirsty you are already 2 percent dehydrated. The best way to prevent dehydration is to replace fluids as you use them by drinking small amounts of water at regular intervals rather than to stop and drink a large quantity at one time.

If there is plenty of water but food is scarce, compensate by increasing your fluid intake to 6 to 8 liters of water per day. In extreme conditions of little food and much physical activity you could also suffer from a loss of electrolytes (body salts) and supplemental sources may be required. A solution of a 0.25 teaspoon of salt diluted in 1 liter of water will provide a day's worth of salt to replenish the lost electrolytes.

If there are no renewable sources for drinkable water, you may need to ration the available water until another source is found. In a survival situation, a minimum intake of a half a liter (0.5 liter) of a sugar-water mixture (2 teaspoons per liter) per day will prevent severe dehydration for a week or more provided you limit physical activity and are protected from the extremes of climate.

---

### Common Signs And Symptoms Of Dehydration

- Dark urine with a very strong odor
- Low urine output.
- Dark, sunken eyes
- Fatigue
- Emotional instability
- Loss of skin elasticity
- Delayed capillary refill in fingernail beds (Press lightly on your fingernail so that the color becomes lighter, release and the color should almost instantly return to normal)
- Trench line down center of tongue

The escalating effects of dehydration are as follows:
- A 5 percent loss of body fluids results in thirst, irritability, nausea, and weakness.
- A 10 percent loss results in dizziness, headache, inability to walk, and a tingling sensation in the limbs.
- A 15 percent loss results in dim vision, painful urination, swollen tongue, deafness, and a numb feeling in the skin.
- A loss greater than 15 percent of body fluids may result in death.

The average healthy person can live 3 to 5 days without water before expiring.

---

## Storing Water

Storing water for long periods can be a problem. The easiest solution is to purchase pre-packaged bottled water. You can also store emergency tap water in plastic containers that can be found in most stores. Make sure that they are appropriate for water storage. If not, there is the risk that chemicals will penetrate the container and contaminate the water. Glass bottles are also safe, but are more difficult to store and too easily broken.

Carefully wash the container and let it completely dry before filling it. Add some chlorine bleach, about ten drops per gallon of water. This will kill most microorganisms, without having too much impact on the taste.

Fill the container completely to the top, to force out all the air. Store the water off the floor, in a place where it cannot freeze (frozen water will expand and break the container), away from direct sunlight, and away from chemicals.

A last minute solution, is to fill the bathtubs and sinks with cold water. It is best to ensure the bathtub and sinks are clean and disinfected first. In an emergency, one source for approximately four liters of water is the toilets' holding tank. (The water in the tank above the bowl.) Warning this water will need to be treated.

## Water Treatment

If fresh water becomes scarce, you may have to use water from questionable sources even water that has a bad smell and taste and may be contaminated by bacteria and parasites that cause diseases such as dysentery, cholera, typhoid, and hepatitis. In a survival situation you may need to use this water but you should filter and treat the water first.

First, filter out any foreign materials such as leaves or dirt using a piece of cloth or coffee filter. Strain the water into a pot or can and bring to a rolling boil for at least one full minute. Let cool for thirty minutes. This will kill any microorganism that could cause illness.

However if you are unable to boil the water you can resort to chemical treatments. There are two types of commonly available chemicals used to treat water - iodine and chlorine.

Iodine is sensitive to light, which is why it is always sold in a dark bottle. It works best if the water is over 68° F (21° C). (Warning: some people are allergic to iodine, persons with active thyroid disease, or pregnant women and cannot use it as a form of water purification.) Add 5 drops of Liquid 2% Tincture of Iodine per quart when the water is clear. Add 10 drops per quart when the water is cloudy.

Chlorine has long been used to disinfect water and can be used for persons with iodine allergies or restrictions. The most common complaint is the chemical taste in the treated water.

| Treating Water with a 5-6 Percent Liquid Chlorine Bleach Solution | | |
| --- | --- | --- |
| Volume of Water to be Treated | Treating Clear/Cloudy Water: | Treating Cloudy, Very Cold, or Surface Water: |
| 1 quart/1 liter | 3 drops | 5 drops |
| ½ gallon/2 quarts/2 liters | 5 drops | 10 drops |
| 1 gallon | 1/8 teaspoon | ¼ teaspoon |
| 5 gallons | ½ teaspoon | 1 teaspoon |

After adding the chemical to the water, swish it around to help dissolve the chemical. Splash some of the treated water onto the lid, spout, and the threads of the water bottle so that all areas are disinfected. Allow the water to sit for at least 30 minutes after adding the chemical to allow purification to occur. The colder the water, the less effective the chemical is as a purifying agent. It is best if water is at least 60° F (16° C) before treating.

You can improve the taste of the treated water by pouring it back and forth between containers, or you can add a pinch of salt per quart or adding flavorings such as lemonade mix.

Halazone tablets are another convenient and inexpensive water purification method used by wilderness survivalists. However, there are two disadvantages. Reliable disinfection requires six tablets per liter for 1-hour contact, resulting in a bad taste to the water. In addition, the tablets rapidly lose effectiveness when exposed to warm, humid air.

## Food

Your home emergency kit should also contain enough food for a minimum of three days for each person in your family. Foods that require minimum preparation and have a long shelf life such as canned, powdered or dehydrated, and preserves are most practical. Be sure to include some power bars, dried fruit and snack foods not only as portable nutrition but also as a sweet treat to improve morale. If you have pets, you should store some pet food as well.

If the power and gas have been cut off you will have to improvise ways of cooking. Alternative cooking sources include candle warmers, fondue pots, or a fireplace. Do not use charcoal grills and camp stoves indoors since they produce carbon monoxide and need outdoor ventilation. You can eat commercially canned food right out of the tin without heating, or you can heat the contents in the can itself. Just remove the label, wash and disinfect the can, and open the can before heating.

Although you can live 3 to 6 weeks without food, you need a certain minimum amount of calories to function. Without food, your mental and physical capabilities will deteriorate rapidly, and you will become weak and unfocused.

The average person needs 2,000 calories per day to function at a minimum level. In extreme weather conditions and vigorous activity such as hiking through the wilderness may require you to consume up to 6,000 calories per day to prevent starving. An inadequate caloric intake will lead to starvation and cannibalism of the body's own tissue for energy. Food also provides vitamins, minerals, salts, and other elements essential to good health. Possibly more important, it helps morale.

# First Aid Kit

Ideally, you should have a commercial grade first aid kit that is large enough to care for all the members in your household.

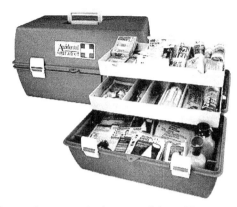

Quality store bought kits are adequate but you should add other items to your kit such as medical and prescription needs. If you require daily medication, keep a minimum three-day supply in your kits. Keep these in the original bottles with the doctor and pharmacy information on the label. If you require glasses, an extra pair of prescription glasses should also be included. Other items you might want to include that are not normally found in first aid kits are:

- multivitamins, and natural antibiotics such as Tea Tree Oil and GSE (Grape Seed Extract)
- antibiotics, if you have been prescribed an antibiotic for a previous infection, ask for a second refill and then store these for emergency use only
- prescription pain killers (for serious injuries over-the-counter pain relievers will be inadequate)
- water purification tablets
- magnifying glass, (to see and remove glass shards and slivers)
- dental cement (great for emergency fixes involving broken teeth or fillings)
- Suture Kit, (for immediate life threatening wounds)
- Surgical scalpel
- potassium iodide (to treat radiation sickness)
- baking soda used for chemical and radiation decontamination
- Clip-on mini flashlight (handy for treating injuries at night)
- A comprehensive first aid manual

Also, be sure to complete one or more of the standard first aid and CPR courses taught by the Red Cross or St. John Ambulance organizations. There is no excuse for not learning such essential survival and life saving skills.

## Tools And Equipment

In addition to the food, water and medicine, you should also store some equipment that may be useful in an emergency. These include:

- Flashlight and extra batteries
- Portable radio to monitor weather and public service broadcasts. A multi band emergency hand rechargeable radio is best.
- Safety candles or oil burning storm lantern (oil lamps can be run on cooking oil)
- Propane camping style cooking stove
- One or more coolers. Inexpensive Styrofoam coolers will work just as well. These can be used to refrigerate perishable food items after a power outage for several hours (See Blackouts p. 210)
- A multi-tool, handy for opening cans and bottles and small emergency repairs
- A crowbar, used for opening doors and windows that have become wedged in their frames, breaking locks and chains, or digging an escape hole through a wall or roof
- Dust mask, plastic sheeting and duct tape to make emergency repairs and to cover doors and windows in case of bio/chemical disasters.
- Decontamination supplies including soap, water, bleach, and baking soda.
- Packaged moist towelettes, garbage bags and plastic ties
- An adjustable wrench or pliers to turn off water and or gas valves
- Pencil and paper, to leave behind notes to rescuers or family if you need to evacuate.
- Deck of cards, and a couple of books to pass the time waiting for the storm to blow over or rescuers to arrive

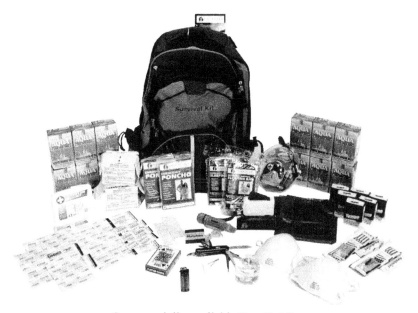

Commercially available Bug Out Bag

## Emergency Travel Kits

Several types of disasters such as floods, wildfires, or earthquakes may require you to evacuate the area quickly and seek shelter elsewhere. An **Emergency Travel Kit** (also called a Bug Out Bag) is one that contains the supplies needed to survive for 72 hours while traveling. This kit should be prepared in advance since time may be of the essence.

The kit is best packed into one or more daypacks since as a last resort you may have to travel on foot in the event that roads are obstructed, or fuel for vehicles is unavailable. To avoid duplication with the Home Emergency Kit, pack the recommended travel equipment and supplies into one or more backpacks, and those items specific to the home kit in another container. If you plan to stay then you can use the supplies from the travel kit. If you need to travel, you can grab the backpack travel kits quickly and load them in the car, or strap them on and move out on foot.

## Recommended Kit Contents

- Enough food and water to last for seventy two hours
- Energy bars, tea, sugar, and coffee
- Map
- Compass
- Flashlight or headlamp
- Extra clothes: at minimum, a pair of gloves, hat, windbreaker or disposable rain jacket, trash bag for cover
- Sunglasses
- First-Aid kit
- Pocket knife or multi-tool with knife
- Waterproof matches and lighter
- Compact Fire starter, plus kindling in a zip-lock bag to keep dry
- Small Water filter or treatment tablets
- Pen and paper
- Small zip lock sandwich bags: use as drinking cup with water filter, protect notes left behind, or notes kept
- Whistle
- Emergency blanket: one or more of the tiny synthetic palm-size packages sold at outdoor stores. Space blankets are waterproof, windproof, and can reflect back 80% of body heat.
- Toilet tissue folded flat and sealed in a zip-lock plastic bag
- Insect repellent
- A small fleece blanket can improvise as both poncho, towel and blanket
- Plastic sheet for shelter
- Mirror
- Sunburn protection
- Pet needs
- Self powered radio and self powered lighting or Glow sticks
- Enough Medicine to last an extended evacuation
- Wilderness Survival guide
- Small cooking kit, metal cup plus a folding pan or pot

Ideally, you should have one daypack prepared for each person in the household. Each kit should contain all the items needed for one person for three days. In other words, do not put all the water and food into one pack and all the tools in another. This redundancy is intentional since in the event that you should become separated, each person will be self-sufficient and have an equal chance of survival. Alternatively, if one of the packs is lost or destroyed, you will still have all the tools necessary in the remaining pack or packs. In addition, this allows you to replace items that become lost or broken which helps ensure that you will always have the minimum of tools required to survive.

## Emergency Pocket Kit

An **Emergency Pocket Kit** is a mini-survival kit that is small enough to fit in a pocket. Usually contained in a small tin candy box the size of a deck of cards it contains vital tools you would need if you were stranded without supplies. In a natural disaster or emergency there are many unforeseen events that could separate you from your  vehicle, backpacks, and fellow survivors leaving you with nothing but what you carry in your pocket. Because of its lightness and small size, you should carry your pocket kit at all times during a survival event.

A pocket kit is simply a miniature version of your travel kit. Instead of a liter of water that you would have in your travel kit, the pocket kit contains a condom that can be use to carry scavenged water. Instead of a first aid kit, you have few band aids, antiseptic swabs, and some pain tablets. Shelter and clothing provided by a plastic bag, and instead of food, a bullion cube to add flavor to scavenged greens in a soup. While this kit would be woefully inadequate to survive on long term, it can provide crucial tools that would make waiting one or two days for rescue much more pleasant.

## Recommended Kit Contents

Equipment

- 1 Stainless Steel Case with roller locks - 5 7/8 x 4 x 1 ½ inches (14.9 x 10.2 x 3.8 cm) Or a cough drop tin of approximate size. The following items should all be fitted inside the box. The box itself can also function as signal mirror, drinking cup, and cooking pot.
- 1 - Survival Whistle w/ clip
- 1 - Swiss Army style knife
- 1 - LED keychain flashlight
- 1 - Flint Fire Starter w/ Magnesium Tinder
- 20- Paper Matches - 1 book
- 1 - Button Compass
- 1 - Wire Hacksaw Blade
- 16 ft. Snare Wire
- 20 ft Fishing Line - 20 lb. test - wound on plastic bobbin
- 6 - Fishhooks - assorted sizes
- 3 - Fishing Line Weights
- 8 ft. Utility Cord (Can be wrapped around outside of box.)
- 1 - Tea Candle - 1 ½ Dia. x ¾ in
- 33 ft. Dental Floss
- 1 - Sewing needle and 10ft strong thread
- 3 - Safety pins assorted sizes

First Aid

- 4 - Adhesive Elastic Bandage Strips, 7/8 x 3
- 4 - Butterfly Bandages
- 2 - Antiseptic Swab
- 2 - "Neosporin" Triple Antibiotic Packets - 1/32 oz
- 4 - Ibuprophen Tabs - 200 mg
- 2 - Acetaminophen Tabs - 500 mg

Water & Food

- 50 - Potable Aqua Water Purification Tabs - in bottle
- 1 - Plastic Bag (for water storage or solar still) - 24 x 18 inches
- 2 - Mocha coffee or hot chocolate packets
- 2 - Chicken Bullion Packets
- 2 - Chinese Herbal Tea Bags
- 1 ea. Salt and Pepper Packets

## What To Do During A Disaster

*If you can keep your head when all about you are losing theirs, you'll be a Man, my son!*
Rudyard Kipling

If disaster strikes, remain calm. Remember to breath, relax, and take things one at a time. If you followed the previous advice, you will already know what to do. Put your plan into action. If there is much confusion, be prepared to take a leadership role. Anyone with some disaster knowledge taking charge is better than a disorganized mob.

First, check to see if there are any immediate threats or hazards such as fire, gas or chemical leaks, rising floodwaters, structural instability and impending collapse.

Next, determine whether it is safer to stay where you are, or to move. Generally, in disasters such as wild fires, floods, and hurricanes, shelter is sought by moving out of the path of destruction. In disasters such as tornados, ice storms, power outages, and pandemics, the best recourse is staying put.

Threats from earthquakes are more difficult to assess since much depends on the structural integrity, and possibility of wild fires. If the building you are in seems intact and stable and there are no signs of fire, then it is best to stay where you are. However, if the building appears to have been damaged by the quake, and/or there are fires breaking out, then you must move out since there is a risk that aftershocks may further weaken and collapse the structure.

## If You Stay

If there are no immediate dangers necessitating evacuation the next course of action is to see to the health and safety of your family or group members.

In cases where schools institute procedures to shelter-in-place, you may not be permitted to drive to the school to pick up your children. Even if you go to the school, the doors will likely be locked to keep your children safe. Monitor local media outlets for announcements about changes in school openings and closings, and follow the directions of local emergency officials.

Do a head count to ensure no one is missing. If someone in your family or party is missing, send the ablest member of your group to do a search within 50 yards of your home. You do not want that person to search too far since they may also risk becoming lost. If anyone that is missing is further away, then you may have to wait for Search and Rescue teams to arrive, or organize and equip such a team with your remaining group members. (See Search & Rescue below)

Check for injuries. If you have multiple injures to several people you will need to set up a triage system. Identify the most serious injuries first such as stopped breathing, heartbeat, and severe bleeding. Make sure that these people get help first and are evacuated to medical facilities as soon as possible. If you are unable to evacuate the injured to emergency services you will need to set up a treatment area and apply first aid yourself until medical help arrives.

Change into rugged clothing with long sleeves and long pants for extra protection and wear sturdy shoes. These should be a part of your home emergency kit. Be sure to wear garden or work gloves when searching through rubble.

Call any family members that were away from home when the disaster struck and call your Family Contact and provide information on your situation and what type of help you may need.

Check on your neighbors, especially elderly or disabled persons. Confine or secure your pets. Animals easily panic and can do injury to themselves and others.

Secure your home and immediate area by checking for dangers and hazards. Clean up and remove broken glass and furniture, check on the building's structural stability, secure heavy objects from tipping over, and watch for smoldering fires.

Sniff for gas leaks, starting at the water heater. If you smell gas or suspect a leak, turn off the main gas valve, open windows, and get everyone outside quickly. Use only flashlights until the area is safe. Do not turn on electrical switches or light matches or have any open flame such as candles, gas lamps etc.

Use your telephone (cellular or landlines) only for emergencies. During a widespread disaster, emergency responders need to have the telephone lines available to coordinate their response, so keeping the lines open is important. Also, do not drive or go out of your home unless absolutely necessary. Keeping roads and byways clear of unnecessary traffic will help rescue and relief workers.

If power has been cut, listen to your battery-powered radio for news and instructions. If your area is being advised to evacuate, then do so, even if you do not personally see any potential hazards.

Once any immediate threats have been addressed and there is no need to evacuate, then resume as many of your normal daily routines as possible. This is especially important if there are young children in your home to help alleviate their fears and anxiety.

## If You Evacuate
Keep a full tank of gas in your car if an evacuation seems likely. Gas stations may be closed during emergencies and unable to pump gas during power outages. Plan to take one car per family to reduce congestion and delay. If you do not own a car, make transportation arrangements with friends or your local government emergency services organization.

Before leaving, shut off water and electricity, if you are sure you have time. However, leave the natural gas service on unless local officials advise you otherwise. Once turned off, only a utility representative can restore gas service to your home. You may need gas for heating and cooking when you return home, and in a disaster situation, it could take weeks for a professional to respond.

Call your Family Contact to report where you are going, what route you are taking, and when you expect to arrive. Close and lock the doors and windows and draw the blinds and curtains. Post a note telling others when you left and where you are going.

Take your disaster supplies or travel kits. Be sure to bring your photo identification because the authorities may not allow people to re-enter a disaster area without identification proving they live there in order to prevent looting.

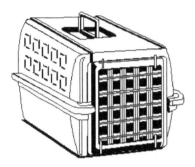 Take your pets with you - do not leave them behind. Pets are usually not allowed in public shelters, so you should go to a relative or friend's home, or find a "pet-friendly" hotel. If there are no other alternatives, you may have to house your pets outside the shelter or in your vehicle in their carrying boxes and ensure they have adequate water and food. Check in on them regularly.

Whether to use travel routes specified by local authorities or take the back roads needs to be decided on carefully. If you live in a big city and the entire city is being evacuated then the roads out will be hopelessly gridlocked in minutes and you will get nowhere. Taking shortcuts and dirt roads may be the only way out. If however you are being evacuated because of flooding or wildfires, then taking the rural routes could lead you right into the disaster.

**Aftermath**

The effects of a disaster can also have devastating emotional impact on survivors. The loss of personal property, loved ones, and pets can cause shock, disbelief, grief, anger and guilt. Memory problems, anxiety and/or depression are also possible after experiencing a disaster. Those especially at risk are children, senior citizens, and people with disabilities.

Children are more likely to become afraid and so it is important to make them feel they are safe. Seniors are more likely to experience disorientation, and the disabled are more likely to worry about having access to their medications and other special needs. In all events, speak calmly and assure everyone that they will all have a safe place to stay, and that all their needs will be provided.

Things you can do to improve morale include:
- Make sure everyone has plenty of food, drinks and rest. Some sweets or other treats are a positive sign that things will be back to normal soon.
- Try to return to as many of your personal and family routines as possible. Do some things together that everyone can enjoy such as have a picnic, play some sports, or play a board game.
- Stay positive and limit the amount of sensational and negative news coverage your family is exposed to. If you go back to inspect a damaged home, leave your children with family or friends. The impact of seeing the destruction would add to their fears.

Also, take extra care with your pets as well. Animals can be come upset and panicked and may scratch, bite or otherwise act aggressively after a disaster. Comfort them by speaking in a calm voice, and ensure they have food, water, and treats if available. Try to find an old blanket or toy they had to reassure them. Keep your pets secured during and after a disaster since they may injure themselves if they were loose to wander into a disaster area.

## Search & Rescue

During a natural or manmade disaster people can become separated from their families and communities and go missing. One of the first post disaster activities is to find and, if injured, provide medical care for those that are lost.

Some knowledge of Search & Rescue (SAR) methods can be useful in locating missing family members before, during, or after a minor disaster, or if you volunteer to join in a larger organized search and rescue effort to look for survivors of a major disaster.

Search and Rescue operations typically have three distinct phases.

## Assessment and Assembly Stage

Gather your family or group, discuss the situation, and collect information about the missing person, such as:

- Age
- Gender
- Physical description, what clothes they were wearing
- Last known location and their intended destination
- How physically fit are they, what equipment or modes of transportation are they using.

If you are searching for someone that is young, physically fit, and those carrying survival equipment you may have to search a wider area since they are more likely to cover greater distances than children, the elderly, or anyone that is injured.

Based on the information gathered, make a list of possible locations to search. For example, in searching for lost children a list of possible locations would include local schools, playgrounds, friend's homes, malls and so on.

Study an area map and review likely travel routes, such as streets, foot or bicycle paths, parks, ravines, trails, and streams. The missing party's personal interests may offer clues; children will tend to head for their schools, teenagers to a park, mall, or cafe. Decide who will form part of the rescue team and who will stay at home or base camp. You always need one person to stay at base camp to handle communications and in case the lost party returns.

Prepare some rescue equipment, which should include communications such as walkie-talkies, or cell phones if service is available, first aid kit, maps and compass and/or global positioning system (GPS) unit, food and water, simple shelter making materials, and signal flares.

## Search Stage

The first rule of searching is, do not make the situation worse by getting lost or injured yourself. Make sure that conditions are safe enough to go out in. Incoming storms, hurricanes, floods, chemical spills, and wildfires may make it too dangerous to mount a search at that time.

During an emergency, your best bet is to form a **Hasty Team**, a few members that travel light and fast and search just the most likely locations. For example, a lost child could theoretically be anywhere within a several square mile area from your home, but to do a grid search, checking every square meter of ground would be slow, and require lots of manpower. It would also not make much sense. A Hasty Team searches just those  areas and routes where your assessment analysis deems the most likely locations, such as the school, playground or community center. The team is given specific targets to search, a timetable so that home base knows when to expect them back, and specific routes to take.

Along the route, searchers should call out for the victim, look for tracks, question potential witnesses, and search for any other clues such as an abandoned vehicle, clothing, and supplies, or campsites. If after searching those targets the missing person is not found, the team should return to home base for debriefing.

## Rescue Stage

If you find the missing person, first do an examination for injuries. If they are conscious, question them on any injuries or pains they may have, and perform an examination of those areas. If time permits, provide first aid to any minor injuries and evacuate the person back to home base.

If there are serious injuries, call or signal emergency rescuers to the scene. Keep the victim warm and off the ground if possible. Warm up a hypothermic person immediately with extra clothing, hot drinks, a fire and close contact with another person.

If the person is unconscious, check for breathing. If not breathing tilt head back, clear the airway of any obstructions, and begin mouth-to-mouth respiration and/or CPR. If a neck or back injury is suspected, move the victim only if he or she is in immediate danger or if profession emergency responders cannot be brought to the site. Consult a comprehensive first aid manual for further information on how to safely transport a severely injured victim.

## USAR

Urban Search and Rescue (USAR) is the term used to describe the location, extrication, and initial medical stabilization of victims trapped in confined spaces usually from structural collapse due to major disasters.

In cases of disasters in urban environments involving widespread structural damage, search and rescue efforts become more hazardous and therefore USAR efforts are usually carried out by fire and rescue professionals. In the event that professional rescuers are unavailable and you have to search for lost friends and family after such a disaster the following describes some essential procedures.

### Assessment Stage

Instead of determining likely locations for a person lost in a geographical area, USAR assessment tries to determine likely locations of survivors in a structure. Gather information on the types of structures involved, the extent of damage, the layout of the building involved, and what hazards are present such as downed power lines, natural gas leaks, flooding, animals, hazardous materials, or unstable structures. Structural damage can be categorized as light, moderate, or heavy.

In addition to walkie-talkies, cell phones, first aid kit, food and water, USAR equipment, should include:

- Construction boots with steel toe and steel sole inserts to protect against stepping on exposed nails and broken glass

- Hardhat with headlight, improvise by using a bicycle or rock climbing helmet and strap on a headlight
- Safety glasses, of the type used in workshops or improvise and use ski goggles to protect against dust and hazards such as fiberglass.
- Dust mask, many building materials are toxic if breathed in as dust
- Leather work gloves and knee pads, for protection when crawling or digging through rubble
- Crowbar, axe, or hatchet, for chopping through debris and leveraging open jammed doors and windows
- Carjack, hand winch, can be used to lift and pull away heavy obstructions

## Search

Searchers should work in pairs known as the *Two-in, Two-out* system. In firefighting, the policy of Two-in, Two-out mandates that rescuers never go into a dangerous situation alone. There should always be at least two rescuers that go together when they enter a location and two when they come out. In addition, two additional rescuers should remain outside the building ready with rescue tools, in order to provide backup rescue if the team inside becomes endangered.

While searching, call out for victims to try to identify their location. Searchers should stop frequently to listen for noises or attempted communication from victims; often this involves all searchers stopping activity at the same time to listen.

Search using a systematic search pattern such as a right/left search pattern (one team searches the left side and one team the right side of a building), or a bottom-up/top-down search pattern. Possible locations of victims inside damaged structures include the spaces that are found between collapsed floors, and the lean-to space created when single wall or floor has collapsed diagonally against another wall. Other possible locations include spaces where victims may have entered for shelter during a disaster - such as under desks or in bathtubs, closets, basements and crawlspaces.

To avoid duplication of search efforts in situations where multiple structures are searched such as after a hurricane or earthquake, the outside of buildings are marked using the FEMA marking systems to indicate buildings that have already been searched. In the United States, markings on the fronts of structures are standardized as follows:

## FEMA Marking Systems

A single diagonal slash indicates that a search in the building is in progress. This is used to indicate searcher locations and to avoid duplication of the search effort.

An X inside a three-foot square means "Dangerous - Do Not Enter!"

**7/15/91**
**1400 hr**

**E-20**    **Rats**

**2 live**
**3 dead**

An **X** with writing around it means Search Completed. Writing around the X gives the following information:

- Time and date the search was completed written above the X
- Search Team's identifier written to the left of the X
- Results of the search (i.e. number of victims or rescued) written below the X
- Any additional hazards such as gas leaks, structural damage, or animals to the right of the X

Marks are made with cans of spray paint usually in Day-Glo orange.

## United Nations International USAR Marking System

Outside of the United States, markings on searched structures usually use the United Nations International Search & Rescue Advisory Group marking system as follows:

- A 1 meter by 1 meter square with G or N (for go or no-go), the team conducting the search, the date and time of the start of the search, and the date and time of the completion of the search written inside.
- The number of live victims removed is written to the left of the square. The number of dead victims found is written to the right of the square. Persons unaccounted for and/or location of other victims is written below the square.
- Additional information on hazards pertaining to the structure is written above the square.

## Rescue

When you find a victim, first check for injuries and administer first aid on site if possible. Before removing the victim you may first have to remove and/or stabilize surrounding debris. This can be accomplished by leveraging to lift heavy objects, or constructing a rectangular wooden framework known as a box crib underneath the object to be stabilized. Leveraging and cribbing can be combined.

Victims who can walk out on their own can be removed using lifts, drags, or carries. Remove victims carefully to avoid any further injury: Where any neck or back injury is suspected, the spine should be immobilized first before attempting to move them. Also, avoid dragging injured victims where the presence of debris and broken glass would cause further injury.

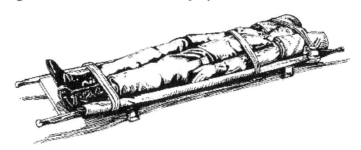

Victim stabilized for suspected spinal injuries on improvised stretcher.

## What To Do If You Are Lost

During a disaster or when evacuating it is easy for you or members of your family or group to become separated and lost. Make sure everyone learns the following basic strategies to use if they should become separated from the main group and are lost.

First, once you realize you are lost, stop, stay calm, and assess your situation. Do not continue to wander around. Look around to make sure you are in an area that does not pose an immediate danger, such as on an avalanche run, near a flooding river, or in the path of a wildfire.

If you are in a group do not split up. Finding a group is easier than looking for scattered individuals. In addition, a group can pool resources and offer moral support.

If you are in a safe location, hunker down and do an equipment check. Note what you or your group are carrying that would assist in a survival situation. This includes food and water, shelter materials, communications, maps and compasses, and survival tools. Your next decision is whether to stay put and wait for rescue, or to try to find your own way out.

## When To Stay And Wait For Rescue

It is best to make camp and wait for rescue if any of the following conditions exist.

Stop traveling when it gets dark. You should ideally stop moving at least two hours before sunset so that you still have enough sunlight to make camp, gather firewood etc. Moving at night in rough or unfamiliar terrain is a recipe for disaster.

If you are exhausted, sick or injured, you need to stop. Exhaustion and injury will affect your judgment increasing your chances of further accidents in addition to worsening pre-existing injuries.

During extreme weather, you should stay sheltered in place. In addition to the hazards from slippery terrain, reduced visibility, and risk of falling tree branches, your food and water requirements increase dramatically. If there are children in your party moving can increase the possibility of separation.

Find or build a shelter that will protect you from wind and precipitation.

Stay near any man made landmarks such as trails, power or railway lines, roads, or dams. These areas are usually searched first.

If it is safe to do so, and you have the tools to do so, build a fire. In addition to warmth and psychological comfort, a fire is visible from a great distance at night and search dogs may be able to lock on the smoke trail and find your camp.

Make you location visible by hanging brightly colored strips of cloth, plastic or paper from surrounding tree branches. If in alpine conditions, set you skis out in a cross, lay out colored ground sheets or excess clothing on the snow.

If you have a whistle or can generate a loud whistle then whistle several times an hour. At night, if you have a flashlight you can shine the flashlight while turning in a circle a few times an hour to conserve the battery. After each light or whistle signal pause, listen, and look for any return signals from search parties. Groups of three are the universal distress signal. Three fires, three blasts on a whistle, three gunshots from a hunting rifle.

If conditions improve and/or you have rested through the night, then reassess the situation. If there is no sign of rescuers, and if you have a good idea where you are and where you can find safety you may decide to try to walk out.

## When To Try To Walk Out

Walking out is an option provided that: You have plenty of daylight, you have a good idea of your location, you know which direction you need to head towards, you know how much ground you need to cover, and no one is injured.

Trying to walk out on your own may also be the only option available under the following conditions.

If the temperature drops suddenly and you do not have additional clothes or shelter materials, you may need to keep moving to avoid hypothermia.

If you did not leave your travel plans with anyone and you are certain that no one will report you missing for several days or weeks. In this case, no search parties will be looking for you and so you must try to find safety on your own.

Points to keep in mind when you walk out:
- Pace yourself, move with caution, you do not want to make the situation worse by becoming injured as well.
- Try to follow marked trails, railway and power lines.
- As a rule, always travel downhill, until you find a river or stream, then travel downstream. Keep following larger stream or river branches downstream.
- Climb a tree or hillock to gain a broader view of your area and look for a possible route to travel by.

To avoid walking in circles, choose a landmark in the distance and direction you want to travel such as a tree or rock outcropping and walk towards that landmark. When you arrive at that landmark, choose another to follow from there.

While moving, stop every hour and use your whistle to signal for possible help. Remember to stop two hours before sunset if you still have not found safety and get ready to make camp again

## **Pandemics And Plagues**

A pandemic is an epidemic of infectious disease that is spread through human populations across a large region such as a continent, or even worldwide. Infectious diseases are caused by the presence of pathogenic microbial agents, including viruses, bacteria, fungi, protozoa, multi-cellular parasites, and aberrant proteins known as prions. Most of these are qualified as contagious diseases (also called communicable diseases) due to their potential of transmission from one person or species to another.

Throughout history, there have been a number of pandemics, such as bubonic plague, smallpox and tuberculosis. Historically, pandemics occur about every 10 to 40 years, so it is likely that everyone will experience a pandemic at least once in their lifetime.

There are two types of pathogenic agents that are the cause of most epidemics; bacterial and viral. Epidemic diseases caused by pathogenic bacteria include; typhoid, tuberculosis, bubonic plague, and cholera. The primary medical treatment used to combat bacterial infections are antibiotics.

Epidemic diseases caused by pathogenic viruses include; smallpox, mumps, measles and a host of influenza type diseases such as Spanish flu, yellow fever, swine flu, and avian flu. The primary medical treatments used to combat viruses are vaccines.

These diseases are spread from person to person through coughing or sneezing, by touching infected surfaces, or through contamination of food or water. Most healthy adults may pass the disease to someone else before knowing they are sick, since they are infectious beginning one day before symptoms develop and up to five days after becoming sick.

201

## Prevention

If you have any forewarning of an impending pandemic, increase your home emergency kit stores from the minimum three days worth of food and water, to three months worth. This will help you to reduce your public exposure time by not having to go out shopping and in case local stores run out of food. Also, add to your medical kit in the event you have to treat sick family members at home. Most hospitals and medical facilities will be overwhelmed in the first few hours of a serious pandemic. If you or anyone in your family becomes sick, your best option will likely be to nurse them at home. If an epidemic or pandemic is reported in your area, take the following steps to help prevent the spread of the infection

### Social Distancing

Quarantine yourself voluntarily if your family members have flu symptoms to avoid infecting others.

Encourage co-workers to stay home if they have the first signs of illness and ask them to remain at home if they have sick family members. Support a human resources policy that allows family members of sick household members to stay at home during a pandemic.

Remove your children from school and day care. Reduce their contact with other children and avoid social activities. Avoid public gatherings and cancel any planned meetings, travel, or social events until the pandemic has burned out.

### Hygiene

Wash your hands. Infectious diseases are spread by the hands more than by any other means. Any surface that has been touched by someone infected could contain the germs or virus that can be transferred to the next person who touches that same surface. Especially likely sources for germs are door handles, stair rails, elevator buttons and ATM machine buttons.

After touching a doorknob or handle, you should definitely wash your hands. If you have just washed your hands in a restroom and then you touch a door handle on the way out you may have put the disease right back on your hands. Use a piece of tissue paper to turn the door handle to exit.

Just having the germs or virus on your hands will not infect you. It is when you use your hands to handle food or when you touch your eyes, nose and mouth that the contagion can enter your system. Always wash your hands when handling food and avoid touching your face until after you have washed your hands. It is always a good idea to wash your hands several times a day - especially whenever you have returned from being in a public place.

## Wear a Mask
If you have to go out in populated areas during a pandemic then wearing a surgical or dust mask can help prevent infection, though this far from foolproof. These style masks will have gaps usually around the nose where airborne pathogens could easily enter. Furthermore, some viruses as so small microscopically that they can pass through these filters. In addition, you need to change these masks regularly so that contamination does not build up on the mask itself.

## Health
Another strategy to prevent becoming infected in a pandemic is to strengthen your immune system. Take plenty of vitamin C and vitamin D every day even if you are not feeling sick. Eating healthy foods and exercising are the two tried and proven methods of staying healthy. Also, do not allow yourself to become too stressed out. Stress has been proven to reduce your body's immunity and make you more susceptible to disease. Living through a pandemic can be a stressful experience. Be sure to take time to relax and find something enjoyable for you and your family to do to reduce stress and anxiety.

Building up your defenses will help your immune system to be as strong as possible so that if you ever do come down with the disease your body has a better chance fighting it.

## Symptoms Of Seasonal Or Common Flu

- Loss of appetite - lackadaisical approach to eating.
- Fever. Childhood flu fevers are often more severe, but it is not uncommon for adults to run a fever in the 100's when they have the flu. Often a low fever - and the weakness and chills it causes - are your first hint that the flu is about to hit you in full force.
- Congestion that turns to a runny nose.
- Sore throat.
- Cough that turns productive.
- Exhaustion and weakness.
- Muscle aches and pains.

All of these symptoms will tend to hit you at the same time. To overcome and treat the flu, here are natural flu remedies for your fast recovery.

### Treatment

**Fluids**: You must replenish your lost fluids in order to provide your body with the strength to get rid of the flu. Drink plenty of water. Orange juice is good for its vitamin C content.

**Sleep**: Sleep is essential to health and the body's immune system. Make sure you get plenty of sleep.

**Food:** Even though you may have a lack of appetite you need to eat and maintain a healthy nutrition to keep your body strong.

**Rest**: Even if you do not feel like sleeping, it is far better to stay in bed and recuperate through relaxation than it is to try to go to work.

**Fever**: Toddlers should be seen by a pediatrician in if a fever continues longer than two days and is accompanied by significant fatigue or any kind of pain

As an adult, if your fever exceeds 103 degrees, or if you have had a fever for more than three days, then you should call your doctor.

## Vaccines

Generally, vaccines are the best protection against contracting the flu. In the event of a pandemic, local medical services will be distributed vaccines and news and radio stations will broadcast information on where you can be vaccinated. However, there are some drawbacks.

Any virus that can reach pandemic proportions is going to be quite a bit different genetically from current strains of influenza, which means that existing vaccines are not likely to help. It typically takes six months minimum to develop and manufacture a new vaccine.

Furthermore, there can also be significant side effects that can be worse than actually contracting the disease itself. As with any emergency, the better informed you are the better you are able to make decisions that will improve your chances of survival. If there is a pandemic, do some on-line research on the nature and severity of the contagion and do not rely only on media reports.

## Antibiotics

Antibiotics are generally used to treat diseases caused by bacterial infections. However, certain bacteria are evolving resistance to current antibiotics. A resistant strain of any of the bacterial diseases could result in a serious pandemic that may be more difficult or even impossible to treat with current antibiotics. Furthermore, if the cause of the pandemic is bacteriological then by the very fact that it is a pandemic, suggests that the strain is already immune to existing antibiotics hence its rapid spread.

---

### Health Tip

There have also been reports of healthy patients developing an autoimmune response known as a cytokine storm in response to some forms of the flu. For those who are concerned about an autoimmune response to the flu, many health experts are saying that taking plenty of vitamin A can help avoid that.

---

## Aftermath

Should the pandemic continue and its effects worsen you may see a breakdown in social services. First, essential services such as police, fire, ambulance, hospital and medical clinics will be overwhelmed. With many people ill and many more afraid to go to work there may not be enough people to run the machinery of a city. Services, such as water, power, and transportation may decline or even cease. Retail food, convenience, and grocery stores may close due to lack of deliveries or out of fear of infection by its workers. Most likely schools, daycares, and universities will close temporarily in order to halt the spread of the infection. Implementing social distancing will result in most social events being cancelled. This means that your best option is to stay sheltered at home.

A pandemic may come in waves, each of which can last for six to eight weeks. This may continue for up to 18 months. Make sure that you have a home emergency kit and follow the procedures for sheltering in place.

# Surviving
## Social Disasters

# Surviving Social Disasters

*When the world is at peace, a gentleman keeps his sword by his side.*
Ho Yen-his 32

The modern urban environment will periodically experience varying degrees of social disorder during which normally available services such as police, fire, and ambulance departments are unable to respond to emergencies. These events include; blackouts, riots, martial law, terrorist attacks and varying degrees of warfare.

During such an event, you may have to fend for yourself for a few days or weeks until the situation returns to normal. Following the previous disaster preparedness guidelines should be sufficient to enable you and your family to survive such events. However, a few extra precautions may be in order.

Since police services may be unavailable extra precaution against home invasion should be instituted. Secure your home and ensure that doors and windows are locked and curtains drawn. If your home has not been previously secured with entry proof devices you may need to reinforce possible entry points by sliding a cabinet against a window or wedging a chair under the door handle.

Move your Home Emergency Kit into the Safe Room and have everyone sleep in the Safe Room at night even if that means mattresses on the floor. If your home is vandalized or robbed, you do not want family members caught in different rooms of the house.

Check and ready any commercial weapons you have such as pepper sprays, tasers, or firearms. If you do not have any commercial weapons remember you can improvise using household objects such as a baseball bat, a can of aerosol spray, or a heavy sock filled with quarters.

Keep candles, lamps or lights low at night. Do not play the television or radio too loudly - you do not want to advertise your presence. Stay indoors and avoid unnecessary travel.

Monitor television and/or internet if available. If these are unavailable you should have an emergency battery or hand cranked radio to monitor news and emergency broadcasts.

## Blackouts

Sudden power outages often accompany storms, natural disasters or can result from system malfunctions. The following steps will help ensure your safety.

Get your flashlight and find the other members of your family or group. Make sure everyone is uninjured and accounted for.

Next, turn off all electrical appliances such as electric stoves or ovens, electric blankets, eclectic space heaters, and air conditioners. The sudden power surge created by having all these appliances on at the moment the power returns can blow a fuse or even create a fire hazard.

Next, go outside or look out your window and check to see if anyone else still has their lights on, or in daytime you can check with neighbors to see if they still have power. This way you can determine if your home's main fuse has blown, or if there is a local or district wide blackout.

Gather candles, blankets if needed, and family together and listen to your battery powered emergency radio for news and weather reports.

## Emergency Lighting

An emergency light is a battery-backed
lighting device that comes on automatically
when a building experiences a power outage.
Emergency lights are standard in new
commercial and residential buildings. There
area also residential versions that you can
purchase and easily install in your home.

Ideally, your emergency lighting should be
left plugged into strategically selected outlets in your home so that
it will turn on automatically if the power fails. Do not forget to
store spare batteries and bulbs.

At very minimum you need a supply of candles. Ordinary candles
are fine, but long-burning candles are recommended. Also
remember to include some waterproof matches and/or a few
cigarette lighters. Also keep a couple of extra flashlights (battery
operated, windup or solar powered).

## Portable Generators

In the event of a power failure, a portable generator can help
restore some semblance of normality, which can ease nerves during
an emergency when the power is shut off for an extended time.

A portable generator only really needs to power the refrigerator, a
few lights, and a radio. This makes the noise and fuel consumption
rates of the larger more powerful generators less practical.
Appliances are plugged directly into the generator's power outlets
using an extension cord. Not all generators run on gasoline, some
run on diesel or propane. Keep in mind that the use of a generator
is a short-term solution due to the amount of gasoline or other fuel
you can safely store. **Warning**: Generators emit deadly carbon
monoxide and so they should be run outside the house where there
is sufficient ventilation.

## Alternative Power Sources

Electricity can be generated using alternative sources like wind
energy or solar energy. However, unless you go through great
expense to outfit your home to function off the grid, these power

sources have little practical use in an emergency blackout. The only exception would be a small solar panel, capable of charging rechargeable batteries used in radios, walkie-talkies, and flashlights.

## Food

If the power outage continues for more than two hours then the food you keep in your refrigerator could spoil. Perishable foods should not be held above 40 degrees Fahrenheit (4° Celsius) for more than 2 hours. To preserve as much food as you can during a prolonged blackout follow these steps.

Do not open the refrigerator or freezer. An unopened refrigerator will keep foods cold enough for a couple of hours at least. A freezer that is half-full will hold for up to 24 hours and a full freezer for 48 hours.

If it looks like the power outage will be for more than 2-4 hours, pack refrigerated milk, dairy products, meats, fish, poultry, eggs, gravy, stuffing and leftovers into one or more coolers. These can be used to refrigerate perishable food items after a power outage for several hours. If it looks like the power outage will be prolonged, prepare another cooler with ice for your freezer items.

If the outage continues for more than a day then eat the perishable food items first and save the canned goods you have stored for after these items have run out or spoiled.

Ideally, you should have a digital quick-response thermometer so that you can quickly check the internal temperatures of food for doneness and safety. If the internal temperature of perishable items has not risen above 40° F ( 4° C) for more than two hours it is probably still safe to eat.

If the food in the freezer has ice crystals and is not above 40 degrees you can refreeze. See **Table 1** for list of perishable food items.

## Riots

Riots can occur almost anywhere and for any number of reasons. You can be caught in a riot in three ways; a riot takes place outside your home or workplace, you are traveling and encounter a riot, or a peaceful assembly or entertainment event turns into a riot. Generally, there are signs of public anger and violence a few days to a few weeks before the actual riot. Reading

the newspapers and following the news may give you a warning about impending protests, rallies, marches etc. Being informed and avoiding troubled areas is always your best defense.

### What to do Indoors

If a riot occurs outside your home or workplace stay inside. Typically, riots occur in the streets or elsewhere outside. Staying inside provides the best protection to wait out the riot. Keep doors and windows locked. Avoid watching the riot from windows or balconies, and move to inside rooms or at least away from windows and doors to minimize the risk of being hit by stones or bullets.

Search for and mentally note at least two possible exits in case you need to evacuate the building in a hurry. Be on the lookout for signs of fire. If the building is set on fire, get out quickly. If rioters are targeting the building and gain entry, try to sneak out or hide.

Check media sources for further information on the progress of the riot. Some riots have been known to go on for days. Contact police to let them know where you are and to request instructions on if and when to evacuate.

### What to do Outdoors

On Foot: Get inside and stay inside if you can. Find a retail store, office building, or coffee shop to get into and off the streets. Look for a rear exit to these buildings that will lead out to a back street where there are no rioters and carefully make you way home.

Try to look as inconspicuous as possible, and slowly and carefully move to the outside of the mob. Stay close to walls or other protective barriers if possible.

Move away from the riot. The more time you spend in the midst of a riot, the greater your chance of being injured or killed. However, in most circumstances it is better to move out of a riot slowly. If you run, you will draw attention to yourself, so it is usually best to walk.

It can be dangerous to move against a crowd, so go with the flow until you are able to escape into a doorway or up a side street or alley. It may also be advantageous to stay with the crowd until you are certain you can safely escape because it will help you remain inconspicuous and improve your odds of survival if shots are fired. In addition, police may barricade side routes and ambush anyone seeking to escape the main mob. You do not want to be the only person trying to get past a police barricade.

Crowd movement is like currents in the ocean. In a large riot, the crowd of people in the middle will be moving faster than on the perimeter. As such, if you find yourself in the middle, you should not try to move in a different direction, but follow the flow and slowly make your way to the outside.

Avoid public transportation. Buses, subways, and trains will likely be out of service, and stations and depots will probably be packed with people. Even if you succeed in getting on a train or bus, rioters may stop it. Subway stations are particularly bad places to be, both because they are difficult to escape and because riot control agents are heavier than air and may drift down into subway stations and accumulate there.

Avoid any contact with riot control chemicals. Police may deploy 'Tear gas'. These chemicals can cause severe pain, respiratory distress, and blindness. Try to stay away from the front lines of a riot, and learn to recognize the signs that a riot control agent has been used. These include popping sounds made but tear gas launchers, hissing sounds from teargas grenades, clouds of white smoke, and sudden surges and movements in the crowd of people.

214

<u>In a Vehicle:</u> Avoid major roads, city squares, and other high traffic areas that are likely to be crowded with rioters. If possible, stick to less-traveled side streets to avoid the mobs.

Do not stop your car. If you can drive away from the riot, drive quickly and try not to stop for anything until you've reached some place you know is safe. If people seem to block your escape route; honk your horn, and carefully drive through or around them at a moderate speed, and they should get out of the way.

Never drive towards police lines as this will be interpreted by the police as an intention to use the car as a weapon against them. Police are trained to protect themselves against deadly threats meaning that they will open fire on you if they think you are going to run them down with a car.

Also, avoid driving towards crowds if possible since this could elicit a violent response. There have been numerous cases of irate non-participants running down protesters. Any pushing though the crowd should be done with patience. Aggressive driving may anger the crowd into attacking you, your vehicle and your passengers.

If you are in a car and the mob surrounds it, get out immediately. Staying  in the car could be a fatal mistake since rioters could roll the car over and set it on fire in seconds.

## What to do at a Public Event
Be prepared. If you know an area is ripe for a riot but you cannot avoid traveling there, take some simple precautions to help protect yourself. Wear clothes that minimize the amount of exposed skin— long pants and long-sleeve shirts. Choose clothing that will help you blend in. Avoid looking conspicuously wealthy, as you are likely to draw the unwanted attention of opportunistic thieves.

When you attend a public event, make it a habit to check for exits and possible escape routes and safe havens. This is a good habit since should there be a fire or terrorist attack you will need to know this as well to evade and evacuate.

Carry some cash with you in case you need to quickly arrange transportation, pay off looters, or bribe police at a checkpoint. If you are traveling abroad, register with your country's consulate and carry your passport and/or visa with you at all times.

If a riot breaks out in a stadium, your response should be based on where you are in relation to the rioters. If you are in the midst of a riot, quickly move to an exit. Do not run, however, and try not to jostle others. If you are at some distance from the action, stay where you are unless instructed to move by police or security personnel. Do not rush for the exits unless you are in imminent danger. People are frequently trampled by stampeding crowds near exits.

## How to Deal With Riot Control Agents

The term "riot control agents" (RCAs) refers to several gases commonly known as 'Tear Gas' or 'Pepper Spray'. Exposure to these chemicals can cause skin, nose, and eye irritation, nausea, and respiratory difficulties within minutes. In rare cases, RCAs can cause long-term health complications, blindness, and even death. The effects generally last less than half an hour but can be extremely uncomfortable.

The first defense is to try to stay out of the line of fire and away from the front lines of the rioters. If the chemicals are released in front of you, you should run straight behind you to get out of range. Try to get upwind of the point of release where there is fresh air.

If RCAs are deployed inside a building, get out as quickly as possible. The chemicals do not dissipate as they would outdoors, and the high concentrations can be extremely dangerous with prolonged exposure.

Get to high ground. RCAs are heavier than air, and the highest concentrations thus tend to be near the ground. Try to get to the highest point possible. This could be up a hill, atop a wall, etc.

If you are caught in a smoke cloud, soak a bandanna or other cloth in apple-cider vinegar or lemon juice and tightly cover your mouth and nose with it. (Of course you would have had to bring these items in the expectation of rioting.)

Finally, avoid wearing oil-based creams or sunscreens, as these aid absorption of the RCAs. If you are exposed to these agents follow the decontamination procedures.

## Chemical Attack

Chemical warfare agents are gases, aerosols, liquids or solids that have toxic effects on people, animals or plants. They can be dispersed by bombs, sprayed from aircraft, boats, or vehicles, or used as a liquid, to create a hazard to people and the environment. Some chemical agents

are odorless and tasteless. Exposure can occur through ingestion, breathing, being absorbed by the skin, and contact with the eyes.

Effects of the agents can include: breathing difficulties, eye irritation, skin abnormalities, nausea, respiratory problems, and chest or abdominal pains. These symptoms can occur immediately within a few seconds to a few minutes, or delayed from several hours to several days.

Precise symptoms would depend upon the agent used, and the severity of the symptoms can depend upon the person's proximity to the contamination. While potentially lethal, chemical agents are difficult to deliver in lethal concentrations and dissipate rapidly when dispersed outdoors.

## Prevention and Defense

Check with your city or town to see if they have an evacuation procedure in the event of natural disaster or terrorist attack. If they do have an evacuation procedure then plan to avoid using these exits. In the event of an attack, the evacuation routes will likely become total mayhem as people panic, particularly in a major city. Depending on the nature of the chemical disaster, you may have to make the choice of evacuating or staying put.

Another thing to check on is whether your city or town has any communal buildings that they plan to use as a shelter in the event of an attack. If your home has no suitable room to use as a shelter, a public shelter could provide the solution for you and your family.

Should you be advised, or otherwise determine, that your best bet is evacuation then follow the procedures listed above. (see p. 189)

## Signs of Chemical Attack
If there is a severe terror alert, monitor the radio and television broadcasts. Local police or emergency services using the television/radio emergency broadcast system will inform you if you need to shelter in place in your area.

Since many chemical agents cannot be seen or smelled you would have to rely on observation and information to recognize that you are in danger. The earliest signs of a chemical attack are birds dropping from the sky, or numerous dead squirrels and rodents scattered around. Birds and small animals are particularly susceptible to poison gas and would be the first casualties of a toxic contamination.

If you see a single person on the ground, choking or having a seizure, chances are that this individual is having a heart attack or epileptic seizure. However, if several people are down, coughing, vomiting, or convulsing, they could be reacting to the presence of a toxic substance.

Evacuate the area immediately and dial 9-1-1. Make sure to tell the dispatcher that a hazardous gas may be present.

## What to do During a Chemical Disaster
Outdoors: If you are caught outdoors during a chemical attack or disaster the most important thing to do is to get a physical barrier between you and the toxic cloud. Get indoors quickly, preferably into a building but even being inside a car will help.

If there is no safe building nearby, try to determine the direction of the wind and move crosswind. If you move down-wind you risk remaining exposed to the gas for a longer time. If you move upwind you risk entering a more dense cloud of the gas. By moving crosswind you have the greatest chance of getting out of the cloud quickly because the gas will move with the wind along a relatively narrow line. Seek higher ground and avoid gullies, valleys and depressions since chemical gases tend to collect in these areas.

If you are in your car, stay inside and attempt to drive away from the cloud (again crosswind if possible). You should not try to shelter in a vehicle unless you have no other choice. Vehicles are not airtight enough to give you adequate protection from chemicals

---

### Emergency First Aid Tip

In emergencies, dry powder such as flour, baking soda, detergents, or even soil can be used to reduce the quantity of chemical agent available for uptake through the skin. Pouring flour onto the chemical followed by wiping with wet tissue paper is reported to be effective against the nerve agents soman, VX, and mustard gas.

---

Indoors: If you come indoors after being potentially exposed to the toxins go immediately to Decontamination procedure (See p. 233 )

If you are indoors, stay calm but make sure to get your family and pets indoors as quickly as possible. If your children are at school at the time of the disaster, they will be sheltered there. Do not try to pick your children up from the school unless specifically instructed to do so. Transporting children during a disaster will likely put you and them in greater danger.

If the best course of action is to stay where you are, take a few precautions to make your home as safe as possible to protect yourself until help arrives or the all clear is given.

Shut and lock all outside doors and windows. Locking them may pull the door or window tighter and make a better seal against outside contamination. Turn off the air conditioner or heater, ceiling fans and bathroom fans too. If you have a wood stove or fireplace close the damper and seal off any other place that air can come in from outside.

Choose a room in your house or apartment with as few windows and doors as possible and/or one that has access to water such as a master bedroom with a separate bathroom. Since most noxious chemicals and fumes are heavier than air the best choice for a safe room would be one above ground floor. (Note this is contrary to the advice given for other natural disasters such as hurricanes, or nuclear events, where the shelter should be low in the home.) In the room you should also have a working telephone landline and/or cell phone.

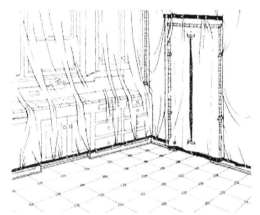

Bring your Home Emergency Kit into the room if it is stored elsewhere. Also, include duct tape, scissors, towels and plastic sheeting. Cut the plastic sheeting to fit windows and doors and use the duct tape to seal the edges and hold the plastic in place. Also, tape over any vents into the room as well as electrical outlets or other openings. Wet towels can be stuffed under door cracks to help keep fumes out.

You can use the sink and toilet as you normally would for hygienic purposes but do not drink water out of the tap. Drink stored water.

Listen to the radio for an announcement indicating that it is safe to leave the shelter. After you are given an all clear announcement, check with local emergency coordinators on how to avoid any contaminants or other hazards that may still be present.

## Aftermath

Immediate symptoms of exposure to toxic agents may include blurred vision, eye irritation, difficulty breathing and nausea. A person affected by a chemical agent requires immediate attention by professional medical personnel. If medical help is not immediately available, decontaminate yourself and assist in decontaminating others. Decontamination is needed within minutes of exposure to minimize health consequences. (see p. 232)

# List Of Chemical Agents

**Arsenic:** Dispersed in aerosol form. Symptoms: sore throat, vomiting, diarrhea, blood vessel damage, heart rhythm abnormalities, a decrease in white and red blood cells and skin abnormalities. Ingesting large quantities of this compound can result in death.

**Chlorine**: Used as a gas. Symptoms: Chest pains, burning throat sensation and in some cases asphyxiation.

**Cyanide**: Used in gas form. Symptoms: Lung problems, respiratory failure, heart problems and brain damage. Even a small amount of this agent, either breathed in or absorbed through the skin, can cause a number of health problems.

**Lewisite**: Blistering agent. Symptoms: Blistering and lesions of the skin, blindness, lewisite shock, chronic respiratory problems and death. Contains arsenic and some of the effects are also similar.

**Mustard Gas**: Blistering agent. Affects people through ingestion, skin contact, breathing and eye contact. Effects include skin abnormalities and blistering, respiratory tract problems, abdominal pain and nausea, swelling and irritation of the eyes, and fever.

**Strychnine**: Used in powder form. Symptoms: Breathing difficulty, respiratory failure, brain death, muscle spasms, and psychological problems.

**Sarin:** Fast acting nerve gas. Symptoms: Paralysis, convulsions, blood pressure extremities, abdominal pains, vomiting, chest tightness and unconsciousness.

**Phosgene**: Choking gas absorbed through skin, breathing and eye contact, Symptoms: Chronic emphysema, chronic bronchitis, fluid on the lungs, breathing difficulty, heart failure, and skin lesions.

## Biological Attack

Biological agents are organisms or toxins that can kill or incapacitate people, livestock and crops. Biological agents can affect a population through natural person-to-person spread of infectious agents such as smallpox, and plague, or it can be released through industrial accident, bio-warfare or bio-terrorism. There are three basic groups of biological agents that could be used as weapons; bacteria, viruses, and toxins.

Bacteria: Bacteria are small free-living organisms that reproduce by simple division and are easy to grow. The diseases they produce often respond to treatment with antibiotics.

Viruses: Viruses are organisms that require living cells in which to reproduce and are intimately dependent upon the body they infect. Viruses produce diseases that generally do not respond to antibiotics. However, antiviral drugs are sometimes effective.

Toxins: Toxins are poisonous substances extracted from plants, animals, or microorganisms. Some toxins can be treated with specific antitoxins and selected drugs.

Biological agents can be used as a weapon using three methods of deployment.

Aerosols: Biological agents are dispersed into the air, forming a fine mist that may drift for miles. Inhaling the agent may cause disease in people or animals.

Animals: Some diseases are spread by insects and animals, such as fleas, mice, flies, and mosquitoes.

Food and water contamination: Some pathogenic organisms and toxins may persist in food and water supplies. Most microbes can be killed, and toxins deactivated, by cooking food and boiling water.

Biological agents tend to break down quickly when exposed to sunlight and other environmental factors, while some, such as anthrax spores, are very long lived.

## Preparation And Defense
### Gas Masks
Many experts advise against purchasing gas masks for the whole family because of the impracticality of doing so. In order for a mask to protect you against a bio-chemical attack you would need to carry the mask with you at all times---24 hours a day, 7 days a week. Since biological agents are not immediately obvious and can have a delayed effect, you would therefore need to wear it at all times to be effective. In

The MSA Advantage 1000 Chem/Bio gas mask (MCU-2/P)

addition, a gas mask needs to be properly fitted to each individual, is expensive to purchase, and requires training to use. Thus for all the time and effort invested for only a minor return in survivability they are not cost effective.

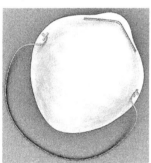

An alternative to a gas mask is a surgical mask or one of the respiratory protection masks recommended for various construction and laboratory tasks. They can help to screen out particulate matter that might be in the air, but these do not provide ironclad respiratory protection. Make sure the mask fits snugly over the mouth and nose.

### Antibiotics
Most authorities recommend against keeping a stockpile of antibiotics because adverse side effects may occur when untrained individuals self medicate and because their overuse can reduce the ability of these drugs to work in serious health emergencies. However, for many types of bacterial infections that can result from any injury including bio-warfare agents, antibiotics can be the

only treatment that could save lives. If you have someone suffering a life threatening infection, and the odds are against you being able to find professional medical attention for three or more days, then as a last resort, a course of antibiotics could save the patient. The danger in taking antibiotics is that a person may be allergic to that specific type. If you stockpile antibiotics, you need to do your research on the types and applications and ensure that whoever is taking them is not allergic to that type.

## Signs Of Biological Disaster

It may not be apparent that a biological agent has been dispersed until people begin falling ill several days later. For most biological agents, the initial symptoms would resemble a flu-like malaise. In such situations, the first evidence of an attack may be when you notice symptoms of the disease caused by an agent exposure, and you should seek immediate medical attention for treatment.

## What To Do During A Biological Disaster

Biological disasters can take the form of infectious diseases or the form of toxic chemicals. If it is an infectious disease type disaster then you will not likely know whether or not your area has been hit or infected until after the fact. Once you have been informed or evidence is such that you suspect some agent is causing illness and death then follow the same procedures as dealing with a Pandemic.

If the biological disaster takes the form of a release of toxic agents they will tend to behave similar to a chemical disaster and so you should follow the same guidelines for Chemical Disasters.

If the exact nature of the biological agents involved are unknown then employ the safety measures for both pandemic and chemical disasters.

---

### Emergency First Aid Tip

In emergencies, a hypochlorite disinfectant solution made from .05% chlorine bleach and water can be used to rinse your skin of infectious agents. However, do not the use solution on your face.

---

# List Of Biological Agents

## Toxins

**Anthrax** in powdered form can cause symptoms that include vomiting, fever, abdominal pain, skin lesions, diarrhea, and ultimately death.

**Botulism** is highly toxic and can contaminate the air resulting in inhalation botulism. Symptoms include blurred vision, swallowing difficulty, respiratory failure, paralysis, and muscle weakness.

**Ricin** can be used to contaminate water supplies, food or the air through aerosol form. Symptoms include breathing difficulty, cough, nausea, sweating, low blood pressure, blue tinge to the skin, respiratory failure, circulatory failure, and death.

## Viruses

**Plague**, symptoms include swollen glands, fever, exhaustion, headaches, breathing difficulty, coughing up blood and death.

**Smallpox** is highly infectious. Symptoms include fever, headaches, rash and skin lesions, backache and fatigue.

**Tularemia** is an organism that can be used in aerosol form to contaminate the environment. Symptoms include ulcers, swollen glands, fever, abdominal pains, vomiting and nausea, diarrhea, weight loss, headaches, fatigue, chills, pneumonia and possible death.

**Viral Hemorrhagic Fevers** Symptoms include fever, muscle weakness, fatigue, dizziness, bleeding under the skin, bleeding of internal organs, bleeding from external orifices, shock, nervous system abnormalities, coma, seizures, and kidney failure.

**Cholera** is usually transmitted via drinking water. Symptoms can include diarrhea, vomiting, cramps, dehydration, shock and possible death.

**Brucellosis** can linger in the environment for a couple of years. Contamination through an aerosol form would be the most likely bio-terrorist route. Symptoms include fever, sweats, fatigue, weight loss, joint pains and headaches.

## Nuclear Attack

*Any event that has a definite probability, however small, that does not decrease with time will eventually occur-next year, next decade, next century, but it will come. Including nuclear war.*
Gwynne Dyer, *War*

The possibility of having to deal with a nuclear disaster in one form or another is not beyond the realm of possibility. Such a disaster can come from a terrorist attack, an attack from a nuclear-armed nation, a nuclear power station meltdown or an accidental, or even intentional, detonation of a nuclear device by one's own government. Whatever the cause or origination of a nuclear event the following procedures can increase your likelihood of survival.

## Preparation And Defense

If a nuclear detonation takes place, it will be too late to start thinking about preparation – all of that has to take place now, however unlikely you think the prospect of a nuclear blast is.

Surviving a nuclear disaster requires advanced planning. There are three stages to a nuclear disaster that require three different strategies. There is the blast stage from which you need to stay put behind solid protection. There is the fire stage from which you will most likely have to flee. Finally, the fallout stage is where the wind carries the radioactive materials from the nuclear detonation through the air to other areas. At this stage you may have to evacuate or stay depending on the circumstances.

The first step is to assemble a Home Emergency Kit should you need to shelter in place and Travel Kits in case you need to evacuate. Check with your town or city to see if there are public fallout shelters and any evacuation plans in such an emergency. Create a plan of action on what you and your family should do in the event of a nuclear disaster.

226

## What To Do During A Nuclear Attack

A nuclear explosion creates a powerful blast wave that can destroy everything around through its enormous force. The initial flash of the blast can be so intense that simply to look right at it can result in blindness and permanent eye damage. It can also result in fire through the ignition of combustible material and this is a particular risk in the area close to the blast.

When the blast occurs, the first step for you and your family is to take shelter during and after the blast. Unfortunately, you will have mere seconds to decide. To survive the impact of the blast wave you are safer below ground level. If there is some advance notice or warning of an impending nuclear event then bring your home emergency kit and supplies down into your basement, crawl space, underground parking garage, or the lowest floor in your home. Stay away from windows and move to the interior of the building to put as many walls between you and the outside as possible.

If you are outside when a nuclear attack occurs, you should literally dive for cover and do not look up at the blast as this could blind you. Find a ditch, run to the nearest building or anywhere that you might be able to find shelter as low down as possible. If you are in a car, you should wind down the windows to avoid possible injury from breaking glass and get down on to the floor of the vehicle, shielding your face and eyes.

The second danger from a nuclear explosion is the risk of a firestorm triggered by the blast and heat of the detonation. Fire is a high risk particularly in areas close to ground zero. If you survive the initial blast but find yourself inside the fire radius you will need to evacuate quickly. Keeping an emergency car kit and a bug out pack ready will be a lifesaver if you have to travel away from the city and survive in the wilderness for several days.

Once the initial explosion is over you will need to be prepared for nuclear fallout. There are two strategies to survive the final fallout stage.

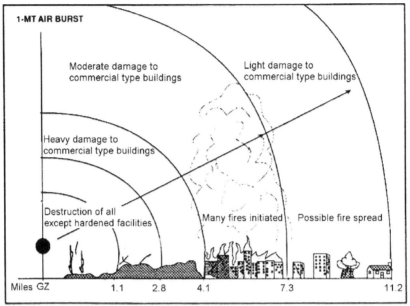

Chart shows range and effects of a worst-case one-megaton airburst on an urban environment.

## Shelter in Place

This requires that you construct some form of fallout shelter. In suburban and rural areas, special fallout shelters can be constructed in the basement or backyard. This can be an expensive project and probably beyond the means and opportunity of most people. A more likely scenario is that you will have to quickly improvise a fallout shelter somewhere in or near your home. If you had your second floor bedroom equipped as a safe room then you can go there and seal the room as you would during a chemical attack. If your bedroom has a walk in bathroom then you have taken care of another problem of being sealed in. You may have to be sealed in for several days so you must ensure you have adequate supplies of food, water, cooking utensils, medical supplies, and some form of human waist disposal.

The fallout from the first 24 hours following detonation is the most dangerous as these particles are still highly radioactive. Fallout can continue for months or even years. However, the fallout radiation levels decrease very quickly, and within a couple of weeks it is just a tiny fraction of the levels at the time of detonation.

In an urban environment you are most likely to have to shelter in place for at least a few days. While evacuating to a safer area that will not be affected by the fallout is preferable to being sealed in a small room for weeks, you may not have that option. In populous areas, the evacuation routes can be damaged or destroyed by the initial blast and the sheer number of people living and working in the city could mean that the streets become too jammed to evacuate. Better to stay put then to run out of gas in an endless traffic jam and become stranded on a highway where you will be exposed and with few resources.

## Evacuate

Ideally, it is better to evacuate the contaminated area and find shelter that is as far as possible from the blast and is upwind from the blast. Wind direction and weather patterns will determine the best direction to head towards. Listen to weather and news reports on your portable radio to plan where you should go. Fallout patterns typically resemble a feather shape with the point at ground zero and the plume going in the direction of the prevailing wind. Most wind patterns in North America follow a west to east direction. If a nuclear explosion occurred west of your current location, and the wind is blowing from the west to east (Westerly Wind) then the best directions to take would be to the north or south to take you out of the plume of fallout.

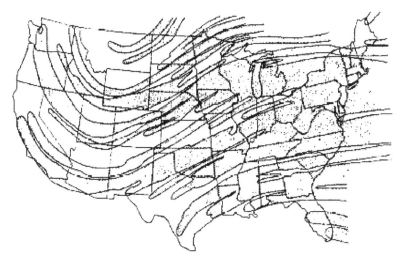

*Fallout areas at 24 hours after detonation*

You may need to stay away for a long period of time depending on the extent and severity of the contamination. It is important to plan to evacuate to a retreat location that would provide both protection against contamination as well as uncontaminated food and water such as bottled water and tins of food that will last for a while. One possibility is to arrange to stay with friends or family in unaffected areas for the duration of the emergency.

If you or your family owns a cabin or cottage away from the affected areas that would be an ideal retreat location, or if you do not own any vacation property you may be able to rent a cabin for the couple of months it would take for order to be restored.

## Aftermath

After either sheltering in place or evacuating to a shelter your next priority will be to treat injuries and address health concerns. A nuclear disaster will create every type of injury from fractures, lacerations, and burns to blindness and radiation sickness. To make matters worse, if a nuclear detonation takes place in an urban environment the destruction to infrastructure and emergency services combined with the high numbers of casualties will mean that medical help may take a long time in coming.

If you followed the advice in Preparing for Disaster, you should have a list of neighbors and their survival talents. Contact anyone nearby that has medical experience for assistance. If there is no medical aid available, then hopefully you have a comprehensive first aid manual and you must do your best to treat medical emergencies on your own. As soon as possible, have everyone examined by a doctor even if no one was injured by the blast. Possible long-term health effects from radiation exposure are another concern and should be addressed by medical professionals.

## Emergency First Aid Tips

Radiation sickness can be identified by symptoms such as vomiting, diarrhea, fatigue, fainting, dehydration, hair loss, loss of appetite and bleeding from the nose, mouth, rectum or gums. Skin reddening, rash, severe burns and peeling are all possible external effects. The first step to any treatment is decontamination, which means removing as many of the radiation particles as possible.

### Baking Soda Bath
For the external cleansing of radioactive particles, soaking in baking soda may help. Baking soda is said to pull out the radiation and help cleanse the body. Bathe only after you have followed the decontamination procedure below.

### Potassium Iodide
Potassium iodide targets the thyroid and slows the absorption of radioactive iodine into the bloodstream. The radioiodine is eventually released from the body through the urine. Potassium iodide should be taken as soon as possible after public health officials tell you. You should take one dose (100mg) every 24 hours for not more than 10 days.

### Prussian Blue
Prussian blue dye clears the radioactive elements cesium and thallium from the body. These particles are then excreted from the body through feces. Prussian blue is available only by prescription. The CDC has included Prussian blue in the Strategic National Stockpile (SNS), a special collection of drugs and medical supplies that CDC keeps to treat people in an emergency. Prussian blue is given in 500-milligram capsules that can be swallowed whole.

### Antihistamines
Antihistamines help alleviate such symptoms as nausea and vomiting and help reduce hypertension and relax patients.

## Decontamination

If you or someone in your family or group have been exposed to riot control agents, chemical toxins, biological agents, or nuclear fallout the first course of action is to decontaminate that person. Decontamination is essential to reduce and prevent further injury to the contaminated person and to prevent that person from contaminating others. The following procedure should work with all forms of contamination.

### Decontamination Area

If you are returning to your home or shelter after being exposed to toxic agents, it is best to decontaminate everyone before entering the living areas in order to prevent further spread of the contaminants.

If you are decontaminating outside make sure you do so downwind of your home and any people in the area. The wind can spread these agents further and contaminate everything downwind of you. If for safety reasons you are restricted to decontaminating indoors, then find a room lower in the home that is the least used and has the least number of windows. A room with a sink and running water is preferable such as a laundry room or guest bathroom. Seal any windows and air vents to prevent toxins from spreading through the ventilation system.

If you are assisting in helping to decontaminate someone else then take the following safety precautions. Wear latex or rubber gloves, surgical mask, protective eyewear, plastic shower cap or bandana to cover your head and hair, and protective clothing such as a raincoat or plastic poncho. After assisting someone else you should then self decontaminate as well.

### Procedure

- Remove all clothing and other items in contact with the body. In most cases, taking off your clothes will remove 80-90% of the potential contamination.

- Contaminated clothing normally removed over the head such as T-shirts and pullovers should be cut off to avoid contact with the eyes, nose, and mouth.
- Remove eyeglasses or contact lenses. Put glasses in a pan of household bleach solution to decontaminate.
- Put contaminated clothing into a plastic bag and tie it off. Depending on the nature of the toxin, these clothes may be washed later.
- Rinse with cold water starting from the head and work down. It is important that you shower; do not take a bath. Do not use warm water since this will open the pores and aid absorption of the toxins into the skin.
- When rinsing your hair make sure to bend forward so that the water runs off your head rather than run down your face where it could further contaminate your eyes and nose.
- Decontaminate hands using soap and water.
- Flush eyes with lots of water.
- Gently wash face and hair with soap and water; then thoroughly rinse with water.
- If pain in the throat makes breathing difficult, gargle with water. Spit out the water—do not swallow it. Do this only if you are able to do so without choking.
- Decontaminate other body areas likely to have been contaminated. Blot (do not swab or scrape) with a cloth soaked in soapy water and rinse with clear water.
- Change into uncontaminated clothes. Clothing stored in drawers or closets are likely to be uncontaminated.
- Once decontaminated, you should seek immediate medical attention.

## Neutralize and Disinfect

After following the above procedures you may still have to take further precautions to ensure you are fully decontaminated and prevent re-contamination.

Neutralize: A solution of 5% baking soda and water will help to neutralize the chemicals on the skin especially the irritant type chemicals normally used in riot control agents such as mace and pepper spray. Concentrate the solution on red or blotchy areas.

<u>Disinfect:</u> For biological agents hypochlorite solutions are effective in the decontamination of skin or other materials. Disinfectants that contain chlorine bleach will destroy most biological agents. Ordinary laundry detergent with real chlorine bleach can also be used.

Be sure to dilute the solution in water before you use it on your skin and rinse the solution thoroughly off your skin after use. You should use a 5% solution to decontaminate equipment and objects and a 0.5% solution to decontaminate your skin.

For biological agent exposure, you will need to wash yourself well with a chlorine solution for about 15 minutes. In the case of blistering agents, about 5 minutes should be enough. Never decontaminate your face using hypochlorite solutions. Wash instead with soap and water.

## **<u>Martial Law</u>**

*A democracy which makes or even effectively prepares for modern, scientific war must necessarily cease to be democratic. No country can be really well prepared for modern war unless it is governed by a tyrant, at the head of a highly trained and perfectly obedient bureaucracy.*
Aldous Huxley

Martial law, meaning military rule, is a set of rules that are implemented when a nations' military takes control of the administration of justice. Martial law is imposed in response to civil unrest or riots, or during wartime when foreign armies force the nominal administration to go into hiding or exile. Only in the case of foreign occupation is there justification for having a country's military assume control. In cases of civil unrest and riots, the implementation of martial law is an ill omen foretelling of tyrannical forces at work within the government. In democratic countries, the government, in theory, exists to provide the greatest common good for the greatest number of people. When large portions of the population become so disenfranchised that they riot

234

it is a sign the government has failed. Under most democratic constitutions a government faced with widespread unrest should resign and call a new election. If instead a government resorts to using the military to control the populace then it has become a dictatorship by any other name. Regardless the reason for doing so, the declaration of martial law is a serious indicator of a dysfunctional and thus dangerous society.

## What To Expect

The first change to expect is that most if not all of your civil or constitutional rights will be 'suspended.' Your freedom of speech, assembly, travel, and right to bear firearms are the first to go. Typically, marches, strikes, and public gatherings of more than three people will be forbidden. Curfews are likely as well as various checkpoints set up at which you would need to provide identification. Gun confiscations using the military and police to do house-to-house searches follow.

Next, restrictions on power consumption, food, medicine, currency exchange, and livelihood may be enforced. Within hours of a state of emergency being declared, grocery store shelves will be bare because of sudden stockpiling efforts or looting. Electricity and fuel may be rationed. Hoarding, the storing of extra food in your home, may be forbidden and house-to-house search teams may confiscate foods stores.

Finally, in worst-case scenarios, whole groups of people will be rounded up at gunpoint and relocated to holding centers or concentration camps.

The dangers you would face under martial law are of being accidentally shot or incarcerated for breaking one of the new rules, or from starvation.

## Preparation

Having a Home Emergency Kit assembled is a vital component to surviving martial law. Restrictions and access to foods and medicines as well as power and fuel shortages are likely. Your kit will provide you with some buffering from the impact of these shortages. Usually the conditions under which martial law is declared will grow over time giving the astute observer some advance warning. If you have reasons to suspect martial law may become a reality, then add to your home emergency kit supplies. Increase your food and water stocks from three days to three months. Do the same for your medical prescription, and pet food requirements. Also, be sure not to advertise the fact that you are stockpiling or taking precautions. Afterwards, many will be enticed to inform on your activities that by then may be illegal.

## Compliance

Most people being law-abiding citizens will face a moral dilemma under martial law. On the one hand, many will want to comply with the new rules, on the other, history has repeatedly shown that during such times of turmoil governments have readily sacrificed innocent civilians to their agendas. Furthermore, under martial law, it is a certainty that little the government through their official broadcasts says is likely to be true. One must judge carefully whether following government regulations is in the best interests of you and your family. For example, would it be better to comply with travel restrictions, or slip off to a family farm or summer cottage and wait until things blow over? Should you agree to evacuate to a relocation center or go into hiding?

Whatever your decisions are, you must at least outwardly follow all regulations. Follow official broadcasts regarding rules and curfews. Speak politely to military and other 'authority figures'. Use the Grey Man strategy of blending into the background and being unnoticed. Carry your identification documents with you wherever you go. Being caught without ID by a patrol or checkpoint can result in detainment and incarceration.

## Stealth

Keep quiet. Do not talk about your political opinions, or actions you are taking to protect your family. A common component to martial law is snitch networks that use fellow citizens to spy on each other and report violations of martial regulations. It is an ugly side of human nature that ordinary people will often betray and inform on their own neighbors and family during dire social conditions. Limit what you say when being questioned by anyone in authority. Follow the same rules for Dealing with Police and never volunteer information.

Avoid where possible any dealings with the authorities. If you know where street patrols, roadblocks, and surveillance cameras are avoid going there. Practice Social Distancing and avoid public gatherings or protests and limit your travel to only the most necessary trips. It is important during such times to attract as little attention to yourself as possible.

## Aftermath

If martial law was declared as a result of a natural disaster, terrorist attack or rioting then it will not last longer than a couple of months and the best advice is to keep a low profile and wait until normalcy resumes. Finally, while martial law sounds like a serious situation it may have little impact on the day-to-day activities of average citizens. Taiwan was under martial law for forty years yet, aside from restrictions on political activities, the average person was unaffected by it. However, there have been historical incidents of governments declaring martial law and using those powers to deprive its citizens of their freedoms and liberties. In such extremes you may have to resort to the advice found in Corruption, War, and Escape & Evade.

## Corruption

*Greed and corruption is the worst malady of society, which is incurable and so contagious that any dealings with it are impossible.*
Ptahotep, Egyptian philosopher, Old Kingdom (2815 to 2294 B.C.)

Corruption is an inescapable consequence of civilization. Seldom in the course of history have there existed states that were not corrupt, and then only briefly. Corruption also poses one of the greatest threats to a civilization, as many ancient philosophers well knew. Much of their advice railed against corruption and the need for society, especially the rulers, to adhere to a code of virtuous conduct - after all, they were supposed to set the example. That the wise advice of moralists was ignored would come as no surprise if one assumes that a corrupt society is the result of a predominantly psychopathic elite. [33]

Corruption causes an attitudinal change of a society whereby the prime motivation is a mercenary self-preservation. No longer motivated by a concern for society, nature, truth, justice, patriotism, honor, or good old honest pride in one's skills, corruption reduces all such concerns to `What's in it for me? Corruption can be instigated by either a rapaciously greedy ruling class, or dwindling resources. Either way the bottom line is always that there is less to go around. The less there is, the more people will be squeezed out of the food chain and perish. The following describes the social symptoms of corruption.

## Signs Of Corruption

Bribes & Kickbacks: A bribe is any form of monetary exchange paid to a government official in order to influence that person's decisions. Police are bribed to avoid criminal charges, judges are bribed to drop criminal cases, jailers are bribed for better treatment, bureaucrats are bribed to process papers, ministers are bribed to hand out government contracts, presidents and prime ministers are bribed to provide monopolies and business concessions. This form of extortion is made to sound less sinister by referring to the bribes as licensing fees, processing fees, administration fees, finder's fees, commissions, and campaign contributions.

The business world's equivalent to the bribe is the Kickback. Here the same pattern is repeated: developers pay kickbacks to landowners, architects pay developers, general contractors pay architects, sub-trades pay general contractors, sellers pay to buyers and so on. Here Kickbacks are referred to as sales commissions, finder's fees, handling charges, administration expenses, and rebates.

<u>Patronage and Nepotism</u>: Corruption also increases the formation of tribal associations. Every racial, ethnic, and religious group establishes an `Old Boy Club' or some other form of `Secret Society', as a means of self-defense against the predation of similar rival groups. This practice contributes to the weakening of the social machine since less skilled and often incompetent people whose only qualification for the position is membership in the club replace skilled and qualified people needed to run the machinery. In addition, when an administrator's primary allegiance is his tribe, his decision-making ability is impaired. What is good for the tribe may not be good for the overall health of the rest of society.

In business, nepotism leads to the ancient principle known in China as the `Three Generation Curse'. The first generation suffers and sacrifices to build the family fortune. The second generation will live off the interest. The third generation will spend the principle and pauperize the family once again. Everyone knows of a family owned business that went downhill after the boss's son took over the business. Seldom is the son as hard working and shrewd as the father. By the time the grandson takes over the reins, he usually has no interest at all in the family business and will spend the company into bankruptcy, or sell off his shares. Instead of the business being run by those best qualified, it is run by those who assume control, not through skill, but by accident of birth. 34

Thus, patronage and nepotism causes the machinery of society to fall increasingly into the hands of under-qualified and inept administrators making bad decisions.

<u>Gangsterism</u>: As corruption increases so does the competition for dwindling resources. Clubs and associations originally started as benevolent community groups become increasingly militant in order to compete. As the competition increases, the clubs and associations become more violent and engage in more activities that are criminal. Those that do not, are swallowed up by those that do. Thus the Tongs, originally Chinese community welfare organizations, evolved into international crime syndicates. Sicilian community defense leagues evolved into the Mafia, while the most successful long-standing gangs evolve into political parties.

Gangsterism is a throwback to tribal societies and even earlier to the time of the great hunt. The structure of gangs mirrors this pattern. There is a loose collection of several dozen to hundred members under an umbrella organization of tribal/clan size within which there are sub-units consisting of four to eight men `crews' who are responsible for the actual crime and violence, the classic hunting pack/squad size formation.

Gangs have always existed within large populations, but their power waxes or wanes because of government policies. As a government becomes increasingly corrupt, there is a corresponding increase in the profit to be had by circumventing government regulations. Naturally, this is illegal and so it is the criminal gangs who are best able to exploit this opportunity. While Triads have always existed in China their enormous power and influence came only after opium became widespread and then banned. Then huge profits from drug smuggling allowed them to buy power even in highest echelons. In America, it was the profits from running liquor during prohibition that allowed local ethnic gangs to coalesce into criminal syndicates.

Government efforts to exert stricter controls on criminal gangs causes the supply to drop and profits to increase, thus fueling even more of the criminal activity they sought to stop. The end game consists of several criminal warlords vying for control of the government. Indeed, it could be argued that what passes for history is but a record of rival gangs fighting for power.

Black Market:. One way to circumvent corrupt institutions is by creating a separate underground economy known a `Black Market'. Here goods and services that are taxed, monopolized, or sold at extorted prices by traditional industries are provided by gang elements to bypass the usual kickbacks to government and business.

The black market has its foundation in excessive taxation or government restrictions on certain goods. Corrupt regimes all make the same mistake, when searching for more money from the populace to compensate for the losses of inept administration and corrupt officials they resort to raising taxes. Modern Governments have thought to disguise these tax increases by calling it different names, licensing, processing, accessing, service fees, but all money paid to a government is, in effect, tax regardless of what you call it. Increasing taxes only works until it reaches a certain bifurcation point - its own critical mass, after which every increase in tax rate results in less money going into government coffers 35 The higher the taxes, the more people will become a part of the underground economy in order to evade taxes. An honest man is not likely to engage in criminal activities to avoid paying a reasonable portion in taxes. However, when the tax levels increase to the point where many people will not be able to survive on what is left, they are forced into a black market economy in order to feed their families. At this stage, corrupt governments will step-up their tax-collecting program using police and military forces. Anarchy and war soon follow.

Once greed and corruption have pervaded all facets of a society then everyone, even decent people, must take part in the system to survive. Honest police officers cannot survive in a corrupt police force, neither can honest politicians survive in a corrupt government, nor can honest businesspersons survive in a corrupt economy.

## Surviving Corruption

For over four thousand years, scholars and philosophers have
lamented and sought a cure for greed and corruption. Everything
has been tried; religion, morality, draconian laws and harsh
punishments but these methods succeeded only briefly if at all.
While a morally upright person can succeed in fighting corruption
within his or her own small sphere of influence, in the larger scale
little can be done other than trying to survive. There are two ways
in which to survive such conditions, the Way of Grass and The
Way of the Chameleon.

*It is the gnarled and useless tree that escapes the axe.*
Lao Tzu

The Way of Grass:  This is the strategy of hiding in plain sight by
becoming as unobtrusive and valueless as grass. Blend into the
countryside, cover the light of your intelligence, and hide wealth
behind the facade of poverty. Lao Tzu who wrote, "The Sage,
while clad in homespun, conceals on his person a priceless jade",
best exemplifies this tactic. To defend against exploitation of your
resources, dress in old clothes, never wear any jewelry in public,
never discuss financial matters, let the exterior appearance of your
home deteriorate, bury or hide anything of value, carry only enough
money for day to day needs. To defend against the exploitation of
your labor pretend to be sick or injured, walk around with a limp,
and act as though you were mentally disabled. [36] In this way, you
can stay under the radar and evade the purges, pogroms, and
extortions that inevitably accompany times of social corruption.

The Way of the Chameleon: This means to be able to change your
appearances and allegiances to fit whatever the situation dictates. In
politics, this means becoming a card-carrying member (under
different names) of every political party or partisan group. In this
way, whichever party seizes power you are able to show a long-
standing membership. If that group is overthrown and the new
power holders begin a purge, then you simply produce another card
showing you are a long time member of that party. By holding
different memberships, without attracting attention, one is able to
be associated with the ruling party and yet avoid political purges. If,
however, you become too pre-eminent with one group you risk

persecution by the next group. Thus, you must ensure that you do not become well known within any organization.

The same method can be applied to community, religious, benevolent, and criminal secret societies. Join the same church, political party, charity organization, sports team, school, and social club as members of the ruling party. Develop connections so you can be forewarned and thus better able to defend against policy and legislative changes, taxation increases, stock market manipulations, rationing, and supply shortages. If you find yourself in dire straights, then having the right connections can help you out of trouble.

Systemic social corruption will always destroy a society in one of two ways; through either civil war or revolution because the majority of citizens can no longer survive under the inhuman conditions, or through foreign invasion when the state is too crippled by corruption to mount a plausible defense against a foreign aggressor. In either case, you should next begin to prepare for war.

## War

*It is a doctrine of war not to assume the enemy will not come, but rather to rely on one's readiness to meet him; not to presume that he will not attack, but rather to make one's self invincible.*
Sun Tzu, *The Art of War*

Around the time that agrarian societies first developed there was also introduced a new concept, ownership of territory. Those ancient skills that were so necessary to the hunt were now put to a different use, the defense or acquisition of territory. Archaeology shows that shortly after the invention of the grinding stone came the invention of defensive walls, after the invention of the plough the sword was invented. War has been a part of civilization since its invention and has plagued every generation since. There is a good chance that you or your children will have to deal with a war scenario. Those who can see the signs and make the effort to prepare ahead of time will have a better chance surviving until peace comes again.

## Signs of Impending War
Before war breaks out there are several social changes that can act as indicators of approaching war. They are as follows:

Social Strife: Increase in angry demonstrations, strikes, marches, rallies, and public speeches arising from a full political spectrum. Every leader knows that regardless of the internal troubles, a powerful outside enemy will have the effect of uniting the people against a common threat and ennobling the ruling party. However, once the threat is removed the internal squabbles will soon resume.

Unemployment: Watch for a dramatic increase in the numbers of unemployed young males. The aggressive energies of young men need the outlets of hard work, sport, and the pursuit of females. When these traditional channels of energy are denied, the inevitable outcome is increased crime and social unrest. The ruling party may be tempted to diffuse a potential rebellion by creating a conflict to draw off extra labor.

Dwindling Resources: Scarcity of resources especially food staples, metals, and petroleum products, leads to high prices that devalue paper currency and rapidly increase inflation. It is no accident that past world wars were preceded by economic recessions. In tribal societies when resources started running thin, aggression was a means of driving away excess population into other unexploited areas. Now there is nowhere else to go so we have to stand our ground and slug it out.

Increased Patriotism: Patriotism is the classical lure used to appeal to the traditional warrior ethic. Look for increased patriotic speeches, flag waving, slogans, songs, marching bands, propaganda, portraits of 'Great Leaders' and 'Heroes of the 'Homeland'.

Increased Militarism: Initially there are military recruitment campaigns, followed by conscription, followed by press gangs.

Look for increasing government spending on the military, greater military influence on foreign and domestic policy.

Choosing an Enemy: Before war can be declared the government must designate an enemy. Traditional enemies are usually ethnic minorities within society or neighboring countries. When war becomes eminent one or more of these 'enemies of the state' will begin to receive greater attention, followed by a dehumanizing process.

Dehumanizing Potential Enemies: In order to be able to kill another human being you must first dehumanize that person. That is you must view the other person as a symbol of something evil and subhuman rather than a real, feeling, human like yourself. In war, this is accomplished through propaganda. The enemy is never portrayed sitting down to dinner with a loving family, laughing and playing with children. Instead, they are portrayed as monsters through the use of slanderous propaganda and rumor campaigns. The truth is that the soldiers of most nations are young naive men that share the same human qualities and desires common to our species. Whenever a government depicts an entire nation or people as evil and warmongering they are employing propaganda to convince the people to support an attack on that country.

## Surviving War

*War is a human paradox in that if one prepares for war, war will come, if one does not prepare for war, war still comes.*
Gwynne Dyer, *War*

War is nothing more than the crimes of rapine and murder carried out on a massive scale. That young men and women are sent off to rape, rob and murder other young men and women without gaining any of the profit or benefits thereof is clearly the work of psychopaths. The presence of war indicates that a society has become completely dysfunctional and that malignant minds are in charge of the machinery of the state. The first step to surviving war is to never join the armed forces, and dissuade anyone in your family from doing so as well.

Wartime can bring some or all of the previously discussed manmade disasters. If the fighting takes place near your home, you may face a chemical, biological, or nuclear attack. If the fighting is abroad you may nevertheless have to deal with martial law and a climate of corruption. Surviving war requires you to adapt the strategies for natural and manmade disasters for each possible disaster as they develop.

As the signs of war point to its imminent arrival be sure to refresh and redouble your survival skills and materiel. Add to you emergency supplies, take extra first aid and wilderness survival training, re-establish connections with friends, family, and neighbors to assist each other both for moral and resource support. Join or establish barter networks and try to find other sources for goods and services for the time when the traditional channels for such become scarce.

Countries at war will use all available resources to keep their armies supplied. This means there is often not enough left for the civilian population. To prepare against such an eventuality one should begin to hoard supplies as the signs of war become evident. Stockpile food, water, medicine, fuel, and seeds - should the war last longer than your stores, you may have to supplement your nutritional needs by growing your own vegetables.

Convert some of your wealth into gold or precious stones, or likely barter items such as cans of coffee, sugar, cartons of cigarettes or shotgun shells. Hide these items in several locations or caches in the event that you or a family member is held for ransom. By revealing one of several hiding places to your extorters, you lose only a portion of your wealth.

The best way to survive a war is to run, hide, and wait for it all to blow over. In order to do this you need someway to travel, somewhere to hide, and you need to provide for all the requirements of daily living while you are waiting.

Should you need to evacuate battle sites you need to prepare travel documents, and transportation. This could include everything from an extra car or boat to an extra pair of walking shoes. You will

need to have stockpiled fuel stores to run the transportation since you may not be able to buy these during wartime. Since the journey may take longer than expected due to interruptions in communications, the mining and bombing of roads etc., you need to carry food, water, extra clothing, temporary shelter materials, and medicine to last through the journey.

Prepare a second safe place to run to should the fighting move closer to where you are currently living. This could be a cabin or farmhouse in the country or another home in another city. Hiding in another city has some advantages; there are better communications, more places to hide, and greater resources. If you have limited funds you could make an agreement with friends or relatives living in another part of the country that, should fighting occur near your home, you and your family could go stay with your relatives until it is safe to return and vice versa.

Also, construct a hiding place at your home or your safe house to store your supplies in. Both friendly and enemy troops passing through your area will send out scavenger teams looking for food and other supplies for the army. As with any group of armed men, you should be wary of having any dealings with them. In addition, able-bodied men and women should stay out of sight since they may be conscripted into the army.

Should the fighting worsen, and as the war lengthens, there is a greater likelihood of atrocities committed against civilian populations. The bombing, shelling and gassing of civilians have been recorded in every major conflict since recorded history as well as large scale enslavement and imprisonment. In such cases, the last survival strategy available to you may be to escape, evade and go underground.

247

## <u>Escape And Evade</u>

*When overwhelmed, you don't fight; you surrender, compromise,
or flee. Surrender is complete defeat, compromise is half defeat,
flight is not defeat. As long as you are not defeated, you have
another chance to win.*
The Thirty-Six Strategies

As much as we may admire other contenders for the title, 'King of
the Jungle', it is modern man that is the unrivaled king of hunters,
the top predator. As children, we learn to play games such as
'Peek-a-Boo', 'Hide and Seek', and 'Tag'. Despite their innocent
appearance, these games are in effect exercises to train our hunting
skills. As these games suggest, man's favorite prey is man. At some
point, many of us will find ourselves pursued by our fellow man,
whether by enemy soldiers in a natural jungle or by criminals in the
urban jungle. To ignore the study of hunting and fleeing is to
ignore our heritage; it is because our ancestors learned and
developed these skills that we enjoy the luxury of world
domination today.

As a rule, the longer you can avoid capture, the greater your chance of survival, however, the longer you stay on the run the greater your chances of succumbing to the elements. Most escapees are caught because they were unable to deal with the everyday problems of survival on the run, not because their pursuers caught up to them. When you are on the run, even minor difficulties can become a major problem; small cuts become infected, cause fevers and threaten gangrene. The best pair of shoes can cause sores so that travel becomes agony. Water, when available may cause diarrhea, and stomach cramps. In the summer, flying insects have been known to drive men insane. In the winter, the cold saps your strength and will to survive. In addition, caloric requirements increase dramatically. Under normal conditions, 2,500 calories per day is adequate to provide enough nutrition to keep one healthy, but on the run, you may need three times that to maintain the same degree of health. Once you are ill from malnourishment or injury, your chances of survival drop rapidly. To be sure, the pursuers are also suffering from the same conditions, but they have the option to return to home base, have supplies delivered, and time to replenish and heal. The primary difficulty when being hunted is to continually have to find shelter and provisions.

To evade effectively one must know what methods would be used in trying to capture you. One must learn the strategy of the hunters. There are three strategies common to hunting; track and kill, ambush, and bait and trap.

## Track And Kill

Track and kill consists of tracking, stalking, and when you have the game in sight, killing. This method requires a great expenditure of energy and is therefore usually restricted to large game where the caloric gains exceed the caloric expenditures. The same holds true in human society. In law enforcement, teams of detectives will track down dangerous offenders such as armed robbers and murderers, but this method is too expensive to use on minor offenders who commit misdemeanors; the financial expense is simply not worth the benefits to society. Tracking and killing is used by the strong against the weak, the many against the few.

Success is dependent on the perseverance of the hunter. The only drawback is time, if the pursued is clever enough to elude capture for an extended time, then the amount of energy expended by the hunter increases. Eventually the expenditure will exceed the reward and the hunt is called off. However, if the hunters are determined at any cost to succeed, then capture is inevitable.

### Tracking Methods

<u>Sight</u>: Sight is our most highly developed sense used to follow the target directly or to see indications of his recent passing such as dust clouds, boat wakes, swinging doors, car headlights in the distance, the smoke or glow of cooking fires.

<u>Sound</u>: If the target is out of sight, or when it is impossible to see clearly, then the brain's focus switches over to auditory detection. People entering strange environments in the dark automatically reduce the amount of noise they make in order to hear more clearly. In the forest one can hear the game crashing through the brush, or splashing across streams, on the street one can hear heavy breathing reflected off the walls of buildings, the sound of cans being kicked along the street, the sudden barking of dogs.

<u>Smell</u>: Tracking by smell is usually accomplished by trained dogs that, depending on the weather, can follow a scent trail up to three days old. However, smell can alert you of the presence of someone nearby. For example, Vietnamese guerrillas seldom ran into an American ambush because they were alerted by the distinct perspiration odor caused by the meat rich diets of the American soldiers.

<u>Signs</u>: Signs are indications in the environment, clues to the direction the game is fleeing. Signs include; tracks and footprints, matted vegetation and broken branches, blood drops if the prey is injured, warm ashes of a cooking fire, warm beds and car engines.

<u>Spoor:</u> An animal's highly evolved olfactory sense allows it to garner a great deal of information by smelling another's droppings. Many animals instinctively bury their spoor to avoid giving their presence away. Humans leave behind another kind of spoor - garbage. Even an amateur detective going through a week's worth of someone's garbage would be able to tell what that person ate, gender, overall health, and the general age of the person. Everywhere people go, they leave behind a trail of garbage, wrappers, containers, papers, cigarette butts, discarded clothing, business cards, and unpaid bills.

## Evading Trackers

There are three tactics to evade trackers: leave no tracks, leave false trails, and wear the pursuers down. A combination of all three methods works best.

## Hide Your Tracks

To leave no trails requires an acute self-discipline to monitor your own movement to reduce the number of clues you leave behind. The following are some general precautions to use in the wilderness.

Walking: Be aware of where you step, try not to leave footprints in soft earth, crush small twigs, matte down grass, or break small branches. Traveling along rocky or swampy ground and along waterways such as streams and rivers are best for hiding footprints.

Resting: Improvise a simple perimeter warning system such as leaving three or four patches of dry twigs along the trail at twenty-foot intervals so that you would be able to hear the approach of anyone following along the trail. Leave nothing lying around ever, you may have to move away quickly and not have time to clean up.

Choose a campsite that is not an obvious choice for shelter, for example, an isolated cabin should be avoided since it would seem an obvious choice to anyone hunting you. Similarly, a small clump of trees in a desert, a small clearing in the bush, a small island in the swamp, all would provide a comfortable shelter, and it is for that reason that these areas are searched first. The rule of thumb is that the more unpleasant the location, the less likely it will be searched. When breaking camp, if no one is aware of your presence, maintain secrecy by cleaning and hiding your campsite. If being pursued, set up booby traps and plant false trails before leaving.

Camouflage: Always try to camouflage yourself, your equipment, and your campsites. This is a last chance strategy in that if the pursuers are able to catch up with you, you may still have the chance to hide. To camouflage yourself, take off your outer clothing and roll them in the mud, stomp them into the grass, soak them in the swamp and kick them around until filthy. Simply stated, to blend in with your environment, you must become the environment. (Also helps to hide your scent.) The same applies to equipment. Check all metal, glass, plastic and other shiny surfaces such as belt buckles, glasses, pack frames, buttons and grommets. A reflective surface can catch the sunlight and signal your presence from miles away. These surfaces should be covered over with material or mud. Also be sure to strap down or dampen any equipment such as cooking pots or tools that is making a rattling noise.

When hunting one always moves up against, or diagonal across the wind so that one's scent does not alert the intended game, however, if being tracked by dogs the opposite is true, move downwind crossing water as often as possible. A simple rule to remember is to 'Hunt with the wind in your face, and run with the wind at your back.'

## Leave False Trails

Never head directly for your shelter. Instead make a couple of changes in direction before heading towards your final destination. False trails should be left anytime one changes direction or comes across intersecting paths. There are two ways to leave false trails - backtracking and misdirection.

Backtrack: Used only if you have already gained a significant lead and can afford the time it takes to go over the same piece of ground twice. Backtracking means to return the same way you came being careful to hide any sign of your return, and then continue in a different direction. Those following you will eventually find your tracks end. The standard procedure for trackers is to continue along in the same direction the tracks had been leading in order to pick up the trail further along. When they are unable to pick up the trail again they will return, this time searching along edges of the path for signs that you may have cut off from the trail somewhere along the way. This costs the pursuers more time and energy. Remember, the more expensive it is to catch someone the greater the chances they give up the chase.

Backtracking is most effective when on soft, muddy, or sandy terrain. Since this type of terrain makes it easy to follow someone's tracks, it is likely that the pursuers are watching for footprints more than any other sign and so are more likely to follow the false trail.

Misdirection: Another method is to leave false clues. For example, if you come to a fork in the trail, drop a personal item such as a piece of garbage or shred of clothing along one path then backtrack and take the other path. Those following will see the item and deduce you went up that path. However, if the trackers are experienced, back track once more and go along the original path where the item was planted. The purpose of this double play is because an experienced tracker would recognize the planted item so near the fork of a trail to be too coincidental, and would choose the other path.

Another tactic is to hang some strips of cloth or a couple of pieces of metal, (spoons, and tin cans) from a tree branch slightly off the trail in the thick foliage, so that when the wind blows through the branches it will make an unusual noise or movement. Those following will waste time carefully checking out the source of the unnatural sound or movement in the bush.

## Wearing Down The Trackers

The third strategy is to wear down the tracker by leaving behind booby traps or, if traveling in a group, leaving men behind in ambush to delay the enemy. Those following will become wary and suspicious of traps or ambushes and this will slow them down. Leaving behind just one booby trap will have the desired effect since, while you are free to move as fast as you can, the pursuers must slow down and cautiously check ever step they take for fear of walking into another trap. Booby traps need not be complex or even dangerous, anything unusual such as some pointed sticks stuck in the ground or a strange looking parcel left in the path will arouse suspicion. Planting even a slight doubt in the mind of your enemy is a great advantage.

## Ambush

The ambush requires less expenditure of energy than tracking and killing and so is used more frequently. The principle advantage of an ambush is the element of surprise, which allows the weaker to overcome the slightly stronger, the few to overcome the few more.

In order to set-up the ambush, the hunter must know the habits of his prey, where and when it eats, drinks, and sleeps, and jungle trails that it uses. Knowing these habits the hunter sets up an ambush in an area he knows the prey will eventually pass by. The drawback to an ambush is the need for concealment, once detected the element of surprise is lost. As a rule, the longer someone must wait in ambush, the more likely that they will be detected. Those waiting will get restless, the limbs become stiff from inactivity, the weather conditions may cause discomfort, eventually they will have to eat and relieve themselves. All this activity increases as time goes on, and will eventually warn off the target. Since there is a limit to the amount of time a pursuer can wait in hiding, an ambush must be set up near an area frequented on a regular basis, such as watering holes, forest trails, dens, and burrows.

## Avoiding An Ambush

Ambushes are planned to coordinate with your routines and habits, to avoid an ambush, avoid routine. Take different routes both to and from home base, alternate the times when you sleep and wake. Do not always go to the same source of supplies and never play the same move twice.

Set up a Red Flag. A 'Red Flag' is any innocuous item that appears commonplace, but which is placed in a specific position so that if someone where to enter the area they would disturb the item's position and alignment. This disturbance would be unnoticed by the intruder, yet would alert you that someone has been there. For example, place a small branch across the trail or entrance to your camp in such a way that anyone entering would move the placement of the branch unconscious of its significance.

Other methods include; placing a piece of scrap paper inside the door jam when you close the door. The paper would drop to the floor unnoticed by someone else opening the door but would immediately alert you that someone has been there If a pencil were placed just so on top of a stack of papers, anyone reading the papers would replace the pencil but would not remember just which way the pencil was pointing. Another method is to sprinkle a light dusting of talcum powder along a tile floor, or on top of filing cabinets, which looks like dust, and will reveal finger and footprints of anyone disturbing the room.

Always approach a base with caution. Check for signs of entry, reconnoiter before entering. Pass by home base as though heading for a different destination so that one can observe the area and then backtrack to home. If your red flag has been tripped, back off and wait. The longer you wait and watch, the greater your chances of spotting an ambush.

When traveling in a group, employ a diamond formation. Send scouts ahead to search for traps and ambushes, have out-riders on the flanks if possible to prevent being cut off, leave a rear guard to use harrying and delaying tactics against possible pursuers.

If you must enter an area where you suspect an ambush, then use the 'Stalking Horse', strategy. The tactic comes from a Plains Indian buffalo hunting technique whereby the hunters get off and walk beside their horses keeping the horses between them and the herd. In this way, they can get within range to shoot without spooking the buffalo. The tactic can be applied in other ways using the basic principle of hiding behind something common and non-threatening. Send in a third party to trigger the ambush and draw the attention, then take advantage of the ensuing confusion.

## Bait And Trap

Bait and trap requires only the energy needed to construct and set the trap. Traps can be used by the weak to overcome the strong and the few the many. Traps can vary from simple to complex constructions capable of tremendous destruction. There are usually two components to a trap, a lure and a trigger. Bait used to lure animals is usually food, bait used to lure humans include money, power, sex, recognition, drugs, and anything 'Free'. Like an ambush, a trap needs to be set near an area frequented by the intended target, but unlike an ambush, a trap need not be limited to the amount of time it waits. The disadvantage of a trap is that it usually cannot discriminate between friend or foe and so poses a hazard to both the intended target and any innocent party inadvertently setting it off.

## Avoiding Traps

Like ambushes, most traps are laid between home and sources of supply. The presence of any sort of bait should alert you to the possibility of a trap. Bait is anything you would want. Military demolitions experts have been known to booby trap food rations, weapons, equipment, and even children's toys. Finding supplies when on the run should always trigger caution. Beware of chance coincidences, unexpected windfalls, and new friends. One must train to develop a natural tendency to resist immediately reaching out for something one wants. The more you want it, the more cautious you should be.

If you suspect a trap, use the scapegoat strategy. The scapegoat suffers the consequences intended for others, in this case, the scapegoat is anything or anyone that will spring the trap and suffer the effects intended for you. This could be a stick thrown at a trip wire, a stray cow chased through a minefield, or a pizza delivered to your house.

## Urban E & E

While the above advice applies to evading in a wilderness environment, the same strategies can be applied should you need to evade in an urban environment.

Few societies have not had incidents of forced labor, conscription, internments, as well as government confiscations of personal property, bank accounts, and illegal search and seizures. History shows that every society undergoes occasional civil disorder and tyranny. For this reason, knowing some of the basic strategies of evading in an urban environment could prove vital to surviving such turbulent times.[37]

## Hiding Your Urban Tracks

In the urban environment, tracks are left in the form of computer records. Every time you use your name there will be a trace left of your activities. The use of credit cards, gas cards, bank accounts, drivers licenses, social security numbers, library cards, video memberships, clubs and professional associations, telephone numbers, health cards, passports, birth certificates, etc. will create a record each time you use them. This information is readily available to anyone with the determination to retrieve it.

Under normal conditions, these records are benign, but during times of civil disorder, such information can be used to track down and exploit targeted groups or individuals.

Monetary Exchange: Never use check, money orders, or credit cards. Pay for things with cash or barter. Never sign your real name on receipts and destroy the receipts you receive. (If you are captured those receipts could help reconstruct your past activities and ensnare others.)

Changing Identities: Use different names for different situations, for example when traveling you may use the name Walker, in restaurants and bars the name Cook, when shopping the name Green. The use of such names, in addition to making it difficult to discover your habits, also helps to serve a reminder to keep track of the different aliases. For example, if you are in a group of people and someone recognizes you as Mr. Cook you would know that you met that person in a bar or restaurant and thus enable you to remember which cover story to use when speaking with him or her. Maintaining consistency in your cover story is important.

Camouflage: As in the wilderness, so in the urban environment you must blend in with the surroundings. If you are heading for the business district, a suit and tie is camouflage, if heading for the country, overalls and boots are camouflage. Continually change your outward appearance, especially clothing. People recognize and remember each other more by what they wear than what their physical features are. It is much easier to identify someone who is wearing a red jacket and blue jeans than by a physical description.

When in doubt, wear the uniform of a technician, doctor, rescue worker, ambulance driver, road crew, forest ranger. A uniform indicates that the wearer is an authority in some field and people are conditioned to obey this authority symbol. However, stay away from police or military uniforms as most armies have a policy of shooting anyone caught in their own uniform. There are also civil penalties against wearing a disguise, but if the disguise allows you to avoid capture, the penalties are mute.

If in a foreign country it is safest to stay in areas frequented by foreigners, a stranger in the countryside is easily noticed. In a pinch one can also feign insanity, pretend to speak to an imaginary friend, never acknowledge the presence of others, in this way people will take you for an idiot, no one will ask serious questions, they will be anxious to ignore you.

## Leaving False Urban Trails

Dead Letter Box: In the business world, false trails are better known as offshore bank accounts, subsidiaries, shell companies, holding companies, and trusts. These are employed by the rich and corrupt to hide their wealth in order to evade paying taxes, creditors, court judgments, alimony, insurance, and other costs.

For those of more modest means false trails can take the form of post office boxes, answering services, and business centers. By doing business under assumed names that can only be traced to a post office box or answering service allows you to monitor anyone taking an interest in you without exposing yourself. If those pursuing overcome the dead letter box obstacle, you can fall back on attorneys to stall pursuers while you seek other means of escape. This is the method most often employed by petty confidence men and small businesses evading creditors.

Transportation: Change modes of travel regularly. Change license plates on cars and/or trade cars in for other makes and colors. When talking to gas station attendants or ticket cashiers casually reveal a false destination. Those following and questioning witnesses will be given wrong or contradictory information. When buying bus or railway tickets, book the ticket for one stop further along the route than your true destination. Anyone wishing to ambush you will rendezvous at the wrong location, or if following you, they will relax their vigilance until nearing the final destination, unaware that your true destination is sooner then expected. Take advantage of their inattention to escape.

<u>Misdirection</u>: This involves creating a fog of misinformation around you. Not telling the truth about where you live, where you are going, or what you are doing. Allow people to make their own conclusions. Anyone hunting you will receive conflicting information about your activities. Without discernable habits and schedules, it is more difficult to track, ambush, or trap you.

<u>Losing a Tail</u>: The first step in losing a tail, is knowing you have one. To find out if someone is following, backtrack and see if anyone backtracks with you. Walk down the street and then pretend you forgot something, cross the street and return in the same direction you came from. Anyone following you would have to turn around and cross the street as well, not something you can do without being noticed. In addition, by walking back you will be able to identify the tail.

Another method is to use reflective surfaces to look around without appearing to be looking around. Stop in front of a store window as though looking at the goods while using the window's reflective surface to scan the background behind you. Pretend to look at your watch and use the glass lens as a mirror, or pretend to clean your glasses to see behind you.

The basic strategy of losing a tail is making the terrain more difficult by leaving behind obstacles. If you are on foot and those following are in a car then use footpaths. Go through alleys, into buildings, stores, shopping malls and lose yourself in the crowd. If those following are also on foot, go somewhere that requires a paid admission, like a subway train or movie theatre. The admission process incurs a non-negotiable time delay, while the tails are waiting to pay for admission, move quickly out a side or back entrance while they are still engaged at the entrance. If the tail is of the opposite sex, go into a busy public washroom and look for a service exit, window, or fire escape. Misdirection can also be used when passing through a room; open the door but leave through a window or another door, or vice versa.

If you are in a rough neighborhood, and you have some acting ability, you could approach a group of people and tell them that you are being followed by an undercover police officer and ask them to run interference. If you are female you can claim those following have attempted sexual assault. If in a wealthy neighborhood you could approach a group of people and claim those following are known car thieves or burglars `casing' the neighborhood and ask them to phone police and run interference.

Avoiding Surveillance: Many countries routinely put their citizenry under surveillance. This includes bugging hotel, conference, and meeting rooms, telephones, and reading mail correspondence. In addition, many different people may be employed as informants such as hotel staff, taxi drivers, tour guides, moneychangers, even beggars and prostitutes. Totalitarian governments also employ the common people in `neighborhood watch' type groups that are charged with reporting all sorts of suspicious behavior. These informants may be encouraged out of patriotic duty, rewarded with money, made to feel they are important, or are doing so to avoid persecution themselves. In the inevitably paranoid society this creates absolutely no one can be trusted.

To avoid eavesdropping devices do not use any electronic communication, or if unavoidable use a prearranged code system that could pass off as innocuous chitchat. The usual subjects include the weather, friends and relations, or business transactions. For example to express `Situation Normal' you could say `The weather seems to be clearing up', or `I spoke to Aunty May', or `We're still making a profit on that deal'. To express danger or a warning the opposite terms could be used such as, `It looks a bit cloudy', or `I spoke to Mr. Black', or `We lost that sale'. It is not difficult to improvise any number of messages around such talk provided both parties have had time to set up the basic groundwork for the code. The same code can be used in written communications as well. If the communication is ongoing however, make sure to change the codes as often as possible since every code can be broken.

## Avoiding an Urban Ambush
In the city, ambushes are set up near homes and offices, bars and cars. The salesperson ambushes his customer at home, court clerks serve subpoenas at the office, the police arrest criminals at their favorite hangout, muggers wait near parked cars.

The rules for avoiding an ambush are the same as in the wilderness. Take different route to and from home base, never head directly to a destination, use extra caution every time one is near home, work place, shopping, and getting in and out of a vehicle. Stop and survey the area before entering and leaving these locations, leave and check `Red Flags'. If anything seems out of place, wait it out or leave.

## Avoiding Urban Traps

The presence of any sort of bait should alert you to the possibility of a trap. Traditionally the bait used to lure prey in the urban environment involved money, sex, or something free

Money: Common ploys include a dropped wallet, a sudden windfall, or a chance to earn money illegally. In con parlance, these traps lure suckers into the con game and are known by such names as `The pigeon drop', `The magic wallet', and `The inheritance game'. Common sense states that everything has its price, making `easy' money or getting more than fifteen percent return on your investment should trigger a warning.

Sex: The second most popular bait. In the field of espionage, it is known as the `Honey Trap' and is used to extort and blackmail the victim into handing over information. In confidence games it is known as the `Badger Game' and is used to extort and blackmail the victim into handing over large amounts of money. If you find attractive men or women suddenly wanting to take you to their room and you are not terribly good looking, be suspicious. The variations on the honey trap are endless.

Something For Nothing: Used in the same way as money but using merchandise or services as the bait. The key word is free. It seems to be an irresistible lure offering something for free.

Drugs: The most effective of traps since once addicted, the victim no longer needs to be lured through artifice but is drawn into the trap over and over again through the urging of his own nervous system, overriding the conscious control mechanisms. The basic trap works as follows, victim is befriended by a gregarious outgoing sort of person who casually introduces the drug to the victim under the banner of *joie de vie*, initially free until the addictive effects begin to take hold. Then the friend turns into a tyrant using access to the drug as his base of power. 38

## What To Do If Captured

*Men rattle their chains to show that they are free.*
Proverb

Whether you are captured by police or military forces, kidnappers, or terrorists the methods of incarceration follow a common pattern. The following are general tactics that can help keep you safe when you are captured.

### Negotiate

If capture seems inevitable, negotiate terms of surrender. The pursuers may not know that they have you trapped and m0ay still expect considerable trouble in apprehending you. Negotiating offers the pursuers an end to the trouble in exchange for better treatment on your behalf, or to stall if you expect reinforcements, or, if time is on your side.

### Cooperate and Play Dead

If you have been caught by surprise and negotiating surrender is no longer an option, then the first tactic is to co-operate, and appear exhausted and injured. In this way, you appear less of a threat, which will allow the pursuers to relax their guard. The tactic is the same as if faced with a charging grizzly bear, lie down and play dead. Expect to be beaten, generally the longer they have been pursuing you the worst the beating. Putting up a brave face and a bad attitude will only make the beating worse. Man the hunter, after a chase, has the urge to kill. Even in the most benevolent of police forces, there will be occasions when a difficult suspect will be taken around back for a 'Lesson in Manners'. By 'Playing Dead', you will not be triggering the instinct to kill the cornered prey. The worst tactic is to fight a last losing battle with your pursuers. Only if you fully expect to be tortured and killed immediately upon capture would you resort to this tactic.

## Stall and Delay
Ask for medical treatment. If you can be transported to a medical facility you increase the possibility of finding an opportunity to escape since security is never as tight as in the regular institutions. You want to avoid as long as possible, being processed through the penal system since the longer you are in custody, and the further along you are processed, the tighter the security. If you are not already injured, fake an injury.

## Let Your People Know Where You Are
As soon as possible make contact with the outside world through family, friends, comrades in arms, and lawyers. Have them contact the authorities to inquire into your situation, post bail, hire lawyers, or bribe jailers. The more people that know where you are, and express their concern for your health to the people holding you, the less chance of you 'disappearing'.

## Make Friends
Most escape plans require inside help, the assistance of other prisoners and guards that means making friends with those who are able to assist you. Try and play on national, religious, and philosophical sympathies, mimic their behavior and use entrainment techniques, of course the best way to make 'friends' is to have money.

## The Grey Man
A form of camouflage is playing the 'Grey man', blending into the background by not drawing attention to oneself through unusual behavior, manner, or dress. Downplay physical characteristics, if strong appear weak, if slim appear fat, change hair color, grow or remove facial hair. Speak only when spoken to and then answer briefly, never volunteer information. Do not look people in the eye, which is often understood as a threat. By becoming innocuous and forgettable you avoid attention. In a penal institution, drawing attention to oneself is a bad idea. In addition, by becoming innocuous, you have a better chance of going missing without anyone noticing right away, which may be vital during an escape attempt.

## Dead man's Trigger Tactic

A Dead Man's Trigger is a spring-loaded hand-held button detonator for explosives. In the classic terrorist scenario the explosives are strapped to the person holding the detonator, so long as the button is held down the detonating circuit is open, but if the button is released, the circuit will close and set off the explosives. It ensures that the person holding the detonator is unharmed since to kill or injure him would cause his thumb to release the button killing the terrorist and those around him - a miniature doomsday weapon. In less extreme applications the dead man trigger or 'Button Down' tactic can work in ways that require you to indicate a healthy constitution also called proof of life. For example, hikers, mountain climbers and canoeists when heading into wild country will register a travel plan with the local forest or park rangers indicating where they plan to go and when they plan to get there. If they do not call in at the expected time, the rangers will begin search and rescue operations.

The key to this strategy is to have something of value, or something that is damaging, to those who seek to harm you, and use this lure/threat to bribe or blackmail them into ensuring your continued good health or release. For example, place incriminating evidence with a third party with instructions to release the material to a pre-arranged channel should you fail to call in every day at a certain time. Another tactic that might work is to rent a safety deposit box and place some fake jewelry in fancy boxes inside. If you are being held for ransom, or in order to bribe your jailers, you could offer them the contents of the box. No one would guess that you would go through the expense and precaution of renting a safety deposit box to store fake jewels. In addition, to get to the box the kidnappers would need to bring you to the bank which could afford you numerous opportunities to escape.

## Escape Tactics

Although the specific details of an escape plan would be dependent on the circumstance, they all employ one or more of following tactics.

266

## Diversion

A diversion timed to occur at the most critical point in the escape is used to draw attention away. Common diversions include, staged fights or riots, false medical emergencies and accidents, alluring women, and the all time favorite, fire. The power of fire is that it cannot be ignored or dealt with later; it is therefore a sure-fire way of attracting attention, causing panic, and drawing off manpower.

## The Tactic Of Injuring Yourself

This is a classic technique whereby one fakes injury or even death to escape. Methods include feigning insanity, or an epileptic seizure, consuming noxious substances to make one ill, and literally shooting oneself in the foot. WWII POW's smoked sugar in their tobacco, which gave them symptoms similar to tuberculosis. Prisoners in the notorious French penal colony at Devil's Island where know to cut their Achilles' tendon in order to avoid the grueling jungle labor that was the major cause of death. Also known in *Grifter* 1 parlance as the 'Blow Off' or 'Chicken Bladder', where a staged but bloody death convinces the sucker that there is no hope to get his money back.

The objectives of this tactic are; to get you moved to a medical facility where conditions and/or opportunities to escape improve, to be relieved of having to do hard manual labor, or to be released because your captors think you're dead or as good as.

## False Flag (Disguise)

Prison uniforms are designed to be noticeably different from the type of clothes normally worn by civilians making it easier to recognize and differentiate prisoners from guards, visitors, and maintenance staff, and to identify escaped prisoners. However, this can work against the system. People usually notice external clothing more than they notice physical characteristics. As long as you do not wear prison clothes, you will not look like a prisoner. The most common escape tactic has been to steal or manufacture a copy of the guard's uniform and walk out at the end of the shift. Other disguises include maintenance, delivery, medical, and religious personnel, or the opposite sex.

---

1 A Grifter is slang for swindler and con artist.

Uniforms can be smuggled in under the clothes of visiting relatives or friends or, if security is too strict, a last resort is to change clothes with the visitor. If outside help is unavailable then uniforms may be bought or stolen from guards. A last resort is to alter the prison clothes. For this you will need needle and thread, clothes dye, and badges, buttons, and nameplates - the little extras that can add authenticity to the disguise.

## The False Double Tactic

This is the classic of escape tactics and is familiar to anyone who has been late for work and has to punch a time clock; that is have some else punch in for you. In prison, this means having someone else stand roll call for you. A variation involves constructing a likeness of yourself to take your place while you escape. The basic premise is to have the authorities believe you are still in custody thus affording you time to make good your escape.

## The Trojan Horse

As the name implies, it means hiding inside something else that would normally be leaving the prison without arousing suspicion. Successful escapes have been made hiding in body bags, coffins, laundry bags, garbage containers, and secret compartments built into various forms of transportation.

## The Tunnel

The last resort of escape tactics is the tunnel. Tunneling involves serious logistical problems; one would need digging tools, a false facade to hide the opening of the tunnel, a way of dispensing of tons of dirt, wood planking to use in shoring the side and roof against cave-ins, a lighting system, and, depending on the length of the tunnel, a way of circulating fresh air to prevent suffocating. Because of the logistical requirements and intensive labor, tunneling is usually a team project, yet despite the efforts required, tunneling has been used in many successful and dramatic escapes.[39]

## Escape Equipment
### Money

Have people from the outside supply you with the currency used in the system. Most successful escapes required bribing a guard to look the other way at the right time. Money is also needed to buy supplies from the prison black market and to buy protection. Without money, your chances of escape are drastically reduced. This is why military Special Forces working behind enemy lines are equipped with gold coins sewn into the lining of their equipment. Other methods of concealing wealth is swallowing precious stones or carrying a capsule containing money in the rectum.

## Keys

Most escapes require getting through locked doors. Even a trained locksmith would have difficult time picking the locks you would find in a security lock up. The best method is to steal the key you need, make a copy, and then replace the original since missing keys will alert authorities to an escape attempt and they will change the locks making the stolen key useless. Another method is to make an impression of the key in modeling clay, calking compound, bar of soft soap or wax. The impression or life size tracing could be smuggled out to cohorts to be copied, or, if you are good with your hands, you may be able to carve a copy from plastic, hardwood, or bone.

## Identity Papers

When on the run you will eventually be required to provide identification papers. These can sometimes be obtained from fellow prisoners or bought or stolen from guards. If you have escaped without papers, the next easiest way to obtain them is to go to a crowded area, wait until you find someone who most closely matches your description, and follow him until you have a chance to deprive him of his identification.

## Maps and Compass

An escape plan requires knowing where to go and how to get there which means you need a map. These can be smuggled or, as a last resort, drawn up from descriptions provided by fellow prisoners or jail staff. If your escape plan involves going cross country you'll need a compass as well. If you can't buy one, the old boy scout trick of using a magnetized needle inserted through a piece of cork or Styrofoam floated on a still pool of water may suffice.

## Provisions

Caloric requirements increase dramatically when on the run. Lack of adequate food and water will make you weak, slow you down, and reduce your mental sharpness making you prone to injuries and mistakes that will get you recaptured. If possible, buy extra provisions and stockpile the high calorie non-perishables like biscuits, chocolate, and dried meat. If extra food cannot be bought through the black market then you will have to save some of your daily rations. Reduce your intake until enough has been stockpiled then eat the full rations again for a few days before the escape date to build up your body's reserves.

# **Table 1: Perishable Food Time Chart**

### **Frozen Foods**

| Food Item | Still Contains Ice Crystals. Temperature not above 40° F (4° C) | Thawed, Held Above 40° F (4° C) For Over 2 Hours |
|---|---|---|
| Beef, veal, lamb, pork, poultry, ground meat and poultry | Refreeze | Discard |
| Casseroles with meat, pasta, rice, egg or cheese base, stews, soups, convenience foods, pizza | Refreeze | Discard |
| Fish, shellfish, breaded seafood products | Refreeze | Discard |
| Milk | Refreeze | Discard |
| Eggs (out of shell) egg products | Refreeze | Discard |
| Ice cream, frozen yogurt | Discard | Discard |
| Cheese (soft and semi soft) cream cheese ricotta | Refreeze | Discard |
| Hard cheese (cheddar Swiss parmesan) | Refreeze | Refreeze |
| Fruit Juices | Refreeze | Refreeze. Discard if mold, yeasty smell or sliminess develops. |
| Vegetable Juices | Refreeze | Discard if above 50° for over 8 hours. |
| Home or commercially packaged vegetables | Refreeze | Discard if above 50° for over 8 hours. |

## Refrigerator Foods

| Food Item | Food Still Cold, Held At 40° F (4° C) Or Above Under 2 Hours | Held Above 40° F (4° C) For Over 2 Hours |
| --- | --- | --- |
| Milk, cream, sour cream buttermilk evaporated milk yogurt | Keep | Discard |
| Butter, margarine | Keep | Keep |
| Baby Formula, opened | Keep | Discard |
| Eggs, egg dishes, custards puddings | Keep | Discard |
| Hard & processed cheeses | Keep | Keep |
| Soft cheeses, cottage cheese | Keep | Discard |
| Fruit juices, opened; Canned fruits, opened; Fresh fruits | Keep | Keep |
| Vegetables, cooked; Vegetable juice opened | Keep | Discard after 6 hours |
| Baked potatoes | Keep | Discard |
| Fresh mushrooms, herbs spices | Keep | Keep |
| Garlic, chopped in oil or buffer | Keep | Discard |
| Fresh or leftover meat, poultry, fish, or seafood | Keep | Discard |
| Lunchmeats, hot dogs, bacon, sausage, dried beef | Keep | Discard |
| Canned meats NOT labeled "Keep Refrigerated" but refrigerated after opening | Keep | Discard |
| Canned hams labeled "Keep Refrigerated" | Keep | Discard |

## **Directory of Resources**

American Red Cross National Headquarters
2025 E Street, NW
Washington, DC 20006
Phone: (202) 303-4498
www.redcross.org/pubs/dspubs/cde.html

National Weather Service
1325 East West Highway
Silver Spring, MD 20910
www.nws.noaa.gov/education.html

Centers for Disease Control and Prevention
1600 Clifton Rd, Atlanta, GA 30333, U.S.A
Public Inquiries: (404) 639-3534 / (800) 311-3435
www.cdc.gov

U.S. Geological Survey
Information Services
P.O. Box 25286
Denver, CO 80225
1 (888) 275-8747
www.usgs.gov

### **US Websites**

Be Ready Campaign www.ready.gov

Agency for Toxic Substances and Disease Registry

www.atsdr.cdc.gov

Centers for Disease Control and Prevention www.cdc.gov

Citizen Corps www.citizencorps.gov

Department of Health and Human Services www.hhs.gov/disasters

Department of Homeland Security www.dhs.gov

Department of Interior www.doi.gov

Department of Justice www.justice.gov

Environmental Protection Agency www.epa.gov

Federal Emergency Management Agency www.fema.gov

Food and Drug Administration www.fda.gov

National Oceanic and Atmospheric Administration www.noaa.gov

National Weather Service www.nws.noaa.gov

The Critical Infrastructure Assurance Office www.ciao.gov

U.S. Fire Administration www.usfa.fema.gov

U.S. Fire Administration Kids Page www.usfa.fema.gov/kids

U.S. Geological Survey www.usgs.gov

American Red Cross www.redcross.org

Institute for Business and Home Safety www.ibhs.org

National Fire Protection Association www.nfpa.org

National Mass Fatalities Institute www.nmfi.org

National Safety Compliance www.osha-safety-training.net

**Canadian Websites**
The Canadian Centre for Emergency Preparedness www.ccep.ca

The Public Health Agency of Canada, www.phac-aspc.gc.ca

SafeCanada, www.safecanada.ca

Public Safety Canada (PS), www.publicsafety.gc.ca/

Public Weather Warnings for Canada,

www.weatheroffice.gc.ca/warnings/warnings_e.html

Weather Office, www.weatheroffice.gc.ca

Canadian Red Cross, www.redcross.ca

St. John Ambulance of Canada, www.sja.ca

Health Canada, www.hc-sc.gc.ca

Environment Canada, www.ec.gc.ca

# End Notes

---

[1] There are several diagnostic definitions such as Psychopathic Personality Disorder, Pathological Narcissism, and Anti-social Personality Disorder, that describe a person that has no conscience.

[2] "If I could have a choice of where to research psychopaths I would like to study those that work at the stock exchange." Robert Hare,

[3] Sociopaths, who comprise only 3-4% of the male population and less than 1% of the female population (Strauss & Lahey 1984, Davison and Neale 1994, Robins, Tipp & Przybeck 1991), are thought to account for approximately 20% of the United States' prison population (Hare 1993) and between 33% and 80% of the population of chronic criminal offenders (Mednick, Kirkegaard-Sorensen, Hutchings, Knop, Rosenberg & Schulsinger 1977, Hare 1980, Harpending & Sobus 1987). Furthermore, whereas the "typical" U.S. burglar is estimated to have committed a median five crimes per year before being apprehended, chronic offenders- those most likely to be sociopaths- report committing upward of fifty crimes per annum and sometimes as many as two or three hundred (Blumstein & Cohen 1987). Collectively, these individuals are thought to account for over 50% of all crimes in the U.S. (Loeber 1982; Mednick, Gabrielli & Hutchings 1987, Hare 1993).

[4] Dr. Hervey Cleckley discussed the "partial psychopath" when he talked about "incomplete manifestations or suggestions of the disorder" in psychiatrists, physicians, businessmen, etc. "Compensated" psychopaths were described as the subclinical psychopath or subcriminal psychopath by the famous Dr. Robert Hare.

[5] Hervey Cleckley (best known for co-authorship of The Three Faces of Eve), a pioneer in the field who provided the first coherent, thorough description of what he called the "psychopath" (and the "partial" psychopath), wrote: "Although they occasionally appear on casual inspection as successful members of the community, as able lawyers, executives, or physicians . . . . [t]he true difference between them and the psychopaths who continually go to jails or to psychiatric hospitals is that they keep up a far better and more consistent outward appearance of being normal."

[6] Since the injury, J.S. fulfilled the DSM-IV criteria for Antisocial Personality Disorder (DSM-IV, 1994). J.S. `failed to conform to social norms' and was notably `irritable and aggressive'. His episodes of property damage and violence were frequent and were elicited after little provocation; e.g. an alteration in routine. He was `reckless regarding others' personal safety'; on one occasion he continued to push around a wheelchair-bound patient despite her screams of terror. His `lack of remorse' was striking; he never expressed any regrets about the nurses he hit. He failed to accept responsibility for his actions, justifying his violent episodes in terms of the failures of others (e.g. they were too slow). He

frequently `failed to plan ahead', leaving the hospital regularly to wander about London with `no clear goal for the period of travel or clear idea about when the travel will terminate'. He showed `an inability to sustain consistent work behaviour'. Since the accident, he could not hold employment due to his interpersonal difficulties. In summary, J.S. fulfilled the criteria for acquired sociopathy except that he lacked premorbid aberrant behaviour.
From: Impaired social response reversal
A case of `acquired sociopathy'
R. J. R. Blair and L. Cipolotti
**Brain**, Vol. 123, No. 6, 1122-1141, June 2000 Oxford University Press

[7] Martha Stout, in her book *The Sociopath Next Door*, identifies what she calls the pity ploy. Psychopaths use pity to manipulate. They convince you to give them one more chance, and to not tell anyone about what they have done.

[8]. Charles F. Bond Jr., Karen Nelson Kahler, Lucia M Paolicelli, *The Miscommunication of Deception: An Adaptive Perspective* Journal of Experimental Social Psychology, 1985, pp. 331-345.

[9]. Named after the Character in Shakespeare's play in which Othello accuses Desdemona of infidelity and mistakenly believes her emotional outburst as evidence of her guilt.

[10] Hess EH, Polt JH (1964): Pupil size in relation to mental activity during simple problem solving. *Science* 143:1190-1192.

Hyoenae, J, Tommola, J, Alaja, A (1995): Pupil dilation as a measure of processing load in simultaneous interpretation and other language tasks. *Quarterly Journal of Experimental Psychology: Human Experimental Psychology*, 48:598-612.

[11] *Primatology*."Eye-blinking is another well-known primate movement. The moment you have the least little bit of stress, the eyelids blink, bang! bang! bang!" (Niko Tinbergen, in a 1974 *Psychology Today* interview)

*RESEARCH REPORTS*: 1. In mental patients, eye-blink rates rise with anxious or tense topics, and with changes to a new topic (Kanfer 1960). **2.** "The eye blink has been found to occur during vocalizations at the beginning of words and utterances, usually with the initial vowel of the word . . ." (Condon and Ogston 1967:229). **3.** The average rate for someone speaking on TV is 31 to 50 blinks a minute--twice the relaxed rate (Tecce 1996).

[12.]"One cannot lie to an aphasiac. He cannot grasp your words, and so cannot be deceived by them; but what he grasps he grasps with infallible precision, namely the **expression** that goes with the words, that total, spontaneous, involuntary expressiveness which can never be simulated or faked, as words alone can, all too easily." Oliver Sacks, *The Man Who Mistook His Wife For A Ha.* Touchstone, 1998*t* The president's speech.

[13.] Sun Tzu's The Art Of War

[14.] There are also physiological causes such as illness and lesions in the brain, chemical imbalances, and the use of various drugs and medicines. These are cases requiring professional medical attention and therefore are not included here.

[15.] Even in social situations territory plays a part, the head of the table is usually reserved for the head of the family, likewise the head of the conference table is usually reserved for the Chief executive, mothers have dominance in the kitchen, children defend their half of the bedroom, their side of the couch and so on.

[16.] The Yanomamo Tribe of Venezuela rainforest has the reputation for being the most violent group with one in four dying as a result of combat. Most of the violence is over the shortage of females. The unequal distribution of male to female ratio is the result of infanticide practiced against females.

[17] Roizen, J. Epidemiological issues in alcohol-related violence. In: Galanter, M., ed. Recent Developments in Alcoholism. Vol. 13. New York: Plenum Press, 1997. pp. 7-40.

[18] This type of breathing technique aids in the production of beta and theta wave patterns associated with relaxation, visualization, and recovery. Abdominal breathing mimics the natural breathing that occurs during the stage of sleep know as REM (Rapid Eye Movement). It is during REM sleep that we dream and it is thought that during this stage that the conscious and sub-conscious minds share information.

[19]. The importance of posture in self-defense is illustrated in a study done in the United States on the effectiveness of self-defense training for women. Although women who trained in a martial art had only a slightly better chance of escaping a violent situation, it showed that these women had far less chance of being attacked. The study indicated that while women have a 25% chance of becoming a victim of violence, women who studied a martial art showed a less then 3% chance. The explanation for this disparity is thought to be attributed to body language. Interviews conducted with convicted rapists, muggers, and purse-snatchers, showed that criminals usually choose easy targets, people who, through their body language, show themselves to be vulnerable. It is suggested that women who studied self-defense projected a more confident posture and corresponding body language that discouraged potential attackers.

[20] Perhaps the most oft-mentioned factor suggested as being relevant to the development of a cheating strategy, especially in males, is being competitively disadvantaged with respect to the ability to obtain resources and mating opportunities. Theoretically, those individuals who are the least likely to outcompete other males in a status hierarchy, or to achieve mates through female choice, are the ones most likely to adopt a cheating strategy. (See eg. Thornhill & Alcock 1983, Daly & Wilson 1983 and Gould & Gould 1989 re: non-human animals, and Symons 1979, Kenrick et al 1983, MacMillan & Kofoed 1984, Kofoed & MacMillan 1986, Cohen & Machalek 1988, Tooke & Camire 1991 and Thornhill & Thornhill 1992 re: humans). In humans, competitive disadvantage could be related to a variety of factors, including age, health, physical attractiveness, intelligence, socioeconomic status, and social skills.

[21] FBI Uniform Crime Reporting 2003
The FBI's Uniform Crime Reporting (UCR) Program's annual publication, *Crime in the United States, 2003*, compiles crime statistics from more than 17,000 city, county, state, tribal, and federal law enforcement agencies.
Here is a summary of the burglary statistics for 2003:

- The Nation had an estimated 2,153,464 burglaries in 2003, a slight (+0.1 percent) increase from the 2002 estimated figure. The rate of burglary in the United States was 740.5 burglary offenses per 100,000 inhabitants, a 0.9-percent decrease from 2002 data.
- Victims collectively lost an estimated $3.5 billion as a result of burglaries in 2003 with an average dollar loss of $1,626 per incident.
- An examination of the burglary data indicated that forcible entry accounted for 62.4 percent, unlawful entry comprised 31.2 percent, and attempted forcible entry made up 6.3 percent of all burglary offenses.
- Most burglaries (65.8 percent) occurred at residences; most residential burglaries (62.0 percent) occurred during the daytime.

Burglary is categorized into three sub classifications:

**Forcible entry** - Defined as gaining entry by the use of tools; breaking windows; forcing windows, doors, transoms, or ventilators; cutting screens, walls, or roofs; and the use of master keys, picks, unauthorized keys, celluloid, or other device which leave no outward mark but are used to force a lock.

**Unlawful entry** - Non-forcible entry is achieved by use of an unlocked door or window. The element of trespass to the structure to commit a theft is essential to classify the act as a burglary.

**Attempted forcible entry** - Attempted forcible entry occurs when a perpetrator is frightened off while entering an unlocked door or climbing though an open window to commit a theft.

278

[22] The Information Reproduced, has been taken from Pamphlets Available to the Public by the RCMP and FBI

[23] Under US law the primary remedy in illegal search cases is known as the "exclusionary rule". This means that any evidence obtained through an illegal search is excluded and cannot be used against the defendant at his or her trial.

[24] The Fourth Amendment to the United States Constitution provides that:
*The right of the people to be secure in their persons, houses, papers, and effects, against unreasonable searches and seizures, shall not be violated, and no Warrants shall issue, but upon probable cause, supported by Oath or affirmation, and particularly describing the place to be searched, and the persons or things to be seized.*

In Canada, Section Eight of the Canadian Charter of Rights and Freedoms protects all individuals from unreasonable search and seizure. For a search to be "reasonable" it must be authorized by law, the law itself must be reasonable, and the manner in which the search was carried out must be reasonable (R. v. S.A.B., 2003 SCC 60). This means that the officer must be acting within the power of a valid statute, and it must be performed on the basis of there being "reasonable and probable grounds" that a crime has been committed.

[25] The number of no-knock raids has increased from 3,000 in 1981 to more than 50,000 in 2005, according to Peter Kraska, a criminologist at Eastern Kentucky University in Richmond, Kentucky. According to the Cato Institute in Washington, DC.
Raids that lead to deaths of innocents are increasingly common;, 40 bystanders have been killed since the early 1980s

[26].Cleary, Thomas, *Mastering the Art of War: Zhuge Liang's and Liu Ji's Commentaries on the Classic by Sun Tzu*, Shambala Publications, Boston, 1989

[27] There are three main chemicals used in pepper sprays you can get over the counter. These are CS (Ortho cloromalononitrile), CN (Chloroacetophenone) and OC (Oleoresin Capsicum.) OC is by far the most effective under normal conditions.

[28.]Michael Field, Scientific America Article, 1979, the physics of Karate. Quote on scientific hand power.

[29].A study conducted in the U.S. showed that most gun battles take place within twenty feet, even within this distance only one out of ten shots fired by criminals hit their target. Police forces with regular pistol practice fared only slightly better with three out of ten shots hitting the target. The reason is thought to be due to the stress and movement that occurs during real life shootings.

[30]. To allow a safety margin, Special Forces teams count the surprise factor as three, one man can take out three with the element of surprise. This is a good rule to apply to any group dynamic.

[31] Attrition warfare is a military strategy in which a belligerent attempts to win a war by wearing down its enemy to the point of collapse through continuous losses in personnel and matériel.

[32.] *Sun Tzu and the Art of Business: Six Strategic Principles for Managers* by Mark R. McNeilly, Oxford University Press, , 2000 p.217

[33] "The result is that all hierarchies inevitably become top-heavy with psychopaths. Since psychopaths have no limitations on what they can or will do to get to the top, the ones in charge are generally pathological. It is not power that corrupts, it is that corrupt individuals seek power." Andrzej Lobaczewski, *Political Ponerology: A Science on the Nature of Evil Adjusted for Political Purposes* (Canada: Red Pill Press, 1998).

[34.] To avoid this curse the wisest of Asian tycoons raise their children in near poverty and forced them to claw their own way to the top. If his own children fail, he will pass control of the business empire to a worthy successor from another branch of the family.

[35.] A bell curve.

[36] A classical example of escaping under the radar by being mistaken for an idiot is the Roman emperor Claudius (10 BC – 54AD ) who survived the purges, poisonings, and executions of his entire family by the emperors Tiberius and Caligula because they thought he was an idiot and thus posed no threat to their power.

37. Since the Second World War the list of countries having employed the above means would include, most if not all third world and communist countries. Even North America has not been immune to several of these abuses starting with the McCarthy hearings on through to current search and seizure laws that allow police authorities enormous powers to confiscate and seize property. Roman emperors were notorious for replenishing government coffers by confiscating the estates of rich senators on charges of treason, easy to accuse, impossible to disprove. Many states have drug seizure laws that are dangerously similar; easy to fake, impossible to disprove, such powers will inevitably lead to the same abuses.

38. Drugs have even been used in the past as a tactical weapon by one nation against another, For example, the importing of cheap opium to China, first by the

European powers, and later by the Japanese `Black Dragon' society during the Second World War. One of the tactics of the Black Dragons was to open high-class bordellos and ensnare local bureaucrats, politicians, and businessmen with women and opium.

[39] As implausible as it seems to tunnel out of a high security prison this is exactly what happened in the famous 1962 Alcatraz escape. American criminals Clarence Anglin, John Anglin, Frank Morris, and Allen West tunneled through their prison cells into a ventilation shaft to escape Alcatraz Island, one of the United States' most infamous prisons. They also used the False Double tactic by putting dummy heads - made of a mixture of soap, toilet paper and real hair - in their beds to fool prison officers making night-time inspections.

## Bibliography

Adams, James, Secret Armies, *The full story of S.A.S., Delta Force & Spetsnaz,* Hutchinson, London, 1987

Alexander, John B., Grollier, Richard, Morris, Janet, *The Warrior's Edge*, William Morrow & Co., New York, 1990

Alexander, Bevin, *How Great Generals Win*, W.W. Norton & Co., New York, 1993

Blainey, Geoffry, *The Causes of War*, The Free Press, New York, 1973

Clausewitz, Carl Von, *On War*, Penguin Books, London, 1968

Charlton, James, Ed. *The Military Quotation Book*, St. Martin's Press, New York, 1990

Cleckley, Hervey M., *The Mask of Sanity,* Emily S. Cleckley; 5th edition (November 1988)

Deshimaru, Taisen, *The Zen Way To The Martial Arts*, E.P. Dutton, New York, 1982

Digest, Reader's, *Facts & Fallacies, Stories of the Strange and Unusual*, Reader's Digest, New York, 1988

Dunnigan, James F., Bay, Austin, *A Quick And Dirty Guide to War*, William Morrow, New York, 1991

Dunnigan, James F., *How To Make War*, William Morrow, New York, 1988

Ekman, Paul, *Telling Lies: Clues to Deceit in the Marketplace, Politics, and Marriage*, Norton & Company, New York, 1985.

Griswold, Terry, Giangreco, D. M., *Delta, America's Elite Counter Terrorist Force*, Motorbooks International, Osceola, WI, 1992

Hare, Robert D. PhD, *Without Conscience: The Disturbing World of the Psychopaths Among Us*, The Guilford Press; 1 edition (January 8, 1999)

Hare, Robert D. PhD, *Snakes in Suits: When Psychopaths Go to Work*, Harper Paperbacks (May 8, 2007)

Kemp, Anthony, *The SAS At War*, Signet Books, London, 1991

Klein, Malcolm W., Cheryl Maxson, Jody Miller, *The Modern Gang Reader*, Roxbury Publishing, L.A., 1995

Lao Tzu, *Tao Te Ching*, Penguin Classics, New York, 1963

Lobaczewski, Andrzej *Political Ponerology: A Science on the Nature of Evil Adjusted for Political Purposes* (Canada: Red Pill Press, 1998).

Machiavelli, Niccolo, *The Prince*, Bantam Book Classics, New York, 1985

Machiavelli, Niccolo, *The Art of War*, Da Capo Press, New York, 1965

Macksey, Kenneth, *The Penguin Encyclopedia of Weapons and Military Technology*, Viking, New York, 1993

McCormick, Donald, *The Master Book Of Escapes*, Hodder Causton Ltd. London, 1974

Morris, Desmond, *The Human Animal, A Personal View of the Human Species*, BBC Books, London, 1994

Morris, Desmond, Marsh, Peter, *Tribes*, McGraw-Hill Ryerson, Toronto, 1988

Moyer, K. E., *Violence and Aggression*, Paragon House, New York, 1987

Musashi, Miyamoto, *The Book Of Five Rings*, Bantam Books, New York, 1982

Nash, Jay Robert, *Hustlers & Con Men*, M. Evans, New York, 1976

Raviv, Dan, & Yossi Melman, *Every Spy a Prince, The Complete History of Israel's Inteligence Community*, Houghton Mifflin Co.1990

Salter, Anna, *Predators: Pedophiles, Rapists, And Other Sex Offenders*, Basic Books (March 30, 2004)

Sifakis, Carl, *Hoaxes and Scams, a compendium of deceptions, ruses and swindles*, Facts on File, New York, 1993

Storr, Anthony, *Human Destructiveness*, Grove Weidenfeld, New York, 1991

Vaknin, Sam, Lidija Rangelovska (Editor) *Malignant Self Love: Narcissism Revisited*, Narcissus Publications, Czech Republic (July 2001)

Wilson, Colin, *A Criminal History of Mankind*, Grafton Books, London, 1985

Wise, Arthur, *The Art and History of Personal Combat*, Arma Press, New York, 1971

Wright, Peter, *The Spycatcher's Encyclopedia of Espionage*, Stoddart, Toronto, 1991

# Index

## A

## B

## C

## T

## U

## V

## W

# Other Books by Stefan Verstappen

### The Thirty-Six Strategies of Ancient China
China Books & Periodicals, SF, 1999,
www.chinastrategies.com/home36

The Thirty-Six Strategies is a unique collection of ancient Chinese proverbs that describe some of the most cunning and subtle strategies ever devised. These proverbs describe not only battlefield strategies, but tactics used in psychological warfare to undermine both the enemy's will to fight - and his sanity.

### Chinese Business Etiquette:
*The Practical Pocket Guide*,
Stone Bridge, Press, Berkeley, 2008,
www.chinastrategies.com/cbe.htm

This essential pocket reference on common business and social protocols for traveling and doing business in China, Taiwan, and Hong Kong, is ideal for anyone doing business with the Chinese, at home or abroad.

### Blind Zen, *A Case Study of Sensory Enhancement for the Blind and Vision Impaired*
Red Mansion Press, SF, 2004
www.chinastrategies.com/blind.htm

Blind Zen tells the story of how a blind woman's efforts to learn self defense led to a unique experiment to adapt martial arts and eastern philosophy to develop new skills and increase self confidence.

### The Little Warriors, Children's Safety
Vol I-VIII, Lulu Press, 2006
www.chinastrategies.com/littlewarrior.htm

This 40 page full color workbook contains 36 safety and street proofing lessons. This Workbook is used in conjunction with the Little Warriors Street Safety Teachers Guide as part of a complete mini-course in street proofing.

## About the Author

Stefan H. Verstappen is a Canadian writer, adventurer, and martial artist. He has worked as a wilderness survival instructor for Outward Bound programs, a street youth councilor, a First Aid and CPR instructor for St John Ambulance, and a martial arts instructor. Since first backpacking through Europe alone at age sixteen he has also traveled the world and spent four years living in the Orient.

For more information on the author visit: www.chinastrategies.com

Lightning Source UK Ltd.
Milton Keynes UK
UKOW06f1454201216
290466UK00001B/102/P